IMAGES
of America

Cincinnati's Northside Neighborhood

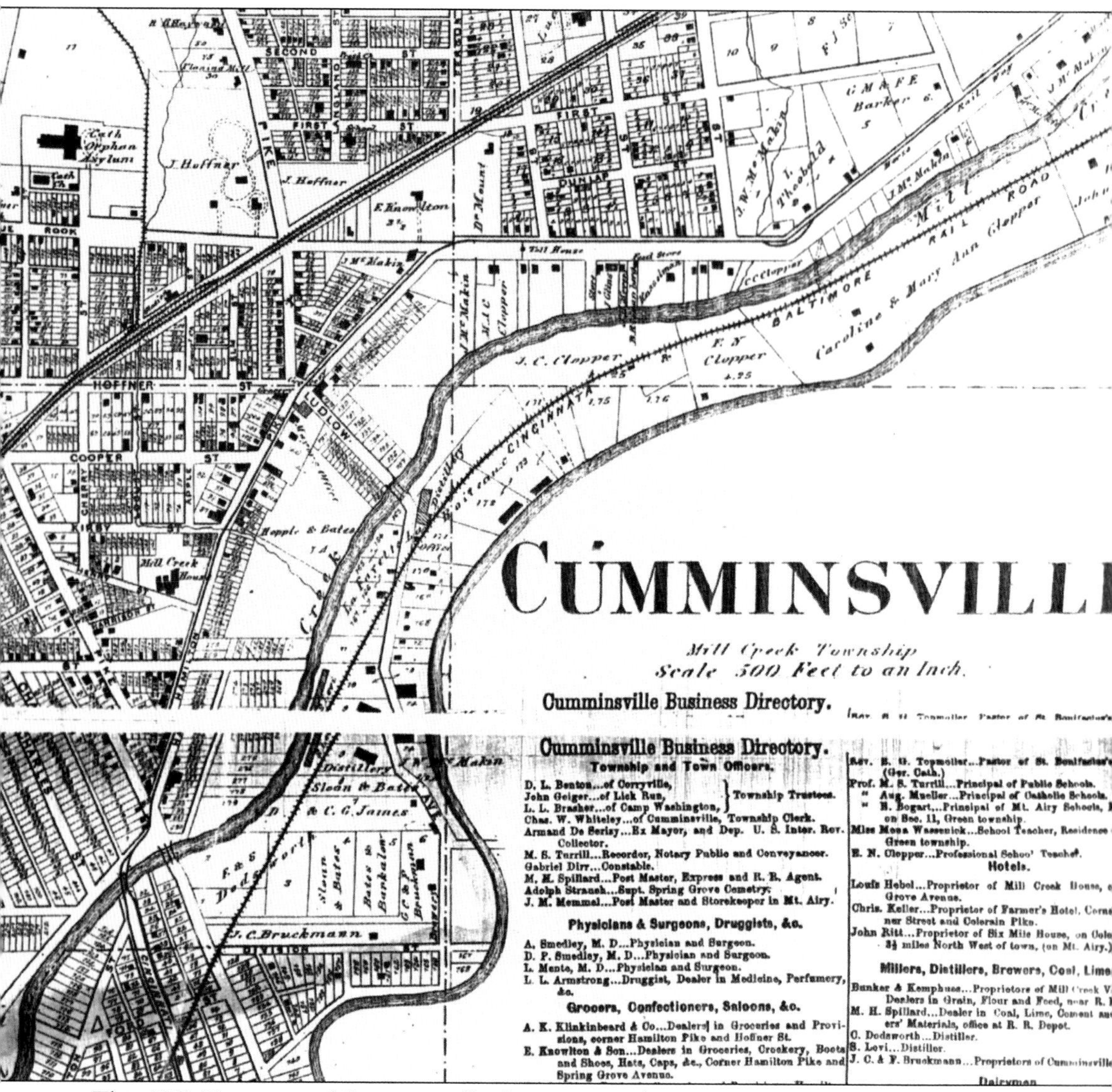

This 1869 Titus map of Cumminsville shows a sprawling post–Civil War village before being split into Northside and South Cumminsville. The Cincinnati, Hamilton and Dayton Railroad crosses the map at a diagonal, and the Mill Creek is now accompanied on the east by Interstate 75. Some old landmarks no longer stand, like St. Joseph's Orphanage, but the street layouts and land usage are much the same as today. (Author's collection.)

On the cover: This Bruckmann family portrait, taken in the 1880s, shows their brewery property on Streng Street. Behind the small cottage and the brewery buildings in the distance is Ludlow Avenue, near today's viaduct. John C. Bruckmann Jr., son of the founder of the brewery, is seen on the left in his goat cart. These brewer's wives have smirks on their faces, indicating an unusually jovial disposition. (Courtesy of Jim Bruckmann.)

IMAGES
of America

CINCINNATI'S NORTHSIDE NEIGHBORHOOD

Dann Woellert

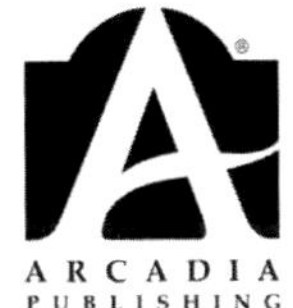

ISBN 978-0-7385-7778-4

Published by Arcadia Publishing
Charleston, South Carolina

Printed in the United States of America

Library of Congress Control Number: 2009931251

For all general information contact Arcadia Publishing at:
Telephone 843-853-2070
Fax 843-853-0044
E-mail sales@arcadiapublishing.com
For customer service and orders:
Toll-Free 1-888-313-2665

Visit us on the Internet at www.arcadiapublishing.com

To John A. Schratwieser

Contents

ACKNOWLEDGMENTS

A 1925 souvenir at the Northside-Cumminsville outing to the Cincinnat Zoo stated, "What makes a community stand out from others? It is the spirit of friendliness and unity which can be seen in the action of its citizens."

I first fell in love with old Northside while researching my family roots. But I also fell in love with a younger Northside as I became involved with the community. Young Northside was open-minded, fun, community-active, supportive, spiritual, and creative. I hope that this work brings about discussion and reminiscing of personal history and good times. It is Northside's fascinating history that makes it so special and diverse today.

I would like to extend special thanks to Donna Erhardt Borgman at Putz Creamy Whip; Al Bocklet; Don Beimesche of the Northside Bank; Trudy Bacchus of Cincinnati Preservation Association; Lucia Stanton Shannon, senior historian at Monticello National Monument; Bruce Demske, Northside Business Association president; Alma Voeckl; Harold Johnson; Rick Schaeper; Fred Deubell, former manager of GAIN News; Linda Bailey at the Cincinnati Historical Society; Robert Meyer, grandson of Meyer Dairy founder; Dorothy Knapp, former co-owner of Mueller's Pharmacy; Sr. Benedicta Mahoney, Cincinnati Sisters of Charity Archives; Sandy Hamilton, loving Northside historic home caretaker; Evelyn Elbe of the First United Church of Christ Archives; Kathy Dahl at Labeautou Woods; Erwin Goedicke, pastor of Northside Presbyterian Church; Cincinnati Public Library Department of Local History and Genealogy staff; Don Heinrich Tolzmann for help translating *Cincinnati Frei Presse* articles about the Cumminsville Turnverein; Diane Brake, enthusiastic Spring Grove Cemetery docent; Matthew Hodgsen and Tom Ford, owners of the Dater House; Louise and Charles Watts; Roberta Lipka Landwehr Watson; Diane and Fred Koch of Koch Greenhouses; Maureen Wood; Joe Taylor at Rotex Inc.; Jim and Carolyn Bruckmann, great-grandson of the founder of Bruckmann Brewery; Jan Holland; Lynn Nelson, Robinson Circus expert; Mike Martini of Media Heritage archives at Voice of America Museum; Clyde Haehnle; Alice Martha Bun Fletcher, oldest living member of the Cumminsville First Baptist Church; Rev. George Southerland of the Cumminsville First Baptist Church; all the enthusiastic Northsiders who offered support, encouragement, positive energy, good food, and good karma; and most especially, Cliff Woellert, for his irreverent sense of humor and portal into my family history; Norma Schaeser Woellert, for her stories of the "old Cumminsville homestead" served over homemade goetta; and the ever-loving support of my amazing parents Roger and Flora Woellert. Unless otherwise noted, the pictures are from my collection.

INTRODUCTION

Northside is one of the most historic neighborhoods in Cincinnati, second only to Columbia-Tusculum on the Ohio River. It boasts two national historic districts—the Hoffner Historic District and the Chase-Pullen Historic District—and one local historic district, the Northside Historic District. Its early-19th-century business district is largely intact, and it has a variety of separately national historic registered private residences.

Northside was part of the larger community of Cumminsville, consisting of today's Northside and South Cumminsville neighborhoods. Several buildings in Northside still have Cumminsville carved over their entrances. However, several nicknames developed for areas within Cumminsville. Goosetown, also called Clopper's Ford, was on the east side of the Mill Creek at the foot of Mount Storm. Hameltown or Hen Peck, in west Northside, sat on the banks of the West Fork Creek, near Colerain Avenue. Frogtown sat next to Spring Grove Cemetery surrounding Springlawn. Presbyterian Flats was the area east of Hamilton Avenue and north of the railroad tracks.

The story of Northside starts at its heart—the intersection of Hamilton Avenue and Spring Grove Avenue, known today as Knowlton's Corner. During the early pioneer days, these were two well-worn Native American trails. Hamilton Avenue followed the path of what was known as St. Clair's Trace, named after Gen. Arthur St. Clair. Spring Grove Avenue followed the path of what was known as Mad Anthony Wayne Trace, who was the general who signed the treaty ending the French and Indian War with Chief Little Turtle.

The first major settler to the area was a surveyor named Israel Ludlow, who was awarded 125 acres in 1789 for his work that encompassed some of Spring Grove Cemetery, Clifton, and Cumminsville. In 1790, Ludlow erected a blockhouse northeast of Hamilton Avenue and Spring Grove, to secure the area from Native American attack. Ludlow's wife was a lady of exceptional education and many accomplishments, and she became so popular among the Miami Indians in the area that they bestowed her the nickname of Athapasca, meaning "the good woman."

An early feud over a shared spring in the second decade of the 19th century between Ezekial Hutchinson, owner of the Hotel of the Golden Lamb, and David Cummins, owner of the Grid Iron Tannery, ended in a change of power to two of the men that helped Cumminsville along its development. Jacob Hoffner bought the foreclosed Hotel of the Golden Lamb and its property to make into his estate and became the philanthropist that donated land and funds for development of community institutions. Ephraim Knowlton bought the foreclosed Grid Iron Tannery and built his general store at Knowlton's Corner, which became the first community meeting spot.

Knowlton had come to Cumminsville in the 1820s to supervise the digging of a portion of the Miami and Eire Canal. As a result, the area became inhabited by rowdy Irish and German immigrants, who gave the area the nicknames "Helltown" or "Happy Valley," depending on their idea of a good time. Saloons, brothels, and beer gardens dominated the businesses at that time.

In the 1850s, the arrival of the Cincinnati, Hamilton, and Dayton Railroad grew the community into a commuter suburb of Cincinnati where people could raise families away from the overcrowded and disease-ridden downtown. With help from Hoffner, who divided his land into suburbs and helped fund the building of several churches, the Masonic lodge, and other businesses, the area soon lost its Helltown moniker.

With the area's large German immigrant "48er" population and abolitionist sympathizing churches, Cumminsville became a pass through stop on the Underground Railroad. The Wesleyan Cemetery was the first racially integrated cemetery in the city, so large groups of escaping slaves, who crossed the Ohio River from the slave state of Kentucky, staged mock funerals and escaped from the river in plain site to the cemetery, where they were given supplies and directions to follow the Mill Creek up to safe houses in North College Hill further north.

Northside had a large German influence to rival that of Cincinnati's Over-the-Rhine. In 1873, 48 percent of Northside inhabitants were German-speaking. The area gave rise to German Lutheran and Catholic churches, German-owned breweries and saloons, German furniture businesses, German *Bauevereine* (or building and loan societies), and German social organizations like the Cumminsville Turner Society. The 1875 *Kenny's Illustrated Cincinnati* proclaimed, "The large number of beer gardens [in Northside] make it quite a resort for the city."

The area supported a wide variety of churches from Catholic, Lutheran, Methodist, Baptist, Presbyterian, and others, each of which contributed to the wholesome community.

Northside's greatest period of growth was from the beginning of the 19th century, when streetcars shuttled people into the neighborhood over the newly created Ludlow Avenue Viaduct. Visitors could patronize a variety of high-quality shops, cafés, and one of three movie theaters for entertainment. From the 1890s through the 1930s, five major circuses pitched their big tops in Cumminsville and had circus parades that caused huge fanfare. The wealthy shop owners around the bustling Knowlton's Corner renamed the neighborhood Northside, to denote its affluence and its geography north of the Cincinnati, Hamilton, and Dayton Railroad tracks.

The proximity to Cincinnati's largest cemetery, Spring Grove, gave rise to supporting monument and funeral business like Dhonau's Funeral Parlor, Miller Funeral Parlor, Spaeth Undertaking, Fisk, Douglas, and Napolitano monuments, and others.

The German ingenuity made Cumminsville a center of carriage and later automotive manufacturing prowess. Early businesses like Dhonau Carriage Company converted to automotive sales. George C. Heilman invented the first gasoline-powered automobile in Cincinnati in 1894 and then sold a line of cars that predated the Ford Model T. Powell Crosley started his American Automobile Accessories Company in Northside, which gave him the funding to start WLW radio station and the Crosley Radio Corporation.

The area being close to the Mill Creek became victim to the severe spring floods that plagued the Ohio valley in 1884, 1914, and 1937, until the WPA-funded flood plan completely redesign the drainage of the Mill Creek.

By the 1950s, industry left Northside, and urban flight resulted in a decrease in home ownership. However, the 1990s has seen a rebirth in historic home renovation and a reclamation of Northside as the eclectic and artsy neighborhood that it is today. The annual Northside Fourth of July parade is one of the most unique parades of its kind in the city.

One

Indian Blockade to Sprawling Village

From the early Native American blockade days in the 1790s, to its incorporation in 1865 as a village, Northside was an important outpost to the city of Cincinnati. Prior to 1811, the area was primarily wilderness and farmland with only a few settlers. Only after 1790, when Israel Ludlow erected his blockhouse, did settlers feel safe to make Ludlow Station, or Mill Creek Station, as it was then known, their home. One of the first early settlers was Robert Badgely, who built his family's log cabin in 1795 at Otte Avenue and Anthony Street. After Ludlow's death, in 1805, Col. Jared Mansfield, Thomas Jefferson's newly appointed surveyor general, set up an observatory in the Ludlow mansion to survey the Northwest Territory with a newly purchased English telescope. The principal meridian that Mansfield created—passing through the mouth of the Great Miami River and extending to the northern boundary of the United States—was the basis for all land surveyed in this country after 1805. This meridian is also one of the man-made artifacts visible from Earth's orbit. In 1811, Ezekiel Hutchinson's Hotel of the Golden Lamb was the first business venture in the area, on the site of Hoffner Park. Ohio governor Return J. Meigs used the Golden Lamb as the meeting place for the first division of the Ohio militia to support the War of 1812. In 1820, the tavern was the site of the first fair west of Pittsburgh. In 1817, David Cummins bought the land across from Hutchinson's tavern, now Knowlton's Corner, and built a large tannery. Brothers Ephraim and Sidney Knowlton came to the area in 1821 to supervise the one-mile stretch of the Miami and Eire Canal that ran through Northside. The influx of workers needed to dig the canal created more business opportunities and helped the little hamlet to grow into a bustling village. The rowdy canal workers soon created havoc, and the neighborhood earned the nicknames "Helltown" and "Happy Valley." Some of the more prominent citizens like Jacob Hoffner began philanthropic measures to create a more upstanding community, by donating land for churches, schools, and more respectable neighborhoods.

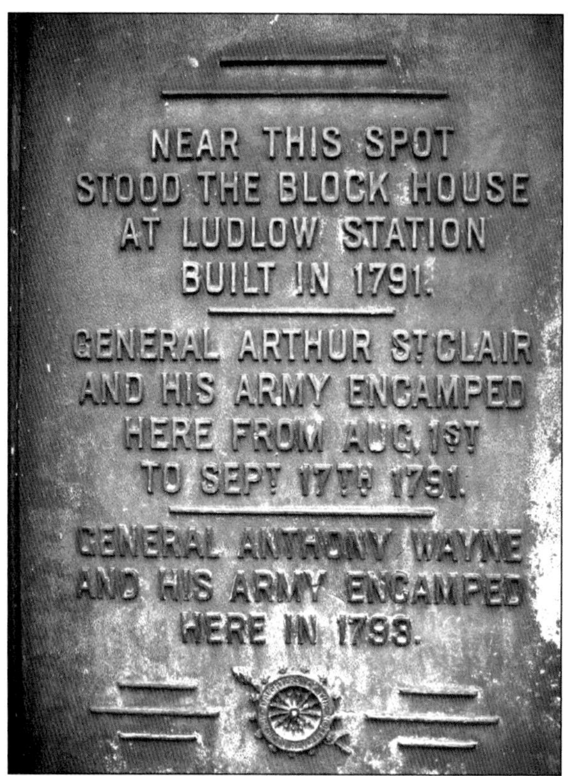

This monument at Knowlton and Mad Anthony Streets was erected in 1916 by the Daughters of the American Revolution (DAR) to commemorate the site of the Ludlow blockhouse. On March 9, 1790, Israel Ludlow, with James Miller, Joseph and Enoch McHendrey, Daniel Bates, Elijah Hardesty, Frederick Patchel, John Nobel Cummins, Jonathan Pierson, Enos Terrace, and Thomas Goudy, formed the first settlement of Ludlow Station in Northside. Built as a frontier outpost to protect from the Twightwee and Pickawillany tribes of Miami Indians, both Gen. Arthur St. Clair and Maj. Gen. Anthony Wayne's armies camped here.

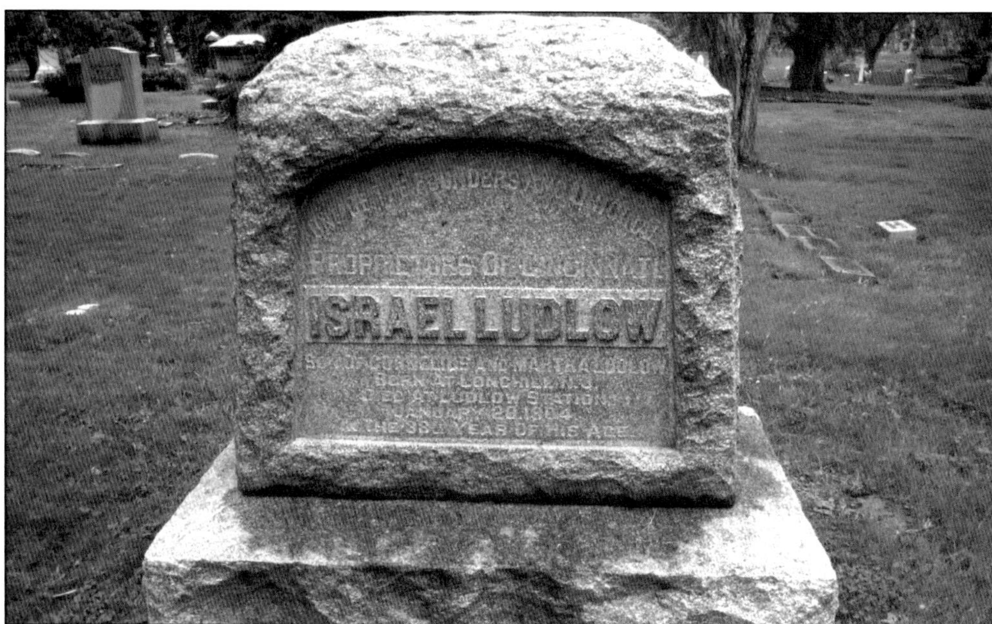

Ludlow (1765–1804) was born in New Jersey but came to Cincinnati to survey the Symmes Purchase. For this work, he was awarded lands that were part of Northside, Clifton, and Spring Grove Cemetery. His monument shown here is at section 113, lot 170 of Spring Grove Cemetery. Ludlow's wife, Charlotte Chambers Ludlow, was nicknamed Athapasca, meaning "the good woman," by the local Miami Indians.

This photograph shows a cross section of the fabled Anthony Wayne Elm that, until 1963, stood at 1315 Apjones Street. Maj. Gen. Anthony Wayne (1745–1796), on his march northward to the Battle of Fallen Timbers in 1794, is said to have rested his troops here and tied his horse to the tree. A monument was erected at the site of the tree in 1929 by the citizens of Northside. When the tree died of Dutch elm disease, it was removed and a section displayed, along with this monument, at the Northside Branch Library. Wood from the tree was taken to the Davis and Seihl Fence Company and made into memorial plaques and mementos that were then distributed almost like pieces of the true cross by the Northside Business Association.

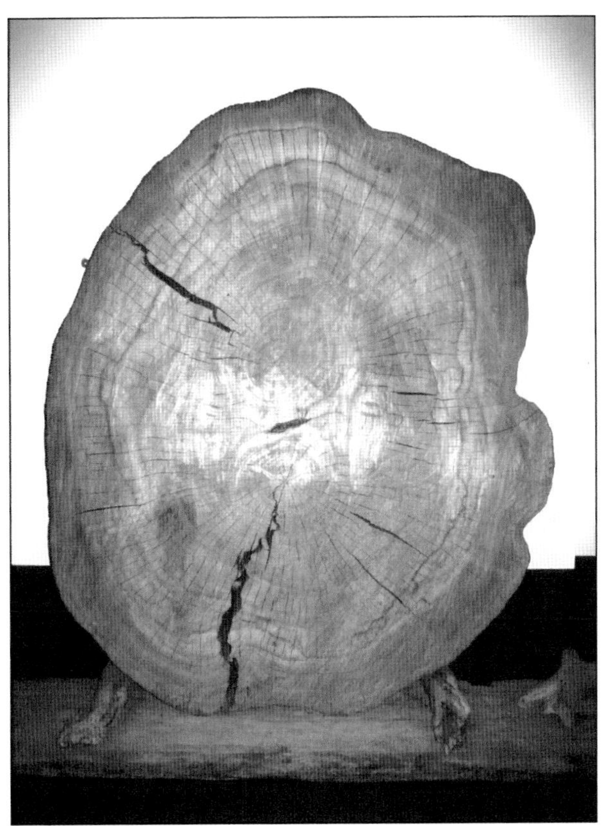

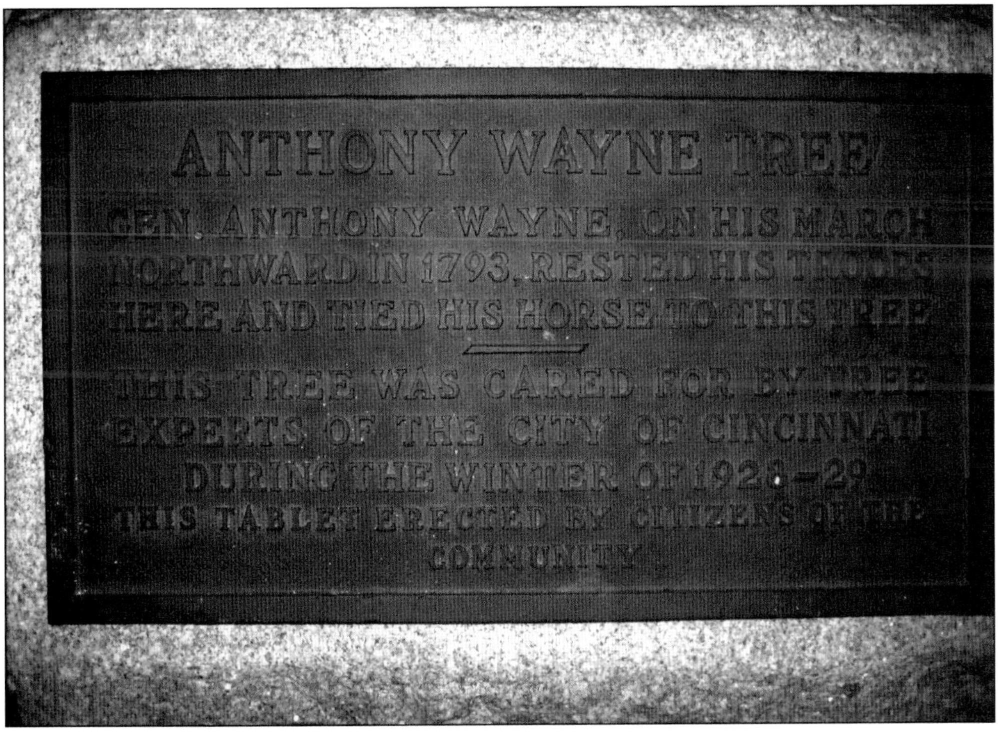

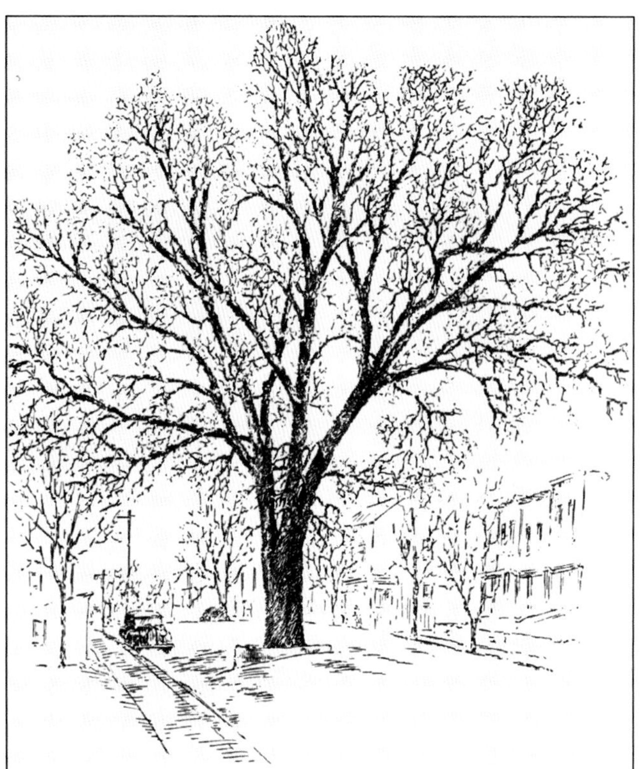

This sketch by Caroline Williams in 1963 for the *Cincinnati Enquirer* shows the location of the Anthony Wayne Elm, in the middle of Apjones Street, guarded by reflectors and a concrete base, before it was removed by the city the same year.

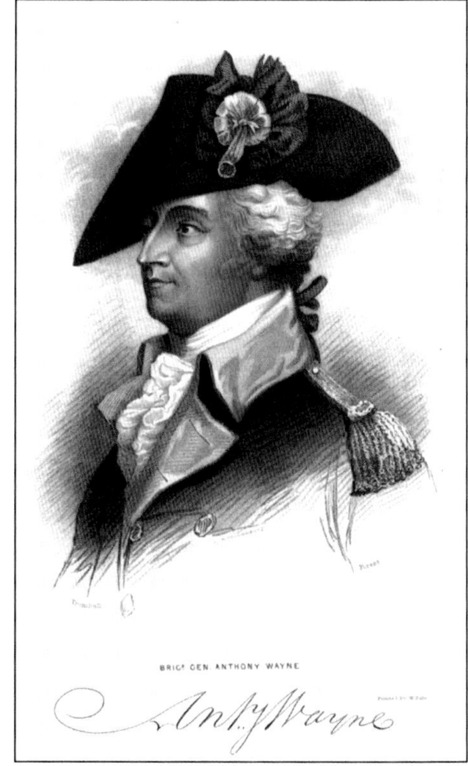

Maj. Gen. Anthony Wayne, signed the Treaty of Greenville in 1795 with Miami Indian chief Little Turtle, ending the French and Indian War. This etching shows Wayne as he would have looked in the days traveling through Northside. He was given the title "Mad Anthony" because of his tactical boldness and personal courage in the field during the Revolutionary War. Mad Anthony Street in Northside is named for him.

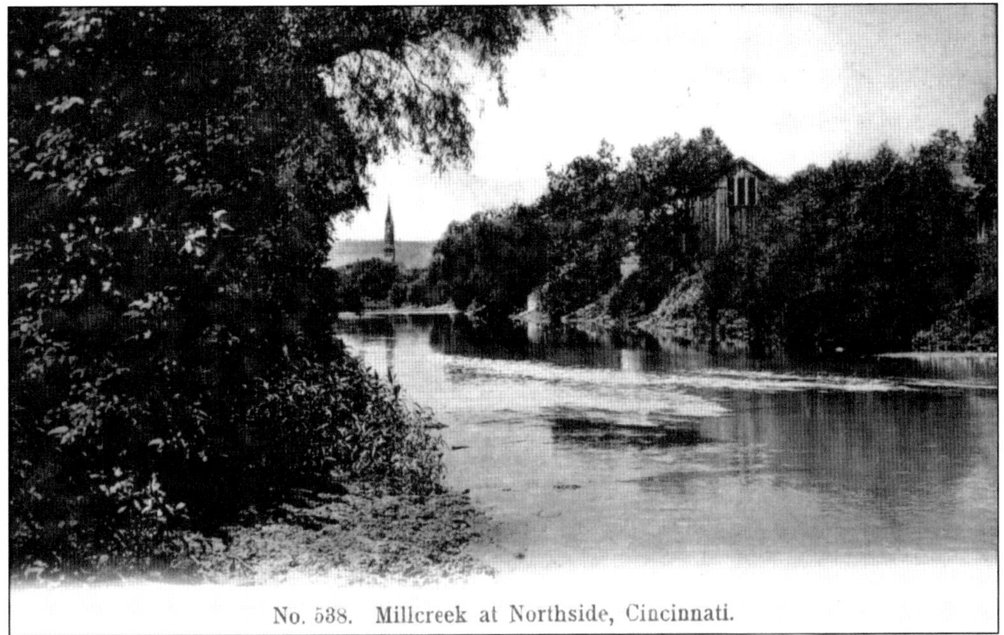

This early-1900s photograph shows the Mill Creek, the lifeblood for early residents of Northside. Its beautiful waters inspired poems like "The Old Spotted Frog." The Miami Indians called it Makatewah, and at the time, it was jumping with bass and salmon. The many natural dams made it a source of income for early beaver trappers, like frontiersmen Scot Spencer and Newkirk Cox. (From the Collection of the Public Library of Cincinnati and Hamilton County.)

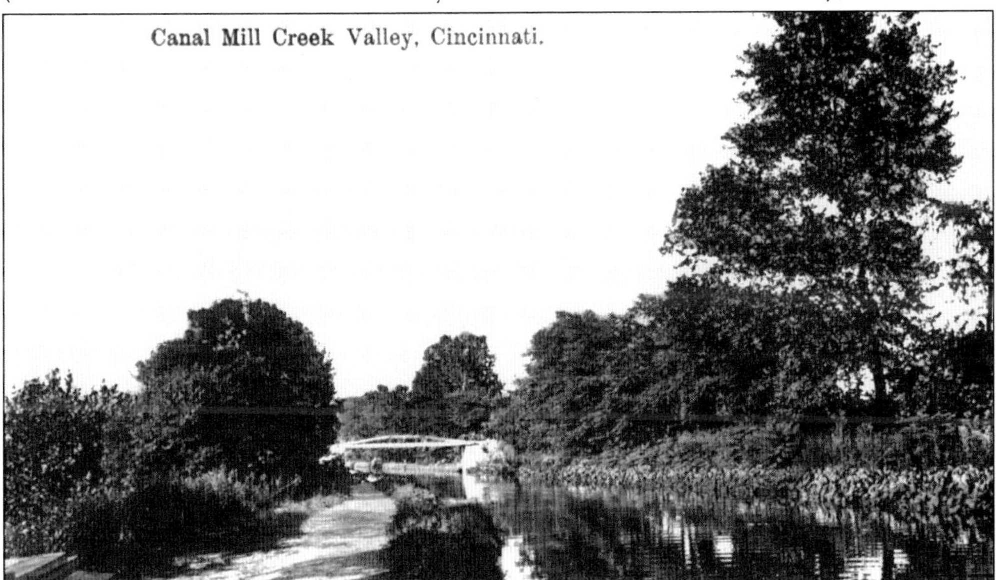

This 1909 postcard shows the Miami and Eire Canal and its towpath winding through Northside's Mill Creek valley. Brothers Ephraim and Sidney Knowlton came to Northside in 1823 to supervise the digging of the one-mile stretch of the canal passing through. They sponsored pleasure cruises on their canal boat, the *Hannibal of Carthage*. In 1825, Ephraim built the Blue Goose Tavern for his canal workers, at the corner of Blue Rock Street and Spring Grove Avenue. (From the Collection of the Public Library of Cincinnati and Hamilton County.)

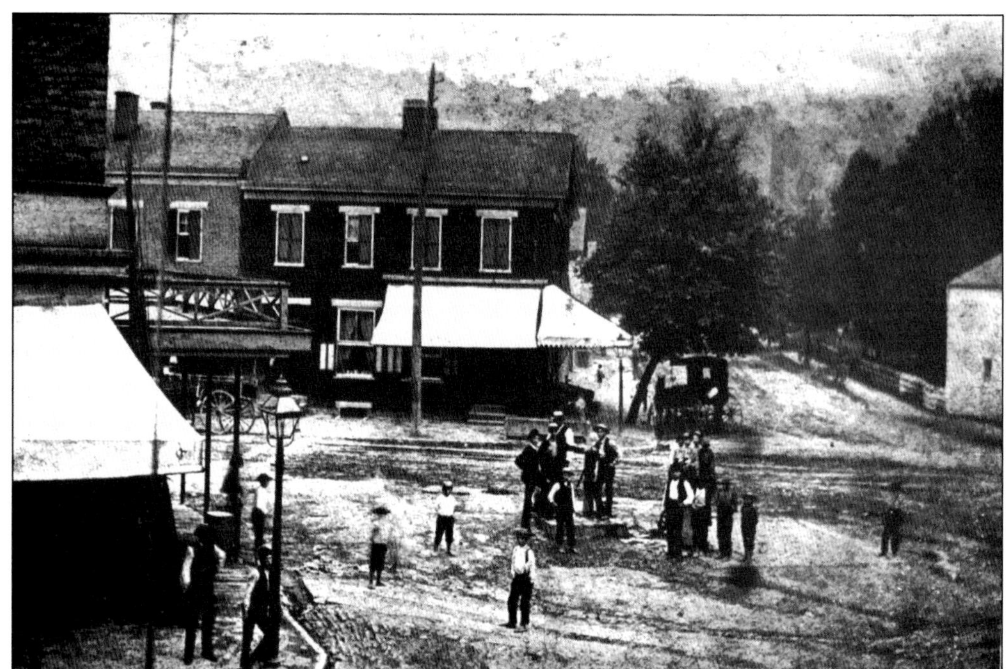

The heart of Northside, shown in this late-1880s photograph, is called Knowton's Corner. It was the intersection of two old Native American trails—St. Clair's Trace, following today's Hamilton Avenue, and Wayne Trace, following Spring Grove Avenue. Both were well traveled by the local Miami and Shawnee Indians and the U.S. Cavalry, who pursued them. The town pump, shown here, dried up when modern sewers were dug in the 1890s for subdivisions.

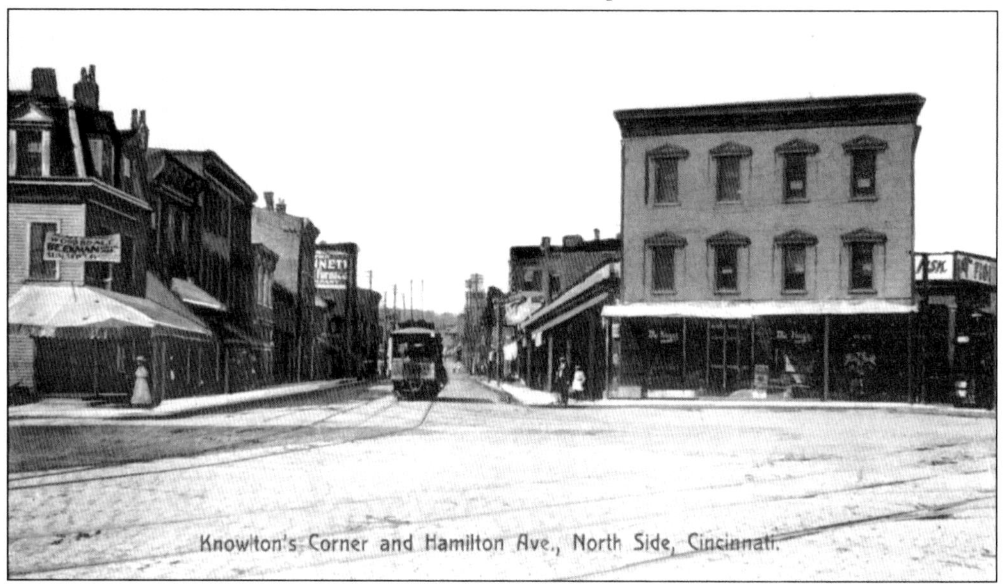

This 1906 photograph shows the view looking north on Hamilton Avenue from Knowlton's Corner. The streetcar on Hamilton Avenue advertises "Home Bake Day at the Cincinnati Zoo." A sign at the left corner building reads "The Last Woodsdale Beekman Mutual Aid Sunday, September 6." In 1982, the City of Cincinnati designated this commercial area a local historic district. (From the Collection of the Public Library of Cincinnati and Hamilton County.)

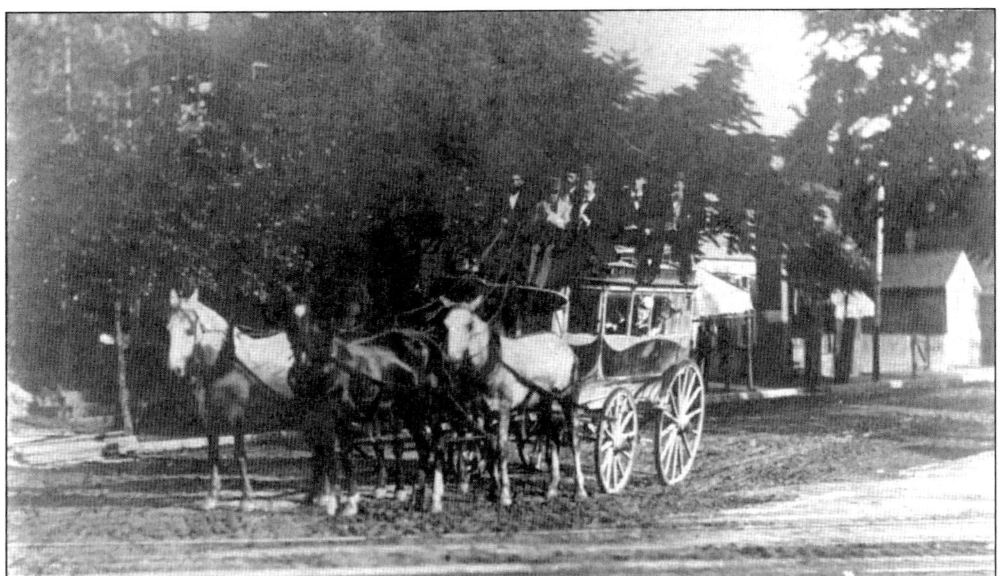

The College Hill Omnibus, owned by Edward Sayre, is shown here in 1872, its inaugural year. It left Knowlton's Corner twice a day at 7:40 a.m. and 5:20 p.m. for a round-trip fare of 40¢. From left to right, the people in this photograph are driver Edward Sayre, Edward Wild, Arthur Upson, Dave Kennedy, two unidentified men, and peering out the windows are Mrs. Josh Pierson and Becky Pierson. (From the Collection of the Public Library of Cincinnati and Hamilton County.)

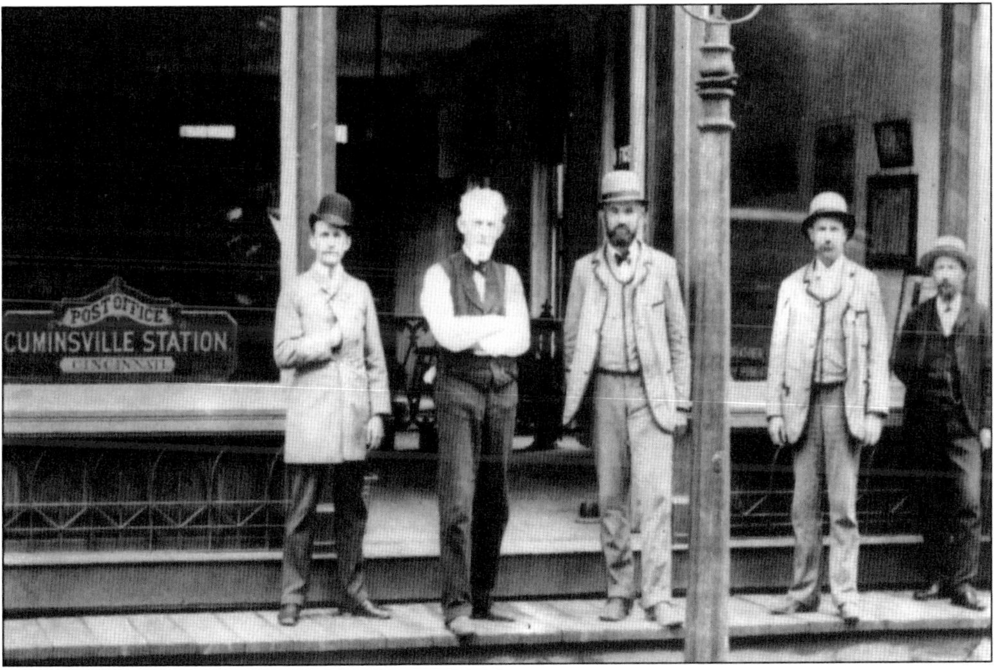

These men in bowler caps guard the Cumminsville Post Office at the Hoffner Masonic Lodge on Hamilton Avenue shortly after its opening in 1885. Note the misspelling of "Cuminsville" in the window. This is the longest continually operating post office in Cincinnati. Ephraim Knowlton, the first postmaster, named this settlement Cumminsville in 1838, after David Cummins, the owner of Grid Iron Tannery. (Courtesy of Don Beimesche.)

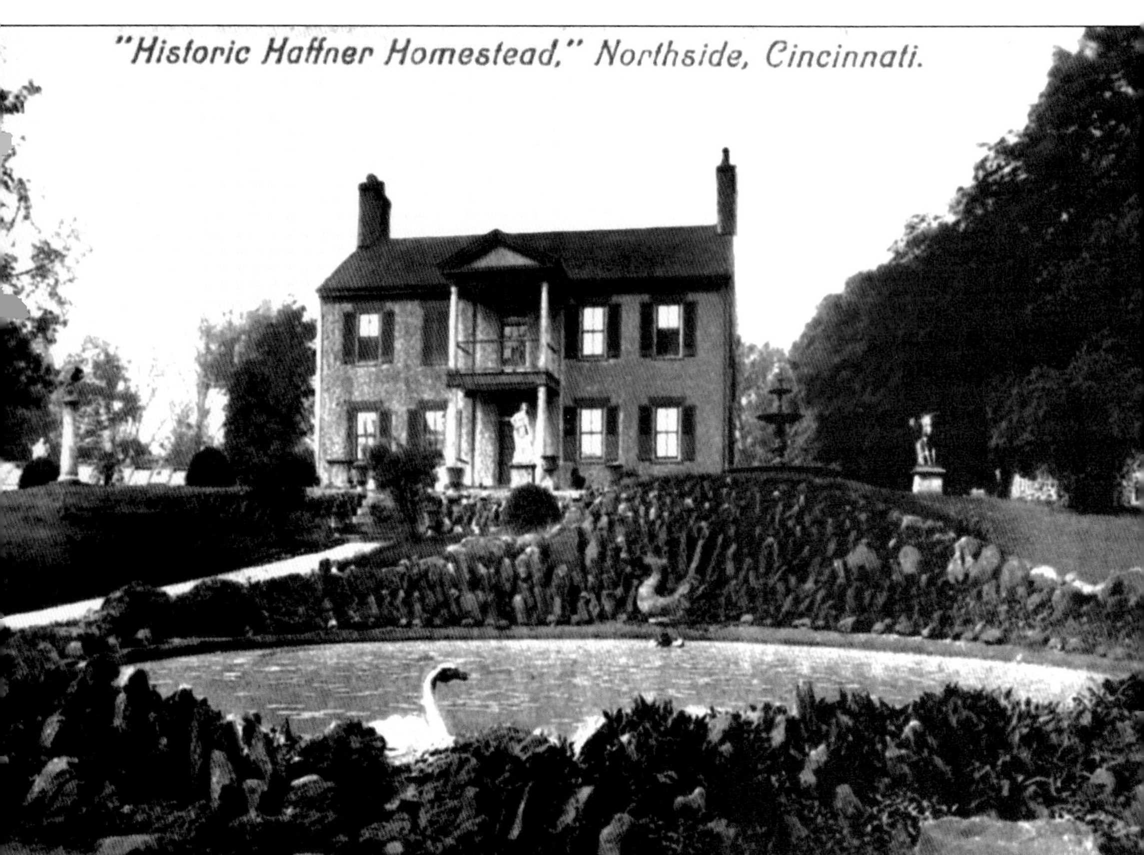

Jacob Hoffner (1799–1894) purchased the Hotel of the Golden Lamb at Blue Rock Street and Hamilton Avenue in 1836. The tavern had been built in 1811 by Ezekiel Hutchinson, and the purchase included the tavern plus 50 acres of farmland. Hoffner lived in Mount Healthy and closely watched the legal squabble between Hutchinson and David Cummins, the tannery owner across Hamilton Avenue from the Hutchinsons, over a shared natural spring. Both Cummins and Hutchinson lost their properties in foreclosure. Hoffner renovated the Golden Lamb into a fantastic estate shown here in about 1900 with six acres of formal gardens that included a greenhouse with bronze griffins, a pool, and more than two dozen statues collected during his travels in Europe. When the property was razed after Hoffner's death, the lions Mic and Mac at the entrance to his estate were donated to the University of Cincinnati, where they guard McMicken Hall, and the stone eagles at the back entrance to his mansion were donated to Eden Park. (From the Collection of the Public Library of Cincinnati and Hamilton County.)

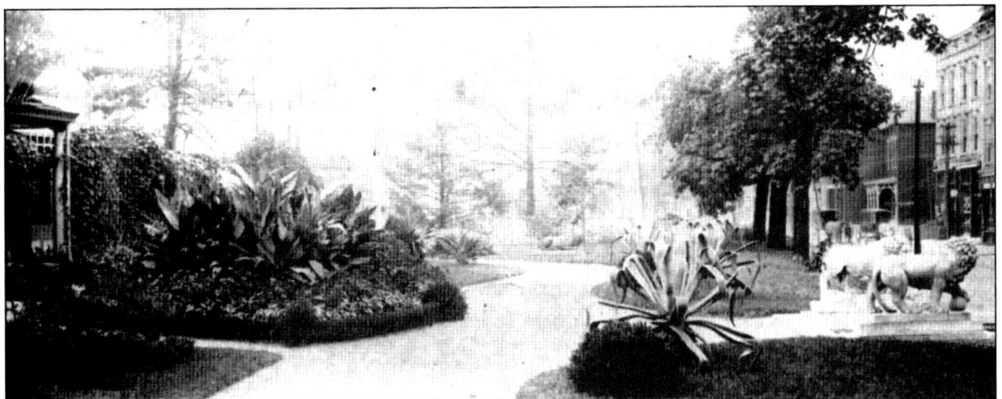

This 1896 photograph of Hoffner's Cumminsville estate, now the Hoffner Playground, shows the statutes of Mic and Mac, who now guard the entrance to the University of Cincinnati's McMicken Hall. The lions were based on the lions standing at the Lonza di Loggia in Milan, Italy. A Cincinnati legend stated the lions growl anytime a virgin passes between them. (Courtesy of Don Beimesche.)

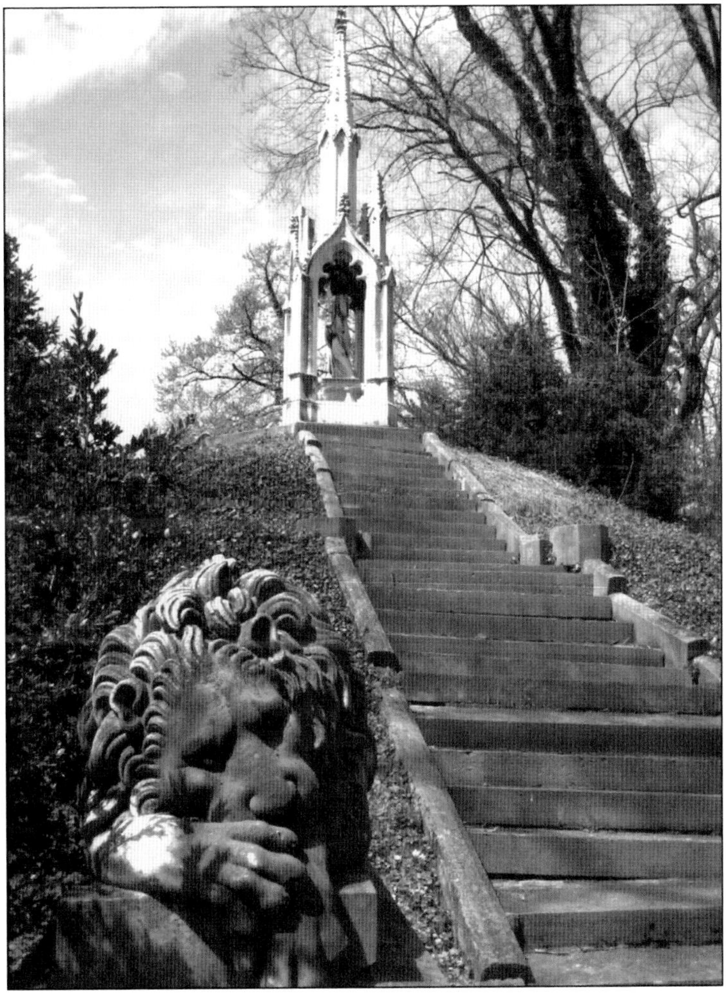

Befitting his great philanthropy, Hoffner's final resting place in Spring Grove Cemetery (section 57, lot 65) graces the highest bluff overlooking Winton Road. The resting lions here mirror the rampant lions that once flanked the entrance to his mansion. The feet of the armless angel at the center of the family monument are adorned with pennies, a tradition of thanks for Hoffner's generosity in Northside.

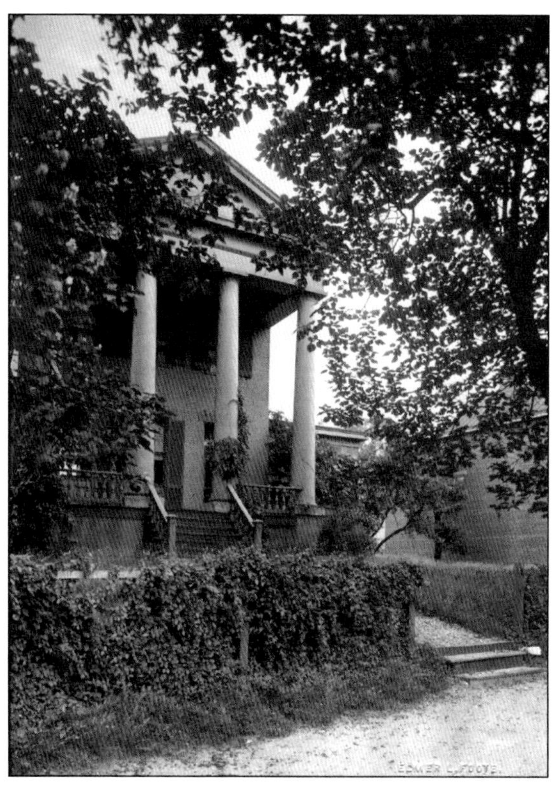

The Willowburn at 1562 Hobart Avenue was built in 1840 by Janet Langland Thomson (1817–1891), daughter of Alexander Langland (1773–1823) and Janet Fergus Langland (1794–1876), early Northsiders. Named for the willow-bordered brook running beside the house, it resembled a Greek temple. Surrounding acreage was divided for homes after the 1880s. The Northside Presbyterian Church purchased Willowburn in 1923, making it their parsonage, but razed it in 1957 for a parking lot. (Courtesy of the Northside Presbyterian Church Archives.)

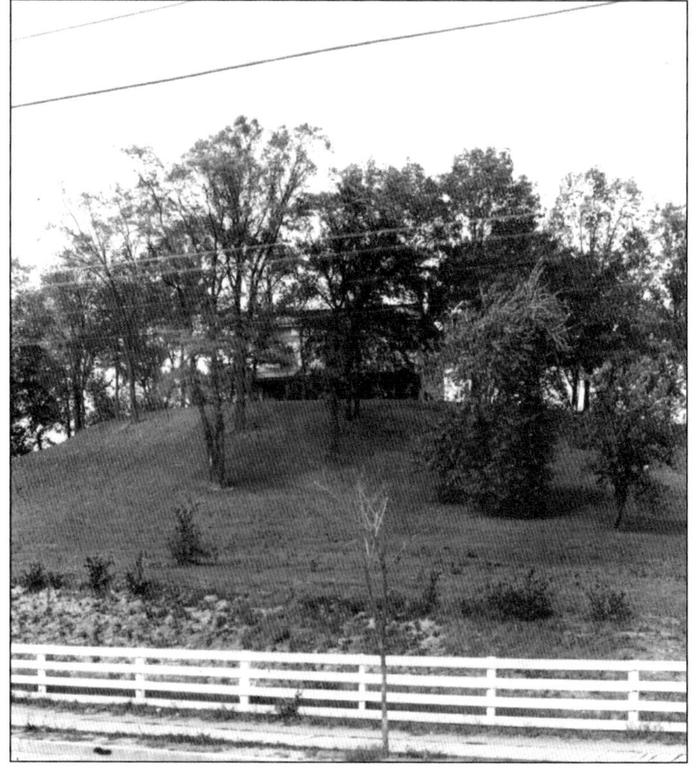

Gen. Henry Blackstone Banning (1834–1881) and his wife Julia Kirby Banning's (1846–1917) home was built in 1843 by Julia's eccentric millionaire father, Timothy Kirby (1797–1876), overlooking Chase Avenue at Gordon Street. Their four children, Timothy (1869–1874), Harry (1870–1944), Ella (1871–1943), and Clinton (1880–1921), never married. Henry served in the Civil War while Julia managed a stagecoach in Northside. (From the Northside Branch of the Public Library of Cincinnati and Hamilton County.)

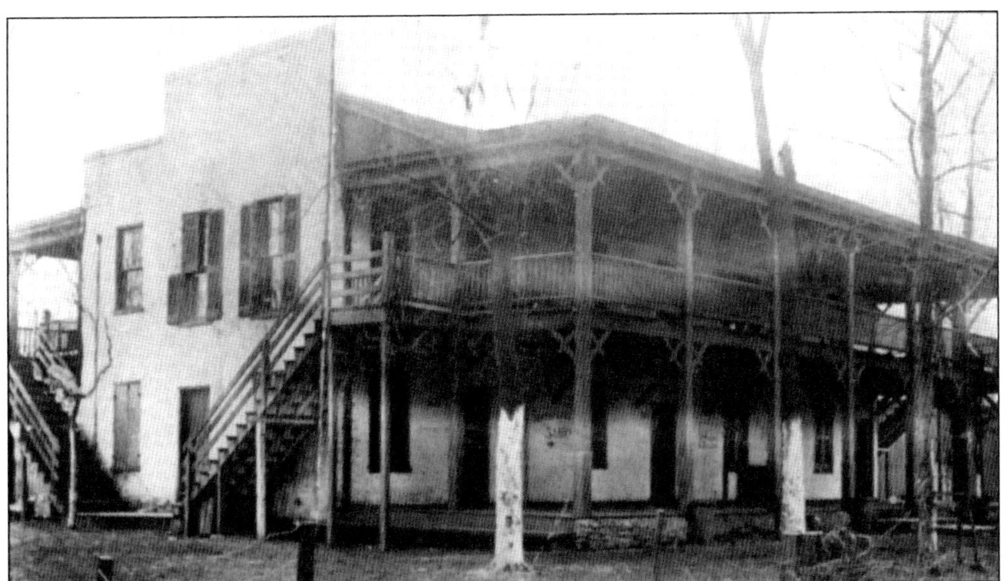

The Millcreek House, built by Ephraim Knowlton (1796–1880) in 1834, was the most notorious roadhouse in Cincinnati. At the corner of Henry Street and Spring Grove Avenue, it held the polls for the presidential election of 1840 and housed Mexican War soldiers. The Cumminsville marshals monitored drunken wrestling matches, cockfights, and relay races outside, while cabaret shows played inside. After years of abandonment, it was razed in 1901.

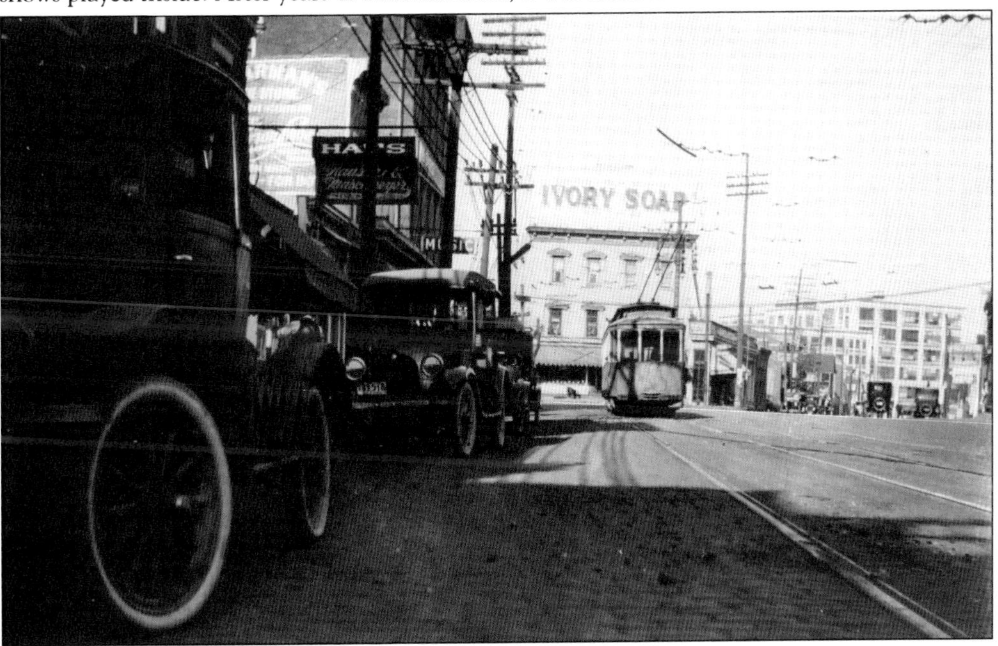

The hustle and bustle of Knowlton's Corner is seen in this 1923 photograph, looking north from Spring Grove Avenue. A streetcar competes with early Model Ts in front of the Hauser and Maschmeyer Menswear store. The American Can building, to the right, had just been built in 1921. The first story of the Knowlton Blockhouse advertises Drs. Judge and Morris, dentists, and an Ivory soap billboard rests on the third story. (Courtesy of the Cincinnati Museum Center–Cincinnati Historical Society Library.)

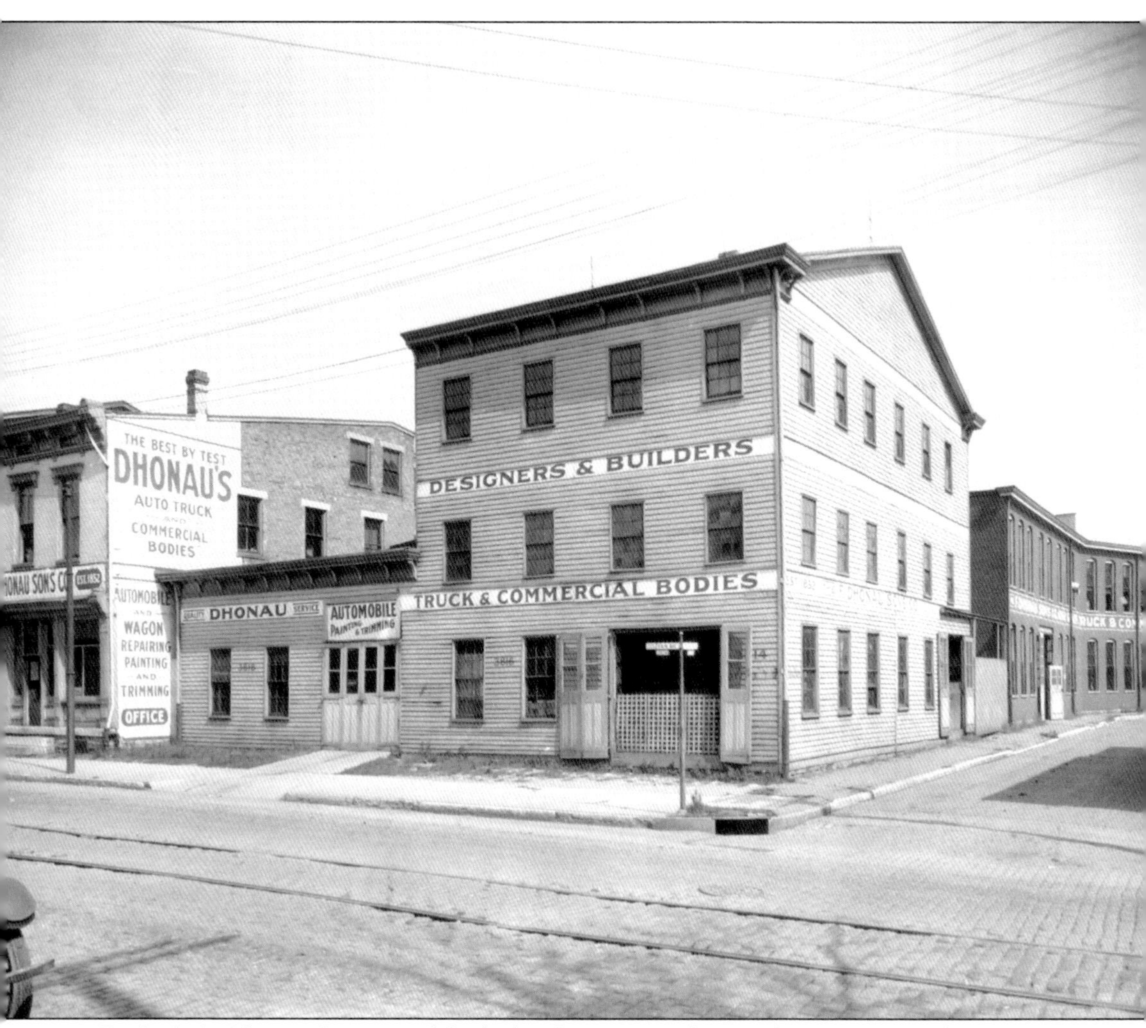

Fredrick A. Dhonau (1829–1903) built this factory complex on the corner of Colerain Avenue and Elmore Street, formerly Dhonau Street, for his carriage manufacturing business. Dhonau emigrated from Soberheim, Germany, to Cincinnati in 1849, arriving in Northside in 1852. He purchased the carriage-making business of William Tozzer and Joseph Lakeman, mayor of Cumminsville from 1869 to 1871, at the same location, who had started making wagons for the U.S. Army during the Mexican War. Fred and his wife, Caroline Eiserman (1832–1907), had 10 children at the family home on 1624 Dhonau Street, nestled within this complex. Fred built the reputation of being the best carriage maker in greater Cincinnati. When he died in 1903, his son Fredrick Jr. (1853–1932), took over the business, expanding into rubber tires, casings, auto bodies, and becoming a sales agent for the Studebaker Company in 1905. Fred G. W. Dhonau (1876–1916), the third generation, took over the business until he was killed, oddly enough, in an automobile accident. In 1921, Powell Crosley Jr. bought the Dhonau facility to build his Marion brand phonograph cases. (Courtesy of Clyde Haehnle.)

Two

Abolitionism and Activism

The Mill Creek valley that runs through Northside was a very well-used escape route for slaves coming across the Ohio River into free territory. It allowed a safe and discreet path to the safe houses in North College Hill, where they could replenish and gain needed supplies for a long journey to Canada. The Northside churches were very sympathetic to abolitionism and aided in these groups' escapes. In the 1830s, the Hall of Free Discussion, near where Dane and Spring Grove Avenues meet, harbored the Lane Rebels, an abolitionist group that was thrown out of Lane Seminary for its strong antislavery debates and went on to Oberlein College. The hall sponsored antislavery debates. The group considered starting an abolitionist commune in Cumminsville based on silk production because of the large groves of mulberry trees in the area. During the Civil War, the a group of women from the Northside Presbyterian Church helped former slaves establish their own congregation in the Northside area by helping to form the First Baptist Church of Cumminsville. As the civil unrest created by segregation began to rise, this strong church community in South Cumminsville was very active in fighting for their rights. Alvina Montgomery (1909–2007) was a strong neighborhood activist and a lifelong member of the Cumminsville Baptist Church. In 1946, she canvassed the South Cumminsville neighborhood for signatures to allow for integration of African American children at Garfield Pool and Wayne Playground and all city recreation parks. She petitioned the city council until she succeeded. "Ms. M" started the Cumminsville Baptist Children's Choir, which eventually became the National Gospel Choir Union, and was given the key to the city of Cincinnati in 1994 by Mayor Roxanne Qualls for her activism. Even today, Northside continues to be a very civic minded and close-knit community.

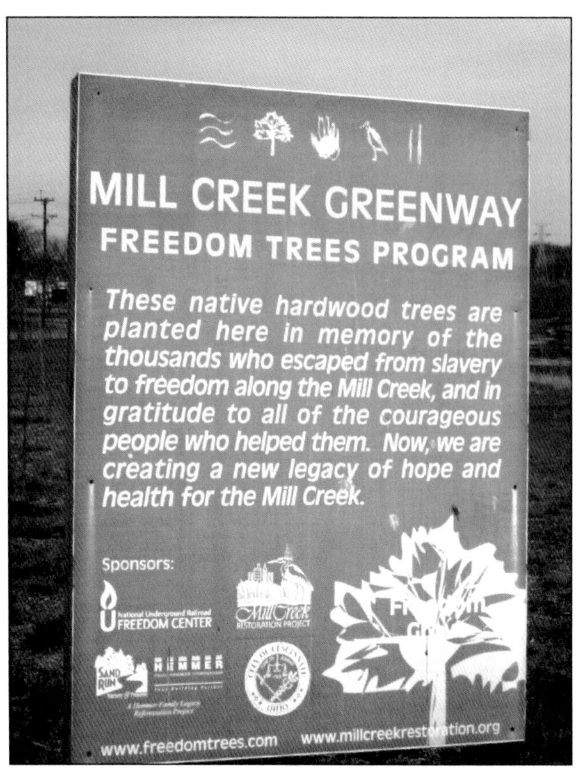

This Freedom Grove sign commemorates the plight of runaway slaves who used Northside's Mill Creek valley as an escape path. The Hall of Free Discussion was built near here by James C. Ludlow, son of Israel Ludlow. Originally it was a meeting place for several liberal Protestant groups, allowing discussion of controversial subjects. Oddly enough, it had separate men's and women's entrances. In 1834, it housed the abolitionist group called the Lane Rebels.

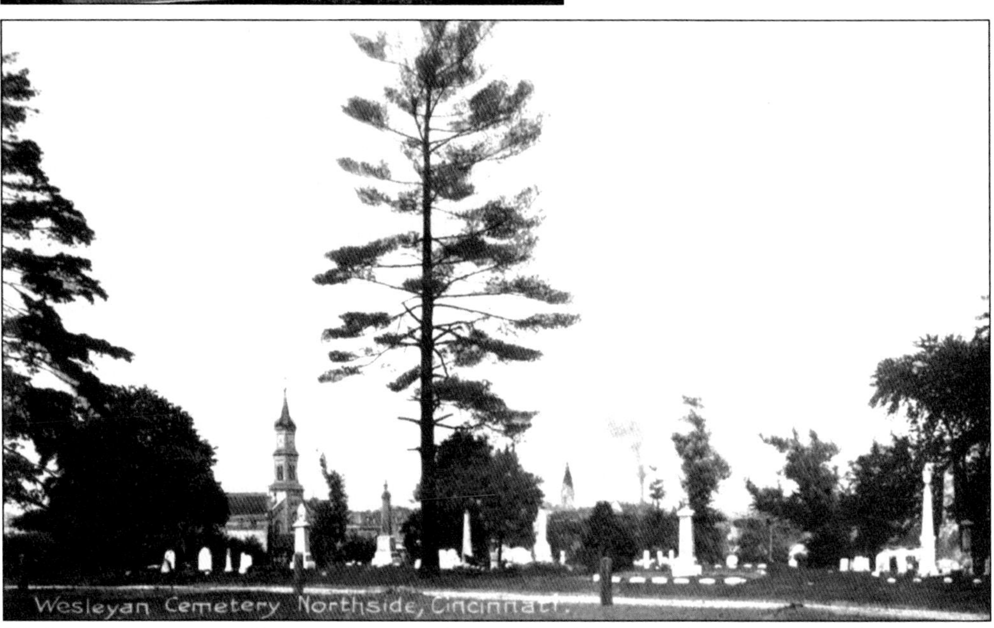

Wesleyan Cemetery on Colerain Avenue, chartered in 1843, was the first integrated cemetery in Cincinnati. A group of runaway slaves known as the Cincinnati 28, aided by Levi Coffin in the late 1840s, staged a mock funeral procession from the Ohio River to the cemetery. They then used the Mill Creek to escape to a safe house in College Hill and on to freedom in Canada. Buried at Wesleyan Cemetery are veterans from all congressionally mandated wars. (From the Collection of the Public Library of Cincinnati and Hamilton County.)

Peter Farley Fossett (1815–1901) was the founder and pastor of the Cumminsville Baptist Church on Streng Street from 1870 until 1901. He was a former slave of Pres. Thomas Jefferson at Monticello. Peter's father, Joseph Fossett (1780–1858), was one of only five of Jefferson's slaves freed in his will, because he was said to be the son of Jefferson and his slave Mary Hemings (1753 to about 1834). Joseph eventually purchased the freedom of his entire family. (Courtesy of Lucia Stanton Shannon, senior historian at Monticello National Monument.)

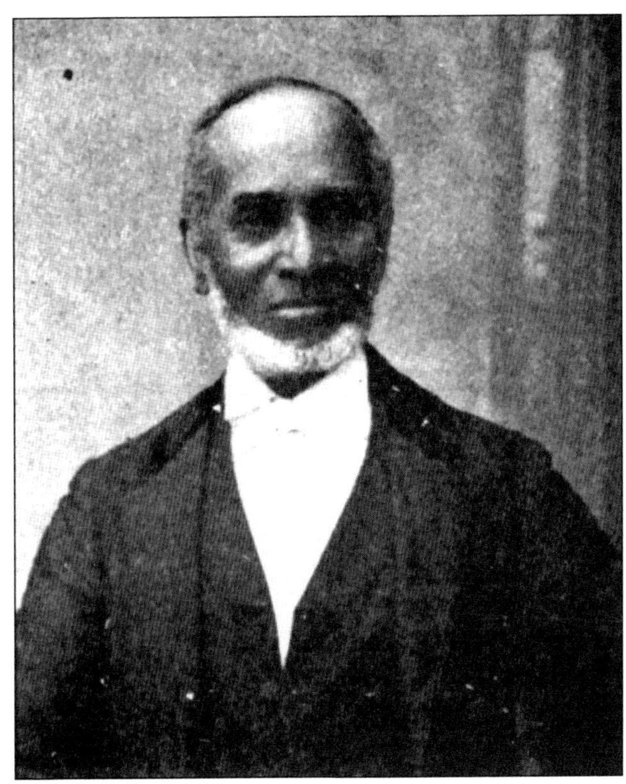

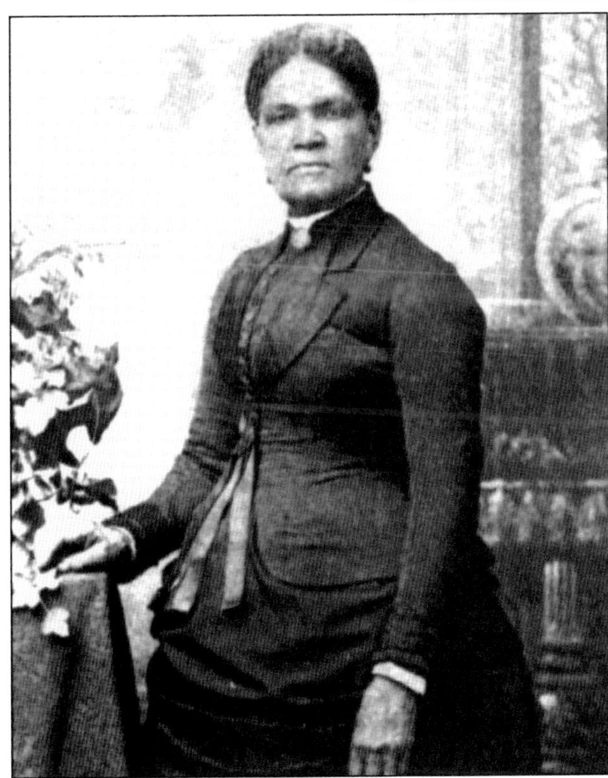

Sarah Mayrant Fossett (1826–1906) was a New Orleans–trained hairstylist before marrying Peter in 1854 in Cincinnati. She supported his Baptist ministry and in 1860, with help from her wealthy clients, sued a Cincinnati streetcar company after a conductor prevented her from boarding, dragging her over a city block. This set a precedent allowing African American women, and eventually men, to ride the streetcars, unique in the country. (Courtesy of Lucia Stanton Shannon, senior historian at Monticello National Monument.)

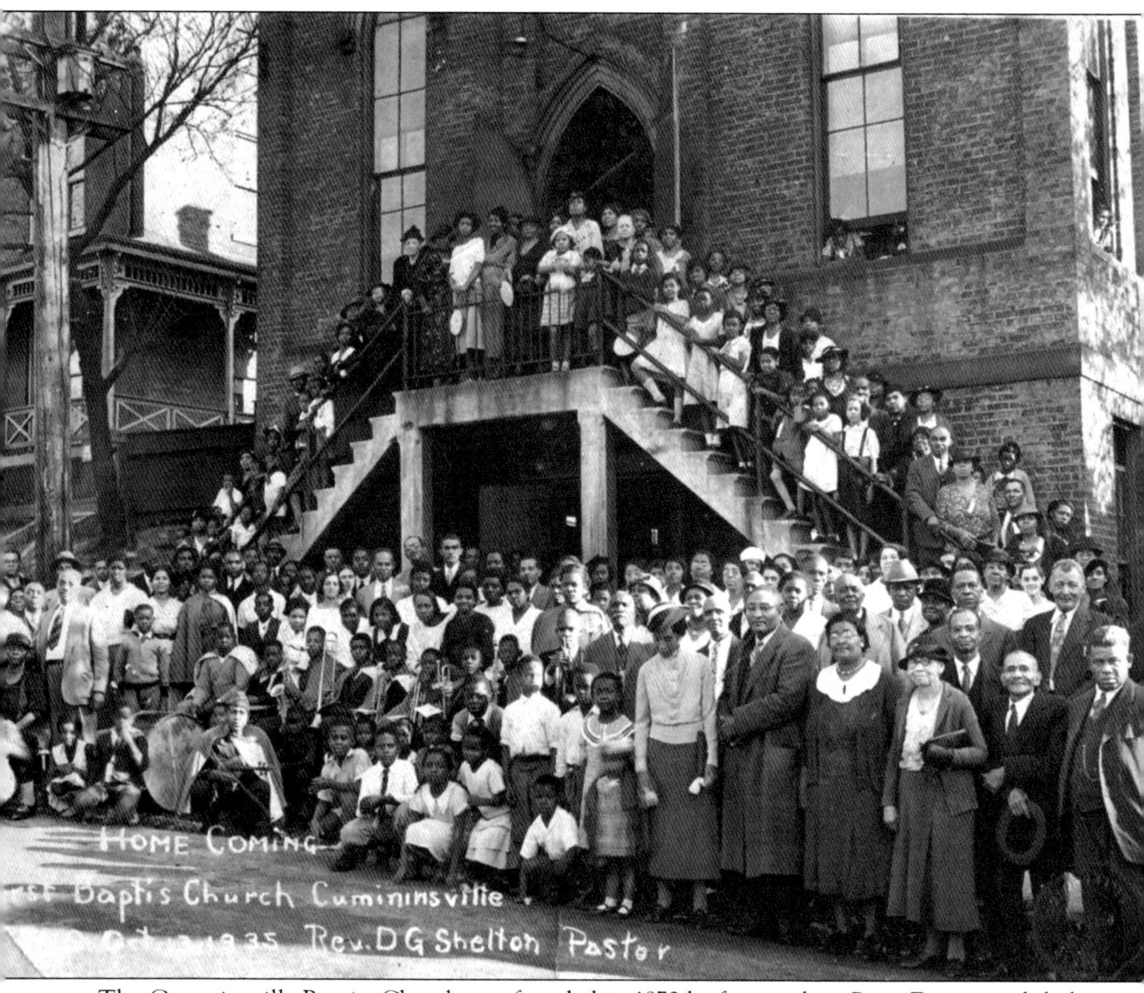

The Cumminsville Baptist Church was founded in 1870 by former slave Peter Fossett with help from a small group from the Northside Presbyterian Church. The church was built in 1878 near the canal at Streng Street on the Clifton side of the Ludlow Avenue Viaduct. This 1935 photograph shows a homecoming in front of the original church on Streng Street. The church was built above grade because of the flooding in the area and was a place of refuge for members during the 1937 flood. It was the first African American church in Cincinnati to be built with their own labor and financing. In the 1950s, the church was purchased by the City of Cincinnati to make way for Interstate 75. A new building was built in 1955 under Rev. Nick Samuels at its current location at 3640 Roll Avenue in South Cumminsville. Throughout its nearly 140-year history, the church has been known for its community involvement and civic activism. (Courtesy of Alice Martha Bun Fletcher.)

Three

NORTHSIDE FLOODS

Northside's proximity to the Mill Creek, a tributary of the Ohio River, was both a blessing and a curse. It provided power for early mills and industry and provided a source of food and livelihood for many early settlers. Those living in the lowest areas, however, dealt with floods nearly every spring. The most devastating of recorded floods was the January 1937 flood, which crested at 80 feet and lasted 18 days, but there were several floods nearly as destructive. Other years where the Ohio River flood stage of 52 feet occurred were January 22, 1862 (58 feet, Spring Grove Avenue was under 4 feet of water); February 15, 1883 (66.3 feet); February 14, 1884 (71.1 feet); March 29, 1897 (62 feet); 1898 (61.4 feet); 1907 (65.2 feet); January 14, 1913 (62.2 feet); April 1, 1913 (69.9 feet); February 12, 1918 (61.8 feet); 1927; March 21, 1933 (61.5 feet); 1936 (59.5 feet); two in 1939; 1940; 1943; and March 7, 1945 (69.2 feet). A sad fact was that the Mill Creek Dam was under construction during the great 1937 flood, whose completion would have saved Northside from the terrible devastation of those waters.

Northsiders dealt with the aftereffects of the 1937 flood in many ways. When wealthy Northsiders had business safes flooded and keys lost, master lock breaker George Stortz came to the rescue for weeks breaking safes. Local grocers did not throw out the cans that had been flooded. Owners sold cans without labels at half price, and housewives would open a can and plan the meal around the surprise within.

Adding to the tragedy of the 1937 flood was a huge fire that started on January 24, 1937, from gas storage tanks that overturned and caught fire in Northside. Called the Black Sunday fire, it burned for 48 hours and took more than 12 hours to tame. Over three and a half square miles burned, 10 factories (including the Crosley factory), and numerous homes, causing an estimated $1.5 million in damages.

Some businesses affected by the floods stayed and rebuilt, and others moved further up Hamilton Avenue and away from the lower Spring Grove Avenue districts. Thankfully the 1937 flood instigated the modern Mill Creek basin redesign to prevent further flooding.

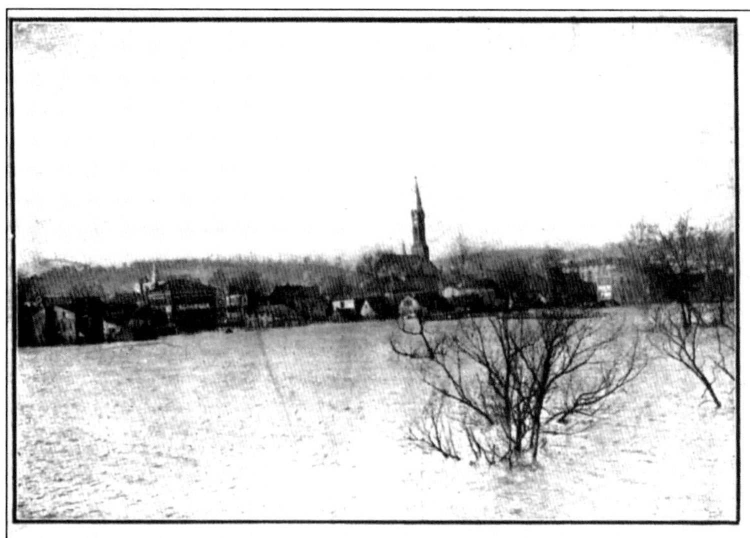

THE FLOOD AT CINCINNATI, OHIO.,
JANUARY 21. 1907. 65 FEET HIGH.
SCENE IN CUMMINSVILLE.
4 MILES FROM THE RIVER.

This photograph shows the 1907 flood on January 21, when the waters were at 65 feet. The line of the horizon follows Spring Grove Avenue and intersects Hamilton Avenue at Knowlton's Corner to the left of the photograph. (From the Collection of the Public Library of Cincinnati and Hamilton County.)

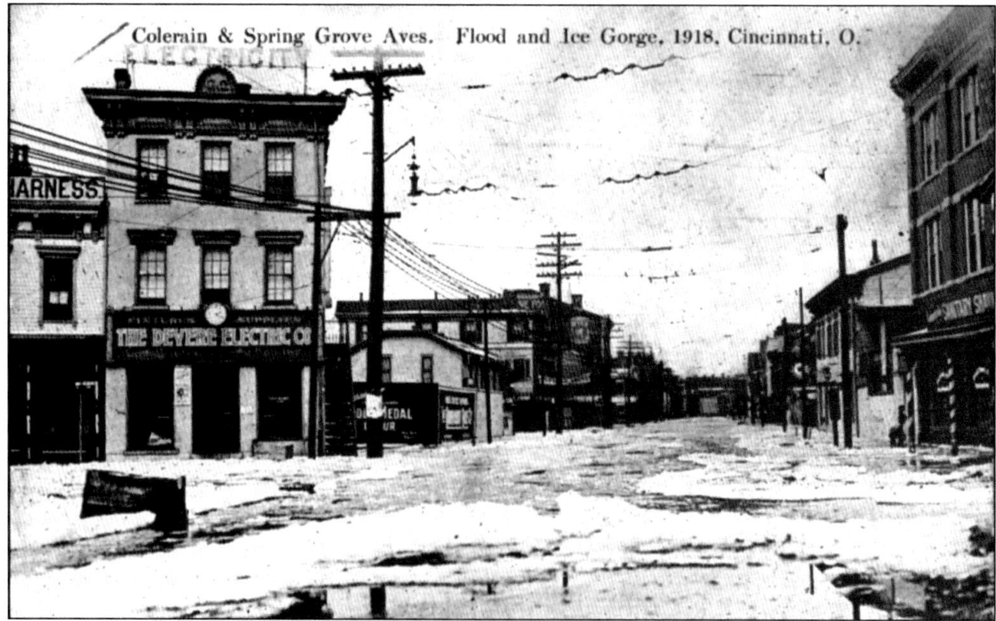

The problem with early spring floods was their potential for freezing. This 1918 flood photograph shows the ice gorge at Colerain and Spring Grove Avenues. The ice gorges floating in the frigid floodwaters sometimes caused as much damage as the flood itself. (From the Collection of the Public Library of Cincinnati and Hamilton County.)

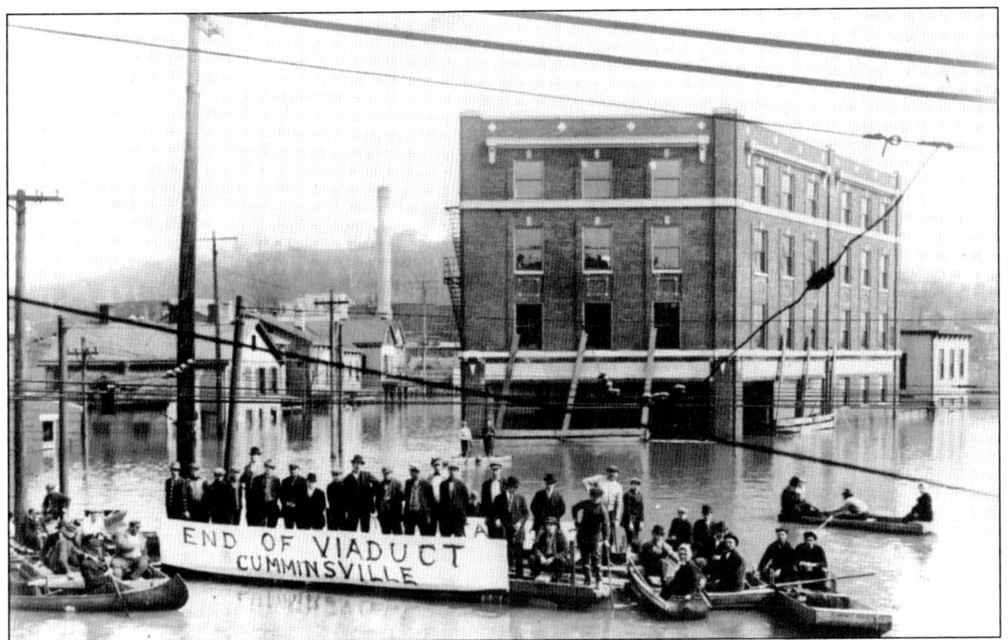

The helpers of the 1913 flood show the deepest depth, at the end of the newly completed Ludlow Avenue Viaduct at Cumminsville. The rescue teams float in their canoes over what now is occupied by a White Castle Hamburgers. At the time, the building behind the workers still housed the Herbert Furniture Showroom, which was newly built that year. (Photograph by Randolph Photographers, from the Mrs. George Schoettle Archives at the Northside Branch of the Public Library of Cincinnati and Hamilton County.)

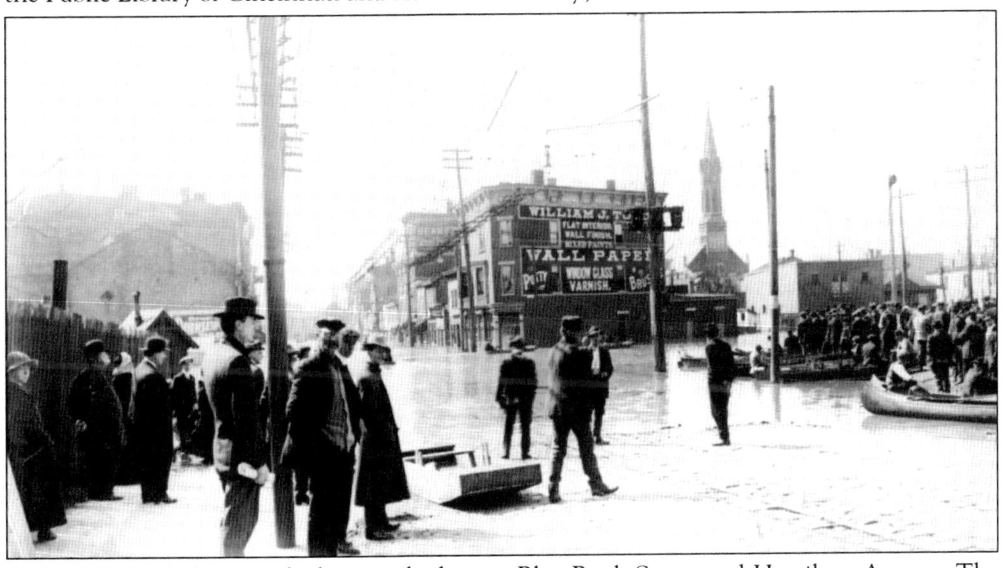

This 1913 flood photograph shows onlookers at Blue Rock Street and Hamilton Avenue. The corner flatiron building on the right was home to the interior decorating business of William J. Todd, who furnished the newly built, grand homes of Northside. The bank of rescue canoes and workers are ready to row into the floodwaters to the right. (Photograph by Randolph Photographers, from the Mrs. George Schoettle Archives at the Northside Branch of the Public Library of Cincinnati and Hamilton County.)

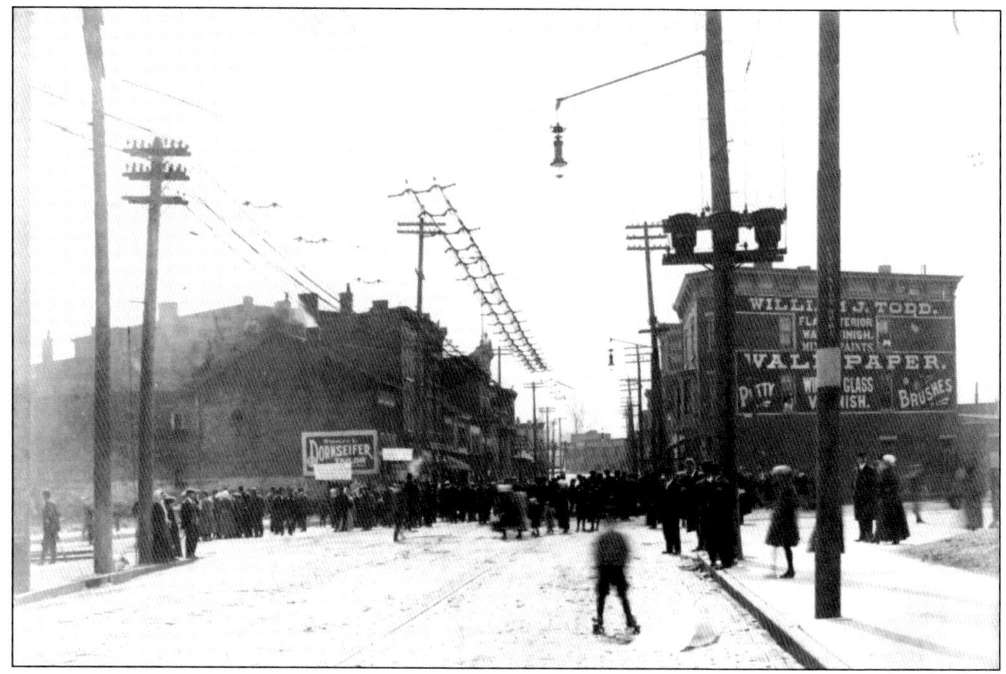

A boy roller-skates into this 1913 flood photograph at the corner of Blue Rock Street and Hamilton Avenue. The sign on the left advertises Stanley L. Dornseifer Tailors at 4046 Hamilton Avenue, now housing Shoetopia. Stanley Dornseifer (1885–1927) started his business in 1908. His uncle Louis E. Dornseifer (1862–1934) operated a jewelry store at 4012 Hamilton. (Photograph by Randolph Photographers, from the Mrs. George Schoettle Archives at the Northside Branch of the Public Library of Cincinnati and Hamilton County.)

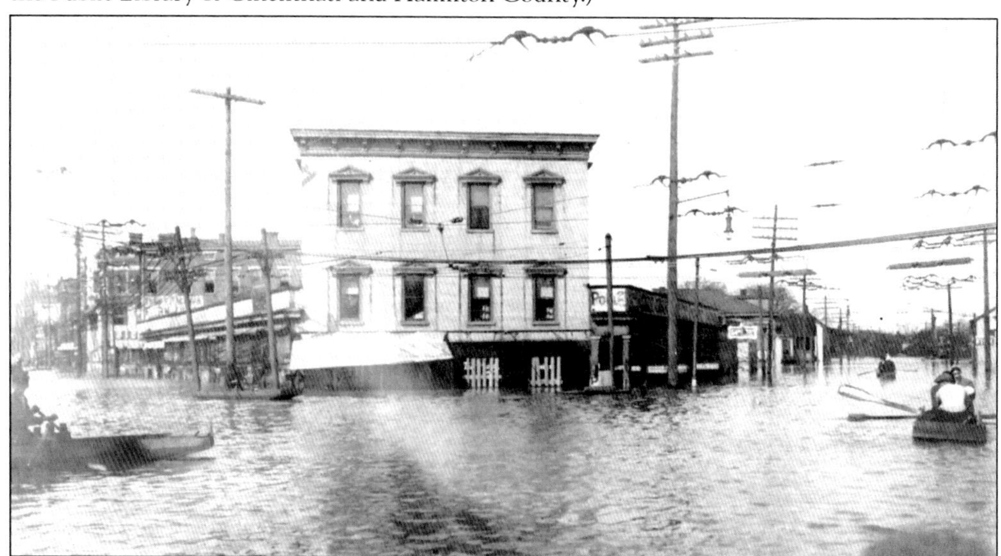

Knowton's blockhouse was nearly 70 years old by the time the 1913 flood submerged its first floor, making Knowlton's Corner look like the canals of Venice. A few years later, an Ivory soap billboard was added over the old stone store, which did not survive the 1937 flood and was razed shortly thereafter. (Photograph by Randolph Photographers, from the Mrs. George Schoettle Archives at the Northside Branch of the Public Library of Cincinnati and Hamilton County.)

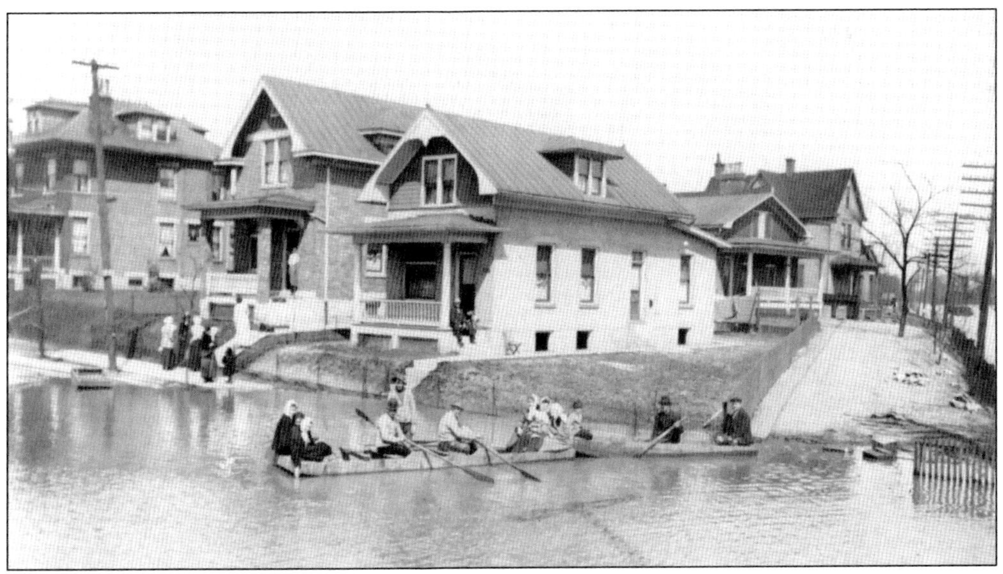

These two loaded canoes of Northsiders seem to be taking a joyride in the 1913 flood, rather than being on a rescue mission. The expression of the older gentleman on the front porch with his dog seems to lament yet another spring flood in Northside. (Photograph by Randolph Photographers, from the Mrs. George Schoettle Archives at the Northside Branch of the Public Library of Cincinnati and Hamilton County.)

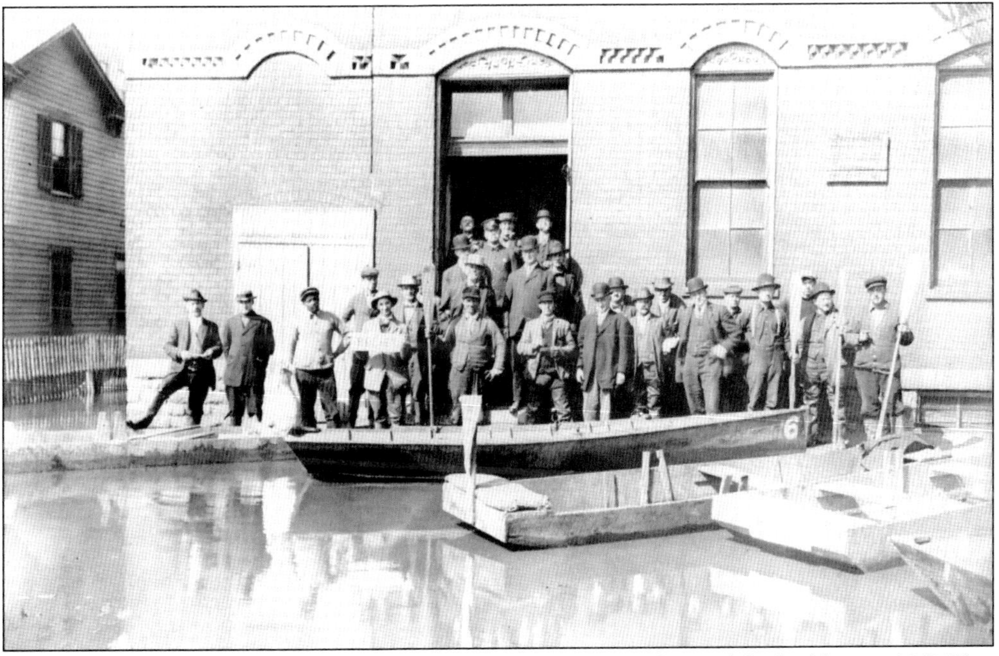

This photograph shows a group of 1913 flood rescue workers in front of the building at 1649 Blue Rock and Turrill Streets. Northside District 10 police lieutenant William Heheman is in the doorway. Heheman became a Cincinnati police officer in 1883 and served Northside's District 10 as police lieutenant from the late 1880s into the 1920s. (Photograph by Randolph Photographers, from the Mrs. George Schoettle Archives at the Northside Branch of the Public Library of Cincinnati and Hamilton County.)

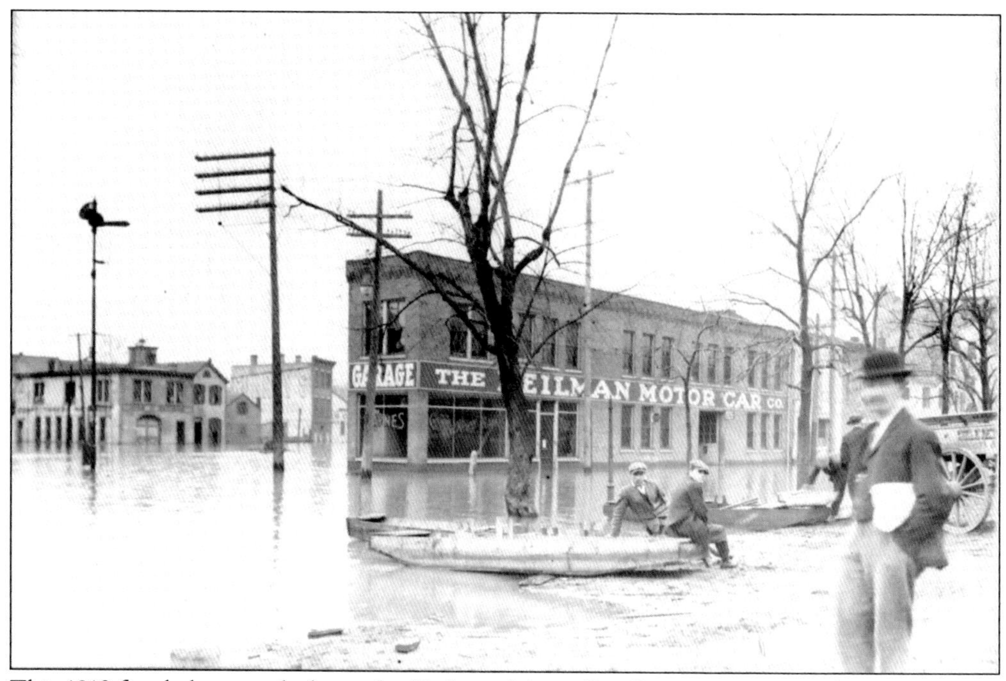

This 1913 flood photograph shows the Heilman Motor Car Company at 1601 Blue Rock Street. John C. Heilman built the first gasoline-powered automobile in Cincinnati in 1901 and built this building in 1911 as a repair garage and showroom to sell the Haynes and Regal line of cars. In 1917, Powell Crosley Jr. purchased the building for his American Automobile Accessories Company. (Photograph by Randolph Photographers, from the Mrs. George Schoettle Archives at the Northside Branch of the Public Library of Cincinnati and Hamilton County.)

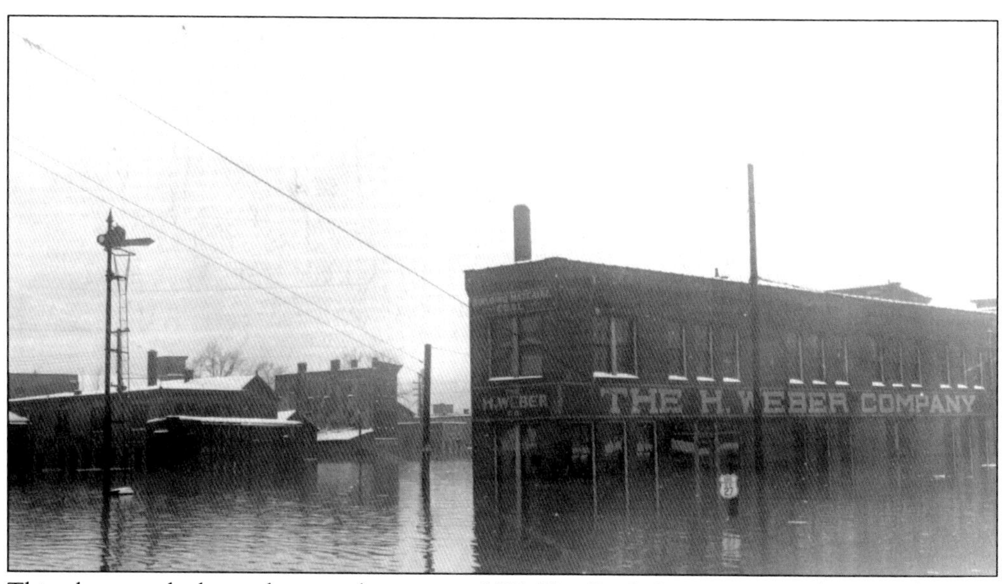

This photograph shows the same location at 1601 Blue Rock Street 24 years later, in the 1937 flood, then occupied by the H. Weber Company. It now houses the business of Ace Doran. (From the Mrs. William Armond Archives at the Northside Branch of the Public Library of Cincinnati and Hamilton County.)

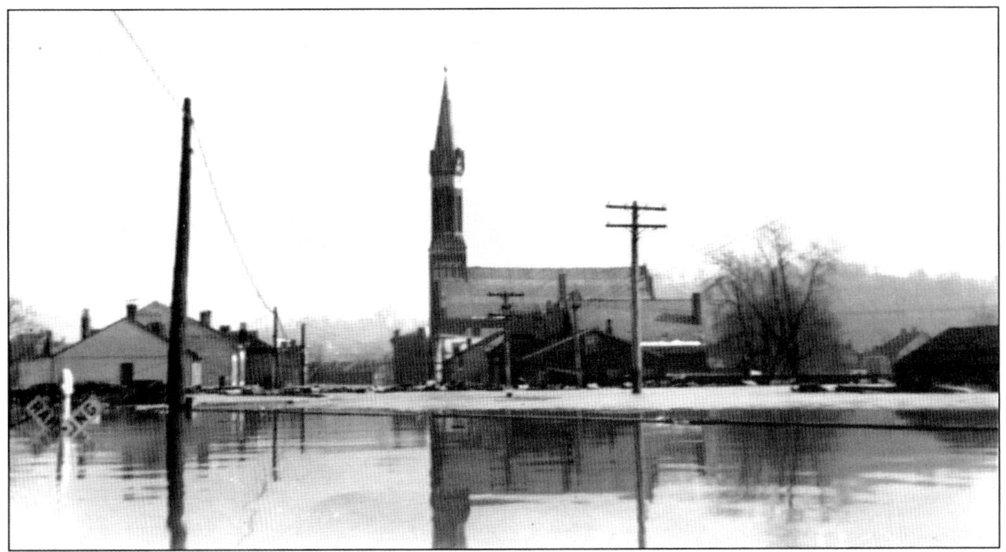

This photograph shows Hoffner Street looking from the railroad tracks toward Knowlton's Corner with the spire of the Hoffner Street German Evangelical Church. Construction of a new gymnasium for the church had begun in August 1936 and was nearly complete when the flood hit in 1937. Damage was repaired and the gymnasium was dedicated in August 1937. (Courtesy of the Northside Presbyterian Church.)

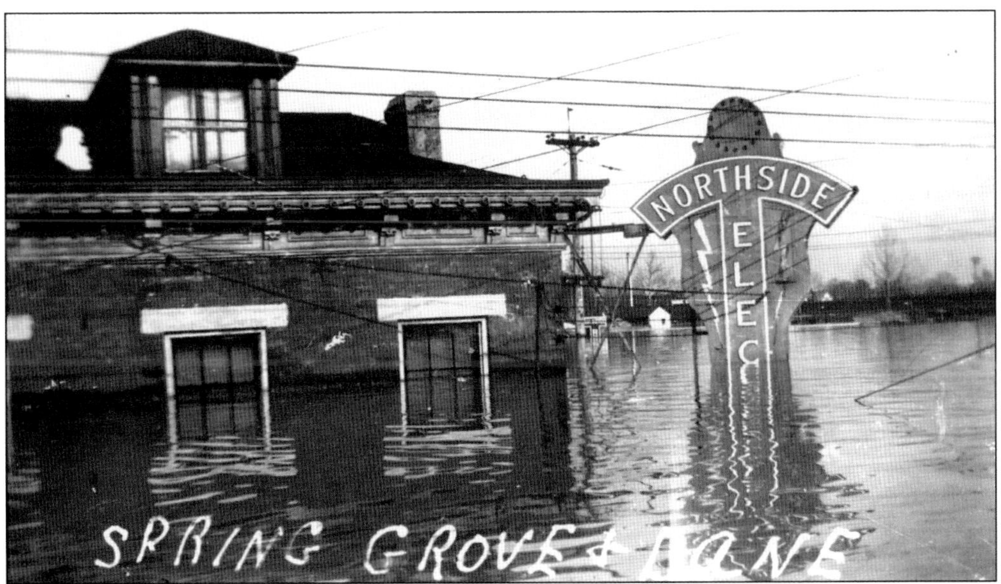

The 1937 floodwaters almost completely submerged the second story of the Northside Electric building at the corner of Spring Grove Avenue and Dane Street. In the 1940s, this building housed Alber's Café and now is home to one of Northside's best venues for live local music, the Gypsy Hut. (Courtesy of the Cincinnati Museum Center–Cincinnati Historical Society Library.)

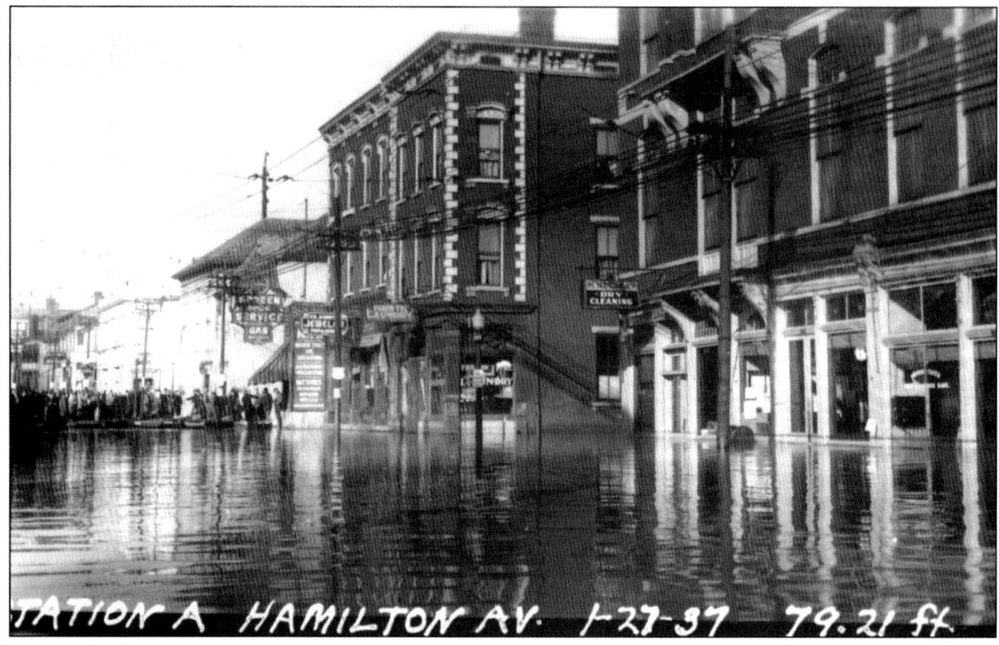

This 1937 flood photograph looks north on Hamilton Avenue on January 21, when the waters had nearly crested at 79.21 feet. The Hoffner Lodge storefront housed Hulbert's Dry Cleaners. Sam Yee Laundry, Ed Schmitt Jewelry, Schneider's Shoe Repair, and Spreen Automotive Parts have since been demolished for a small park. (From the Mrs. William Armond Archives at the Northside Branch of the Public Library of Cincinnati and Hamilton County.)

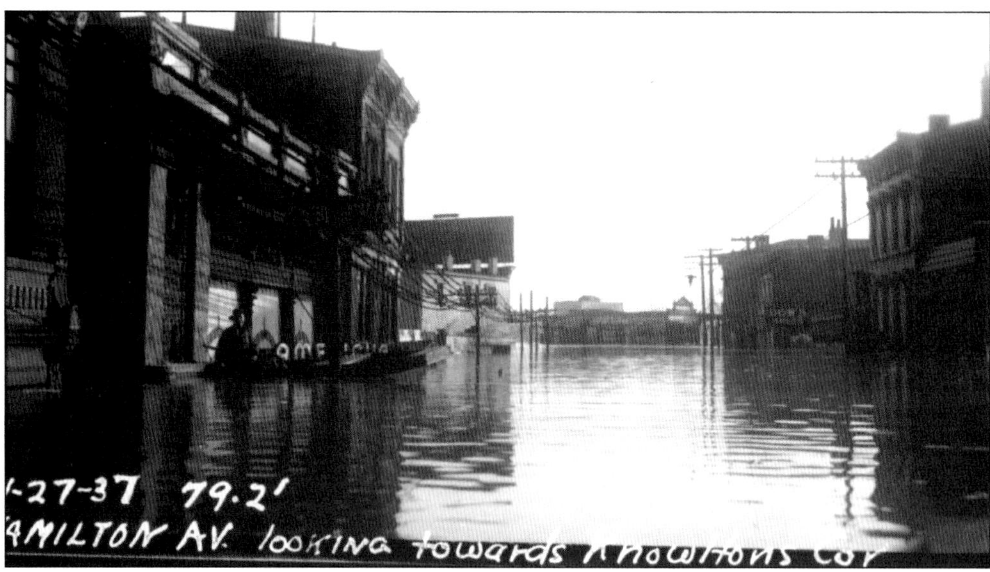

This view of the 1937 flood, looking south on Hamilton Avenue, shows an unidentified rower at the level of the Americus Theatre sign. In the distance, the wall of Siewarts Café building at the Ludlow Avenue Viaduct advertises Red Top Ale and Mergard's Bowling Alleys at Knowlton Street. (From the Mrs. William Armond Archives at the Northside Branch of the Public Library of Cincinnati and Hamilton County.)

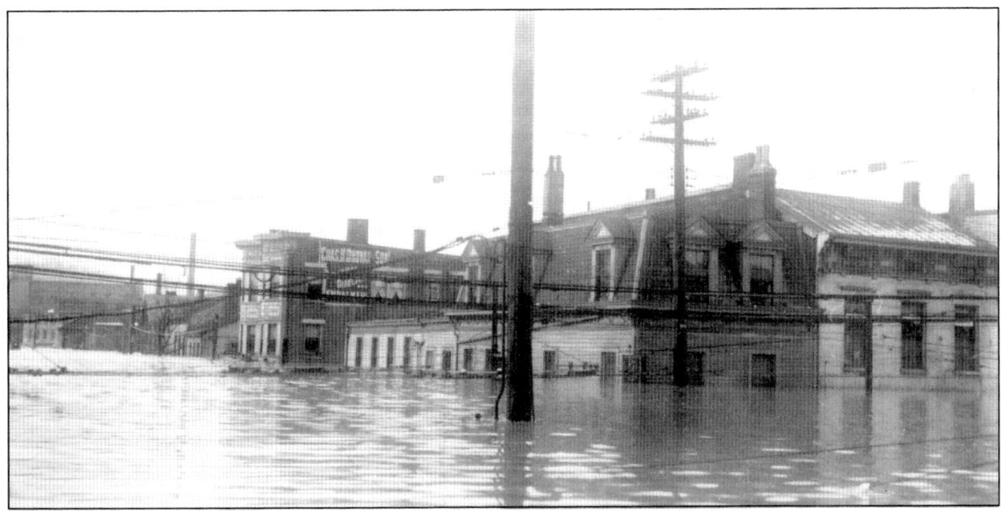

A view of the 1937 flood, looking west along Hoffner Street, shows water levels at the second stories of the buildings and shows the painted advertisement on the side of the Dhonau Funeral Parlors building reading "Charles H. Dhonau & Sons Funeral Directors and Embalmers." (From the Mrs. William Armond Archives at the Northside Branch of the Public Library of Cincinnati and Hamilton County.)

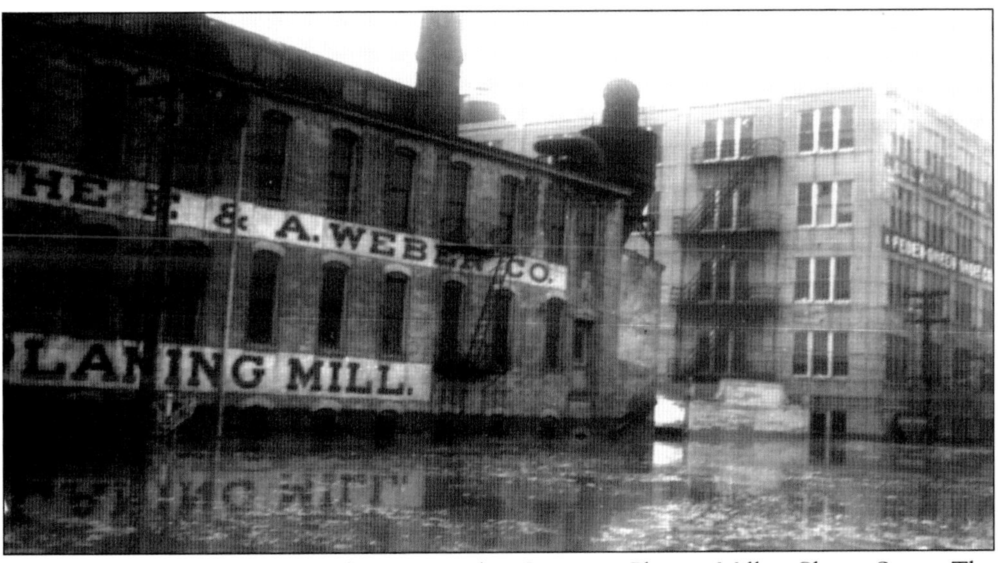

This photograph of 1937 shows the E&A Weber Company Planing Mill at Cherry Street. The Weber brothers got started by building three concrete buildings in Northside, for the Schieffele, Helming-McKenzie, and Wilson Shoe Companies. They went on to build the beautiful Queen Anne homes on the east side of Delaney Street and built their own twin homes at 1675 and 1679 Chase Avenue. (From the Mrs. William Armond Archives at the Northside Branch of the Public Library of Cincinnati and Hamilton County.)

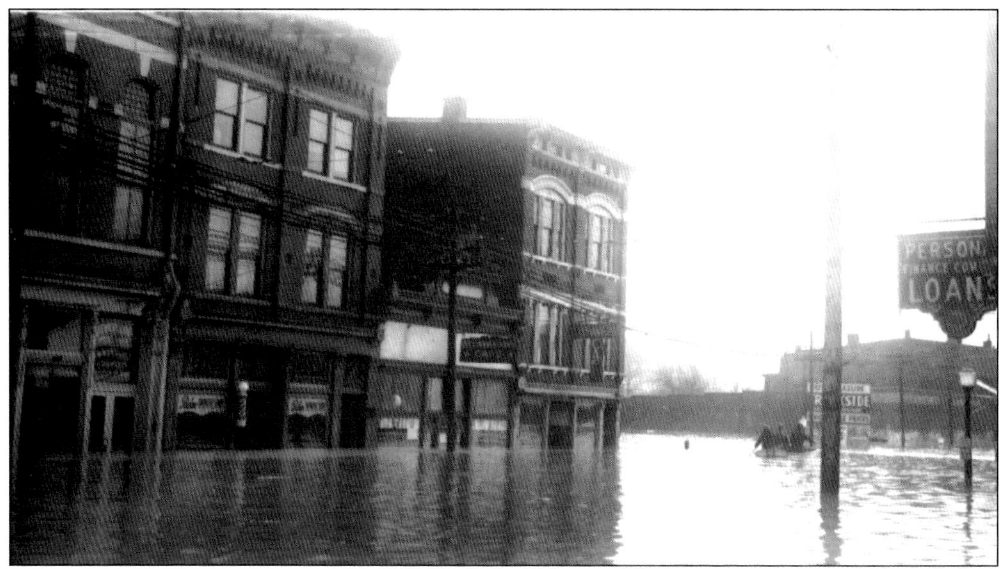

This photograph shows a view of the 1937 flood on January 25, looking south on Hamilton Avenue toward the intersection of Blue Rock Street. The buildings are, from left to right, the Hoffner Lodge, the Palm Barber Shop, the Dillman Brothers Café, now the Blue Rock Tavern, and the Amber Tavern. (From the Mrs. William Armond Archives at the Northside Branch of the Public Library of Cincinnati and Hamilton County.)

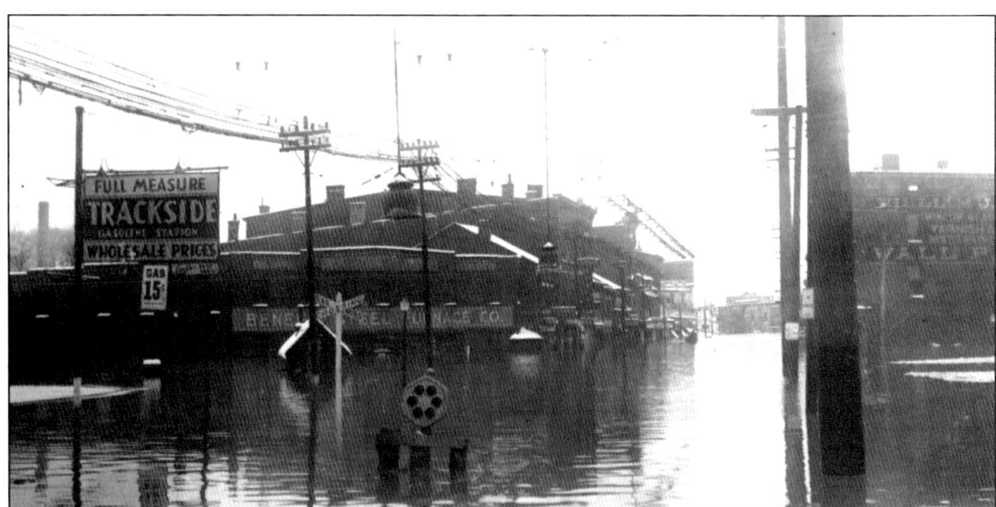

This 1937 flood photograph shows the Benefit Steel Furnace Company at 4048 Hamilton Avenue at Blue Rock Street, now housing Slim's Restaurant. Full Measure Trackside Gasoline sold for 15¢ at the corner, and the station advertised ladies restrooms, an apparently rare commodity at a gas station. (From the Mrs. William Armond Archives at the Northside Branch of the Public Library of Cincinnati and Hamilton County.)

Four

SALVATION AND CIPHERING

The diversity of Northside can be seen in the variety of religious organizations, which coexisted very well in the community. Early in Northside's history, the sense of community was top priority. Philanthropists like Jacob Hoffner donated land and resources for St. Joseph's Orphanage and the German Evangelical Church. Congregations helped and supported the formation of other denominations, even lending them their places of worship. As a great example, the Northside Presbyterian Church supported the founding of the Cumminsville Baptist Church, an African American organization. Charles Miller donated the stone for the building of the Northside Methodist Church, and other neighborhood philanthropists helped form other congregations.

Education was also a very early priority; Northsiders continued to demand the best and most-up-to-date schools for their children. The first real public school in Northside was the Union Graded School, built in 1854 at Knowlton Street. Prior to this institution, grade school classes were held at a log cabin near Westmoreland Street and Innes Avenue, then in the Hall of Free Discussion, and on Spring Grove Avenue in Knowlton's Hall. The first Kirby Road School came along in 1869 and operated along with the Union Graded School. One all–African American school operated in the same period on Dirr Street. Kirby was enlarged in 1876 to accommodate 400 students. In the 1880s, the large public schools began being built—first Salmon P. Chase (1888) and James A. Garfield School (1897) and the second Kirby Road School (1910). The Northside Catholic churches, St. Boniface and St. Patrick's, each had their own private school, as did other organizations, like the Cumminsville Turnverein, which operated a German-language school for the children of its members from 1870 to 1895.

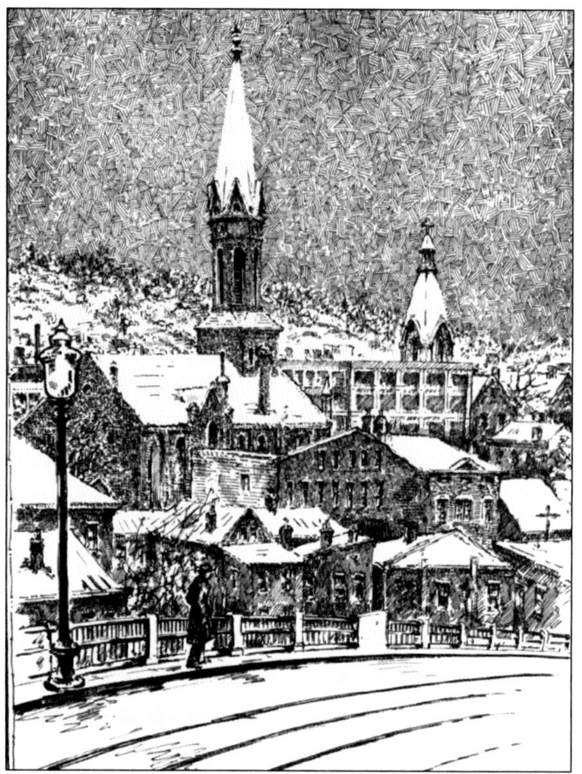

This beautiful 1942 print by *Cincinnati Enquirer* illustrator Caroline Williams shows the snow-capped spires of the Northside churches as seen from the Ludlow Avenue Viaduct. Hoffner Street German Evangelical Church supported Northside's tallest steeple from 1894 until a storm in 1993 destroyed it.

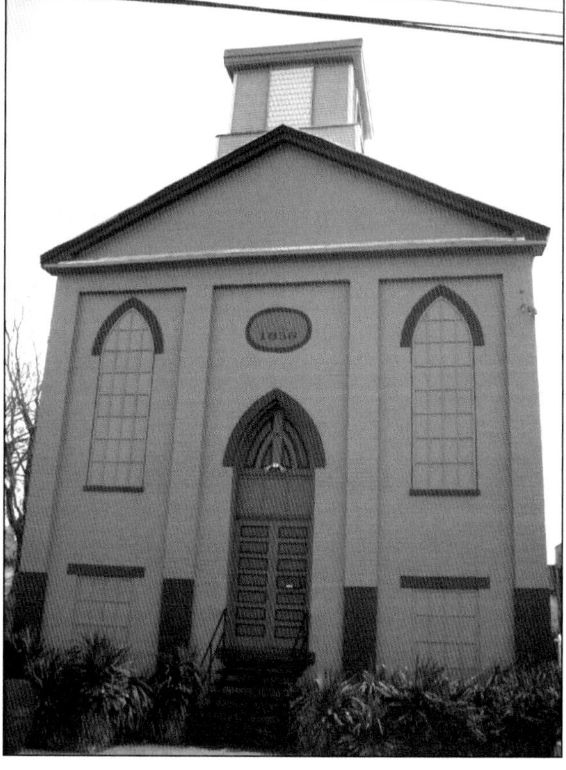

This is the first church of the German Evangelical congregation of Northside at 4014 Apple Street. Jacob Hoffner donated the land in 1856, and parishioner Karl Meyer built it for $2,920. The congregation moved out in 1894 to build a larger church on Hoffner Street. Hoffner bought the building back and presented it to the Grand Army of the Republic (GAR), who removed the steeple to showcase a Civil War cannon.

When the original Apple Street German Evangelical Church was outgrown, the congregation built a new church on Hoffner Street in 1894. The steeple held clocks on each of its four sides with bells that rang before Sunday services and at the death of prominent members. The Fellowship Hall at the street level hosted many parish activities, including the annual Sauerkraut Supper. Men of the parish could hone their skills at the basement shooting range.

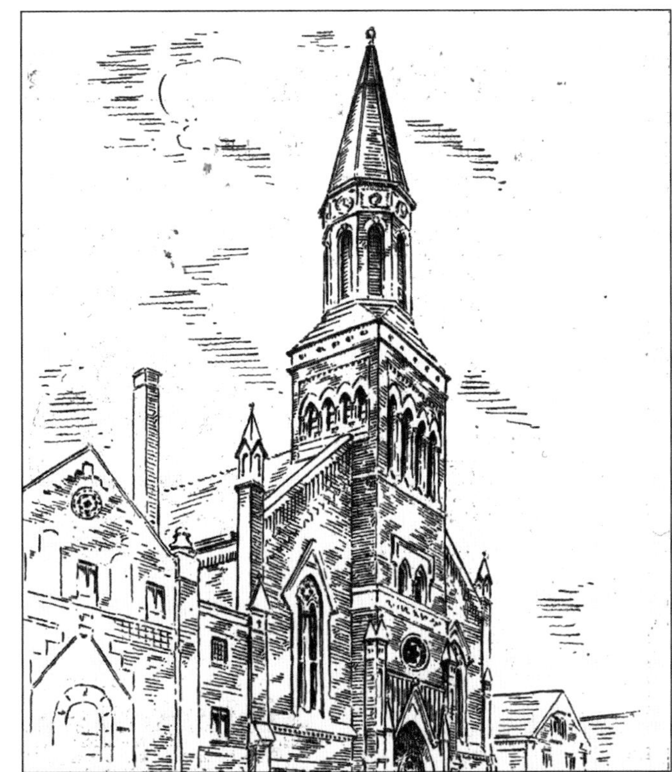

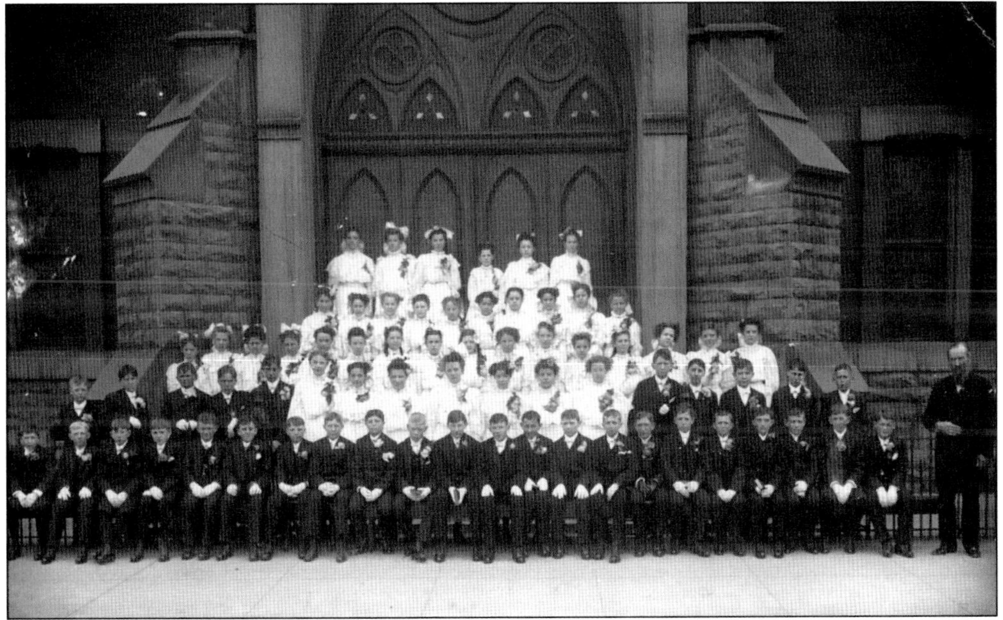

Northside photographer Paul Mueller took this group confirmation picture in 1907. These children stood at the massive doors of the old Hoffner Street German Evangelical Church after their confirmation with their pastor Christian Schenke, who served as pastor from 1879 to 1912. During their ceremony, each child was tasked with reciting a verse of the Bible from memory. (Courtesy of Evelyn Elbe, First Church of Christ Archives.)

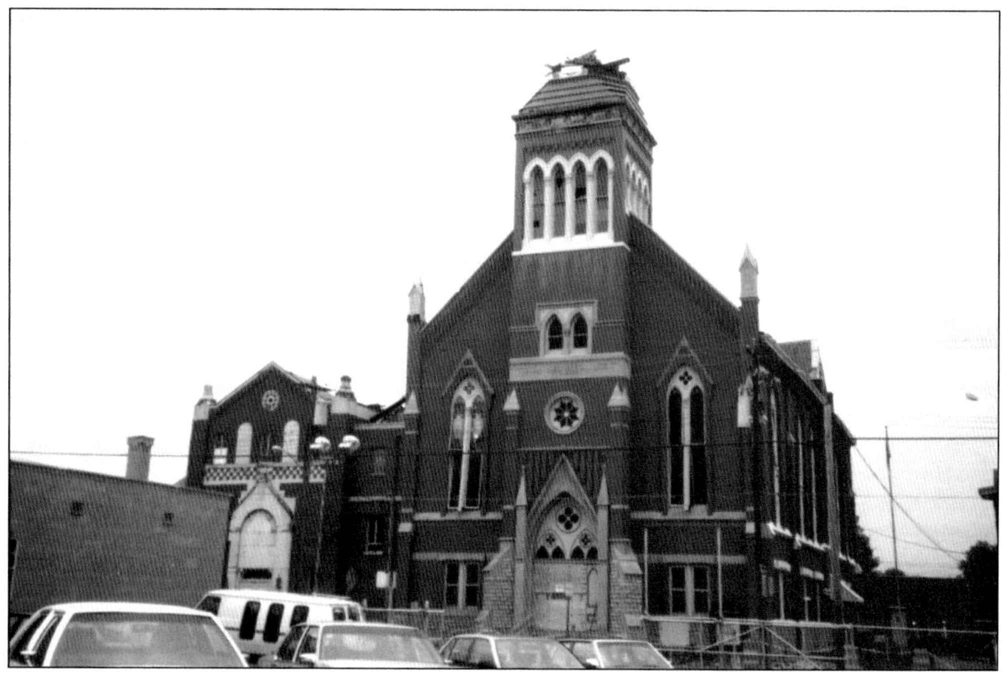

On June 10, 1993, at about 6:30 p.m., a thunderstorm caused the landmark steeple of the Hoffner Street Church to collapse into the church and gymnasium next door. Neither the parsonage nor the home of the Moeschl family on either side of the church were affected. The saddened community watched over the next three weeks as Golsch Wrecking removed the pieces of their 99-year-old church, which hosted countless weddings, baptisms, and funerals. The stained-glass windows and the original 1894 cornerstone were saved and moved to the new church in College Hill, but the wall murals inside crumbled with the brick. One young parishioner dangerously rescued the large German nativity set piece by piece that was stored at the top of the steps in the steeple. (Courtesy of Evelyn Elbe, First Church of Christ Archives.)

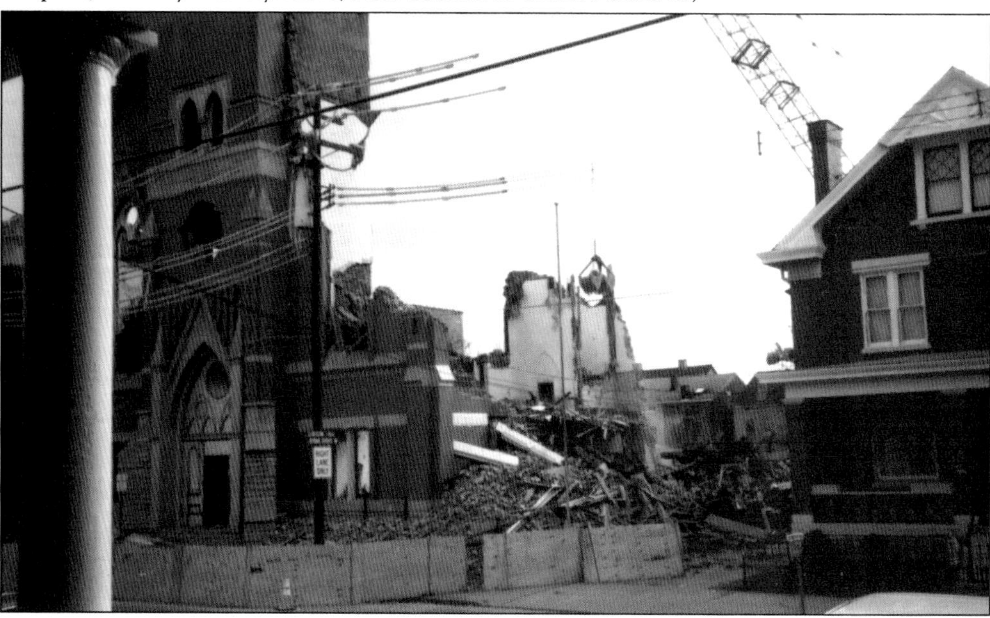

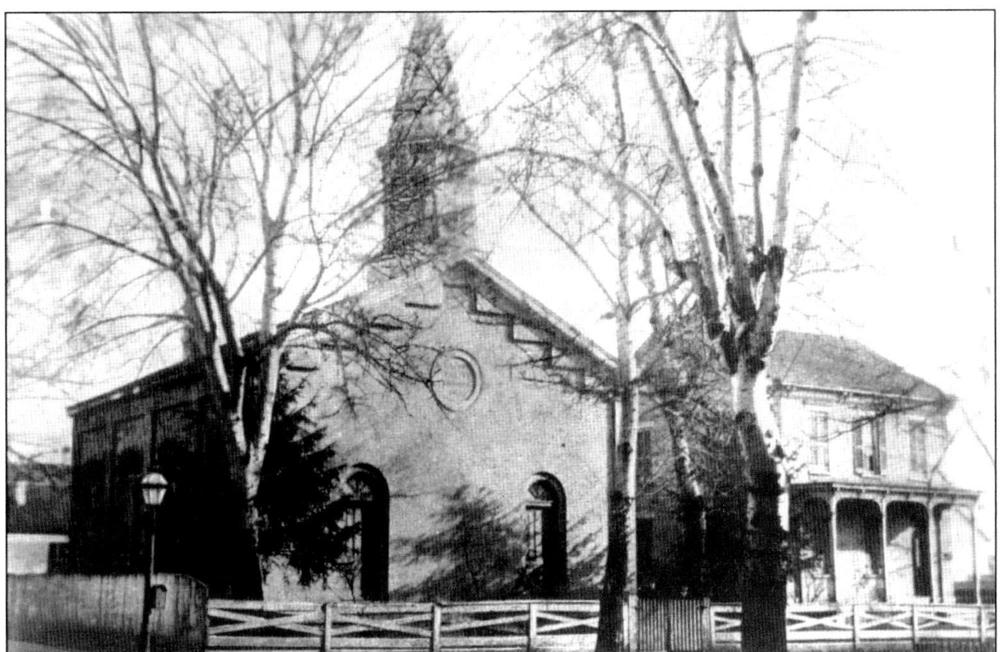

The first church of the North Presbyterian congregation, shown here in the 1880s at Lingo and Langland Streets, was designed by James McClure and built in 1853 for $2,300. The church was razed in 1887, after a larger church was built in 1886. The house to the right behind the white picketed fence was the parsonage, built in 1871 for a cost of $3,689. (Courtesy of the Northside Presbyterian Church Archives.)

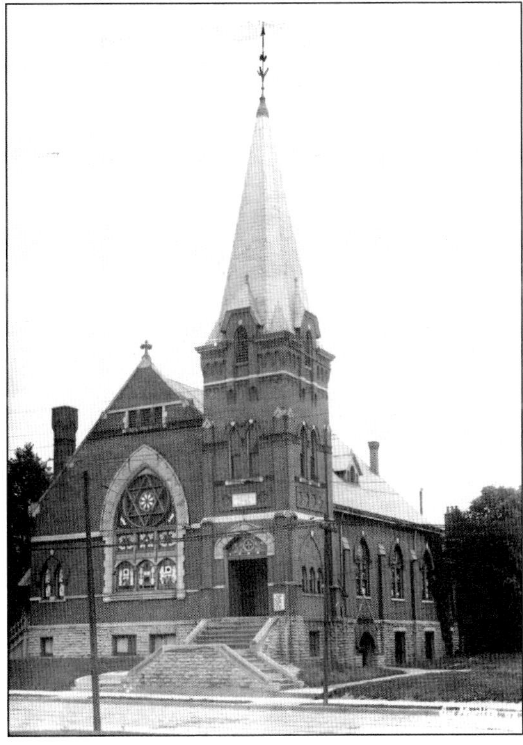

This is a 1908 photograph of the North Presbyterian Church, designed by architect Lonsdale Green for $17,100 in 1886, before the side addition of 1910. This congregation consisted of the many well-to-do Northsiders and included as its early members Ephraim Knowlton and his family, Janet Langland, the Ludlow family, Josiah Lingo, Timothy Kirby, and the Dodsworth family. (Courtesy of the Northside Presbyterian Church Archives.)

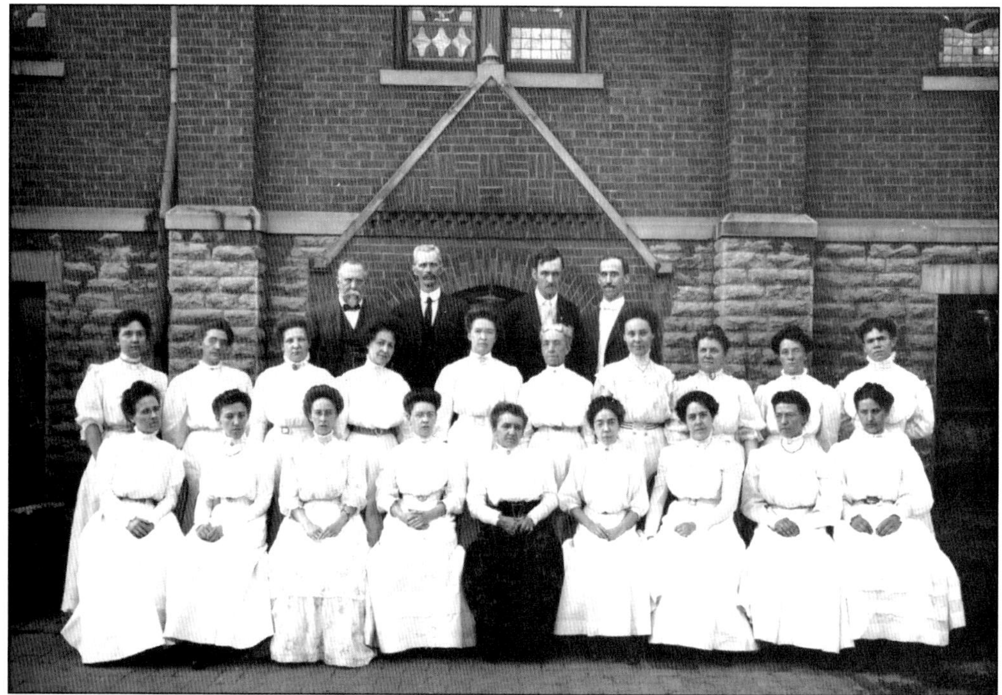

A women's auxiliary Bible study group at the North Presbyterian Church in 1905 shows uniformly high-collared, white-dressed Christian women. (Courtesy of the Northside Presbyterian Church Archives.)

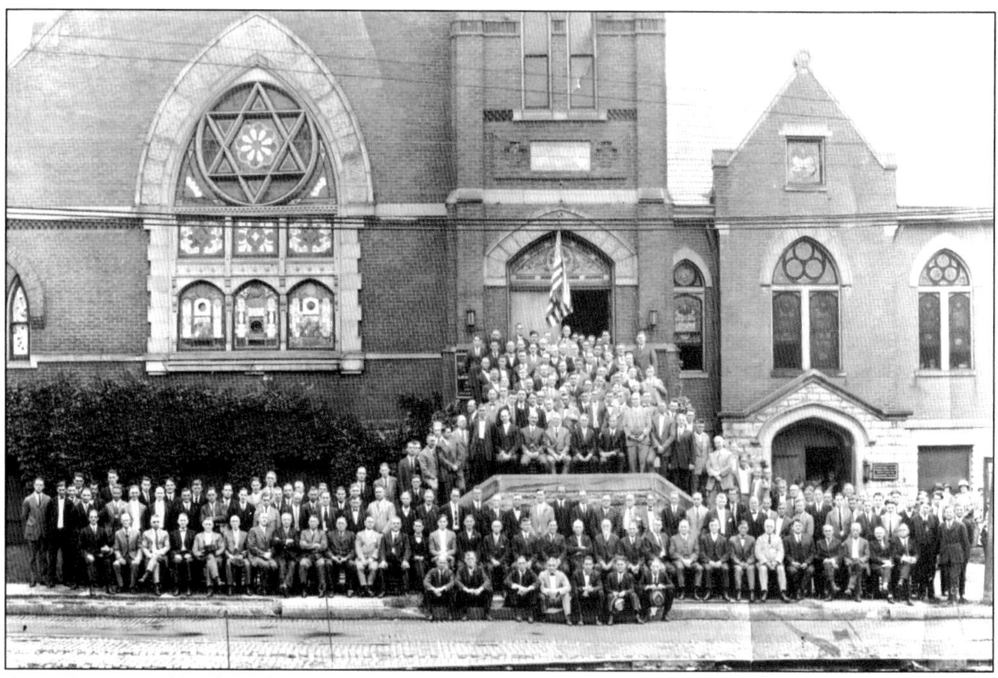

A 1925 men's Bible class photograph in front of the North Presbyterian Church shows the trolley tracks in the street. The men look more relaxed than the women in the photograph above. (Courtesy of the Northside Presbyterian Church Archives.)

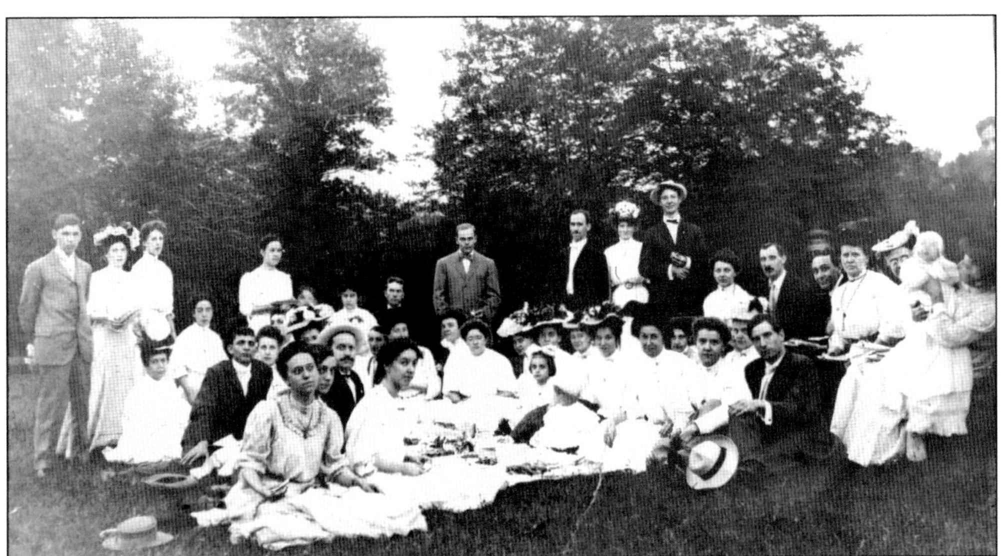

This group of smirking Northsiders is dressed in their Sunday best in 1905 during a church picnic at Mount Airy Forest. Mount Airy was a favorite spot for family and organization picnics in Northside. (Courtesy of the Northside Presbyterian Church Archives.)

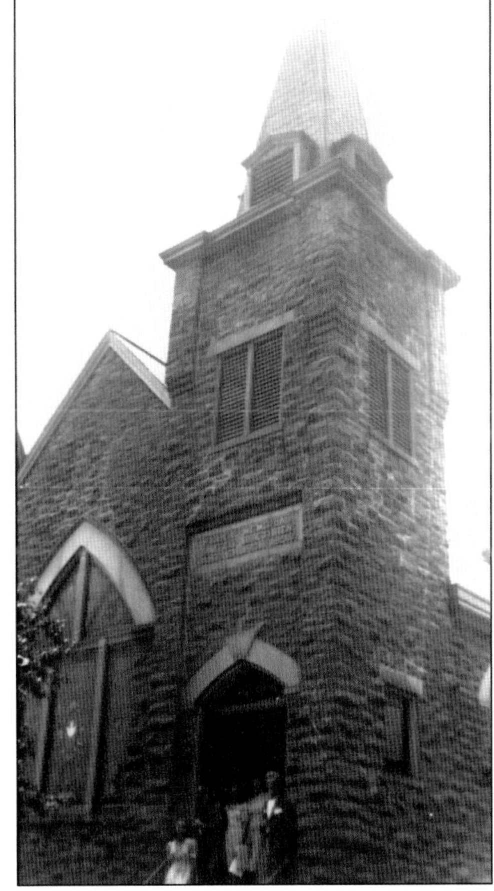

The Willey Memorial Chapel in South Cumminsville at 3736 Borden Street started as a Congregationalist Sunday school. In 1896, the Mount Airy United Brethren Church took charge, and in 1900, under the Reverend James Ungling, the stone church was built and dedicated. This photograph shows a 1941 group at the church. The building now houses the Cincinnati Urban Outreach and Church of Christ organizations. (Courtesy of Jan Holland.)

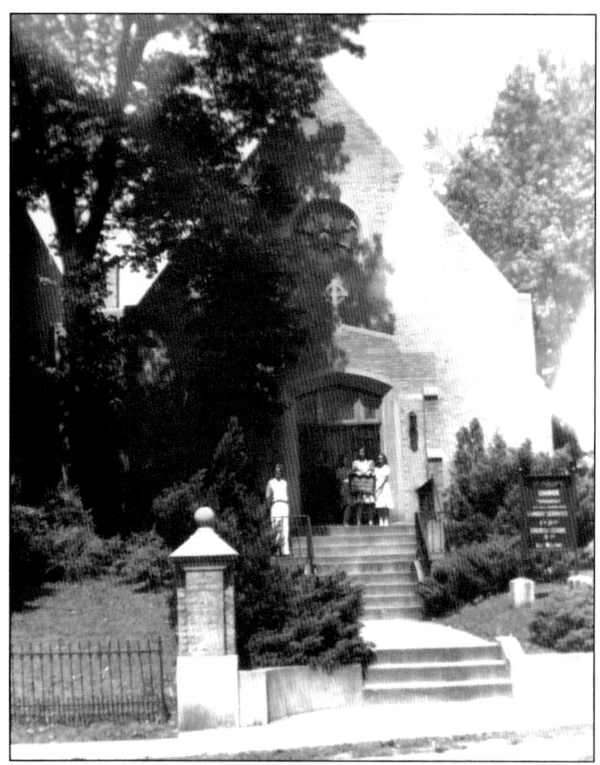

St. Phillips Episcopal Church at 4139 Kirby Road was built in 1872 for $12,000. Modeled after a typical English countryside church, it was first named St. James the Less, but shortly renamed due to an irreverent play by the same title. Timothy Kirby donated the land. The congregation moved out of the church in 2003 and now meets at the Churches Active in Northside (CAIN) building on Hamilton Avenue. (Courtesy of Jan Holland.)

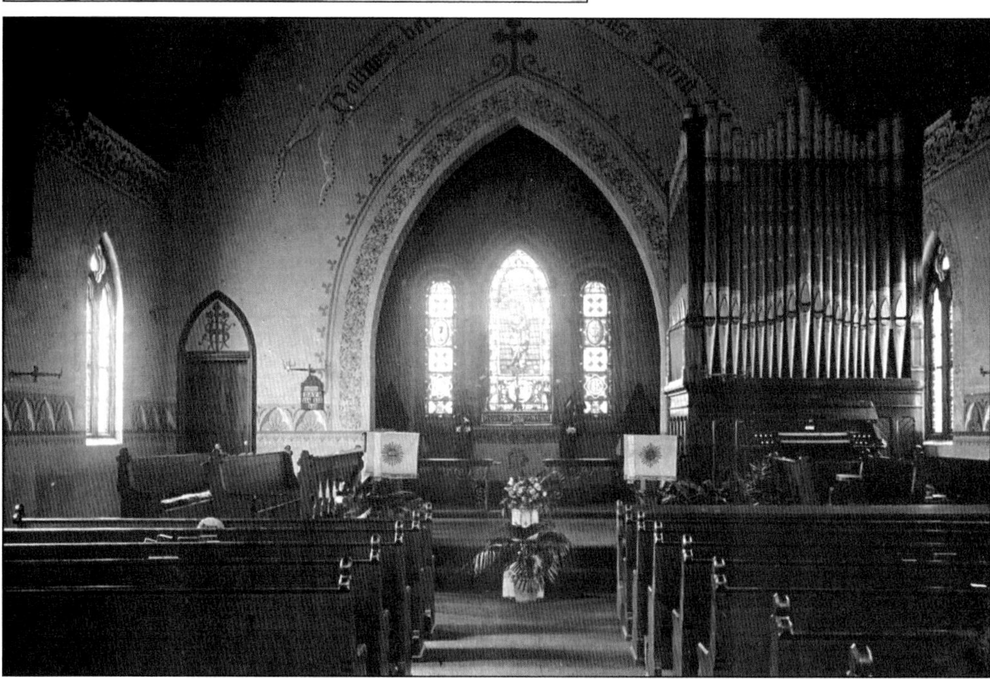

This photograph, taken in the 1930s, shows a newly renovated St. Phillips Episcopal Church with its sparkling new stained-glass window. The carved stone baptismal font in the center of this photograph was made, along with the stone cross on the top of the church, by parishioner James Callahan and is now owned by Jim Bruckmann. (Courtesy of Jan Holland.)

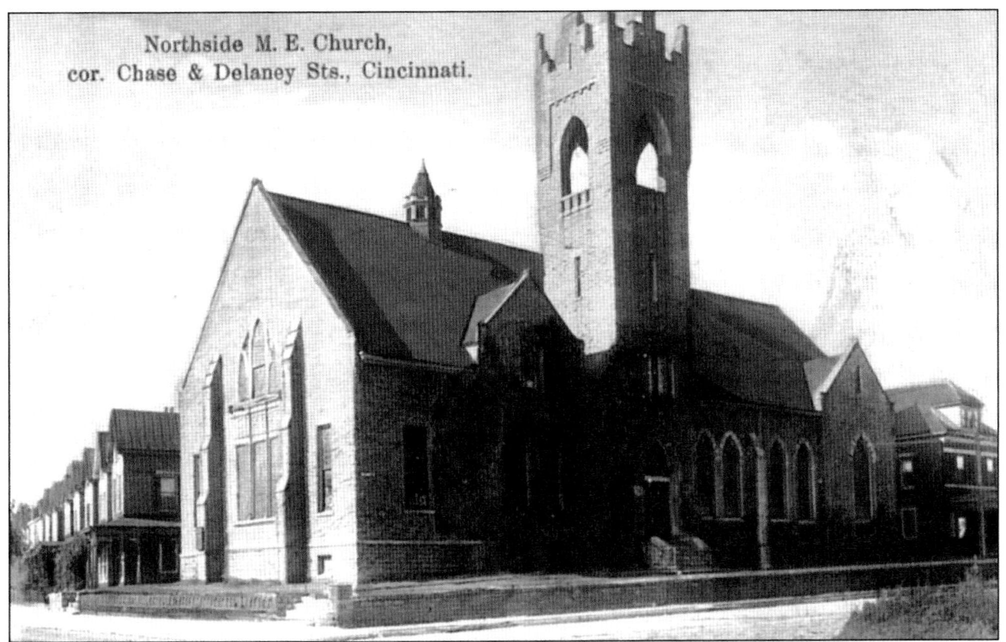

The Northside United Methodist Church was built in 1894 and designed by architect Samuel Hannaford (1835–1911). This congregation's first church at Wesleyan Cemetery was destroyed by fire in 1889. The church purchased the lot on Delaney Street from Julia Banning, and Charles Miller, a Northside undertaker, donated the stone from his quarries. In 1980, the church was listed on the National Register of Historic Places. (From the Collection of the Public Library of Cincinnati and Hamilton County.)

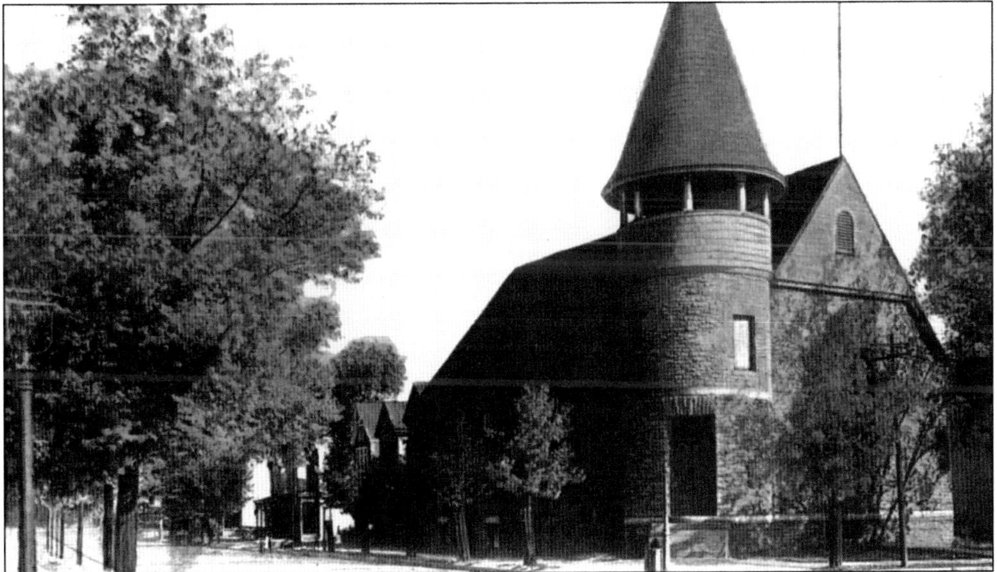

Immanuel Baptist Church, at the corner of Pullan and Hamilton Avenues, was built in 1896 by Cincinnati architect James McLauglin (1835–1923), the architect of Shilito's Department Store. Its modest stained-glass windows and materials speak to the Baptist ideals of simplicity. Throughout its life, it struggled as a mission church. Now it is home to the Word Alive Christian Fellowship. (From the Collection of the Public Library of Cincinnati and Hamilton County.)

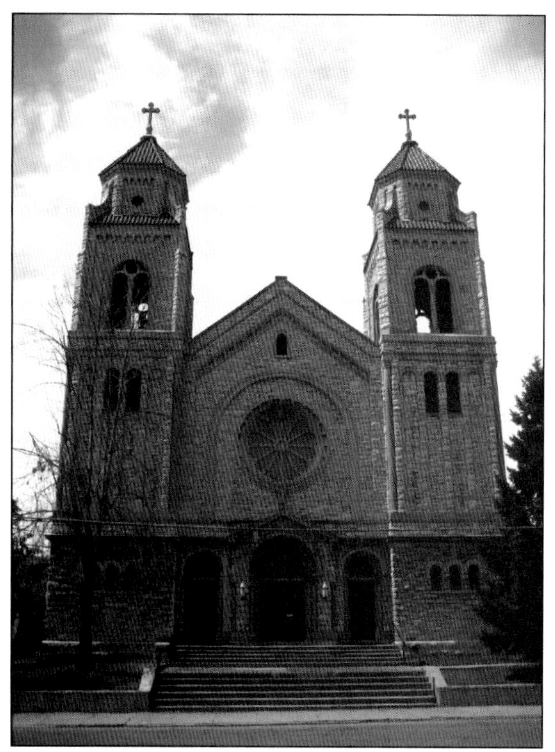

St. Pius Roman Catholic Church, at 1814 Dreman Avenue, was organized on October 3, 1910, as a sister parish to St. Boniface, for the growing middle-class German Catholics of South Cumminsville. This twin-towered Romanesque church, shown here, was built in 1927 by architectural firm Kunz and Beck. The church closed in 1998 due to dwindling membership and then housed Working in Neighborhoods (WIN), a nonprofit working to provide better housing.

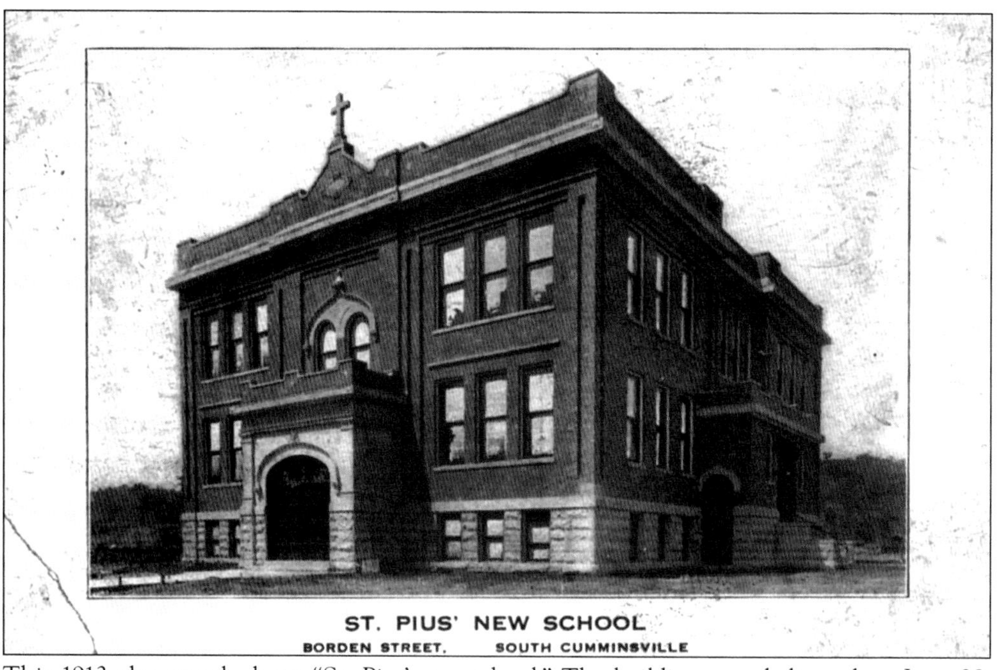

This 1913 photograph shows "St. Pius' new school." The building was dedicated on June 28, 1913, by Archbishop Henry K. Moeller (1849–1925), making it the fifth school in Northside. The school building contained eight regular classrooms with two music rooms and an auditorium seating 750. The children were taught dutifully by the Franciscan Sisters of Oldenburg. (From the Collection of the Public Library of Cincinnati and Hamilton County.)

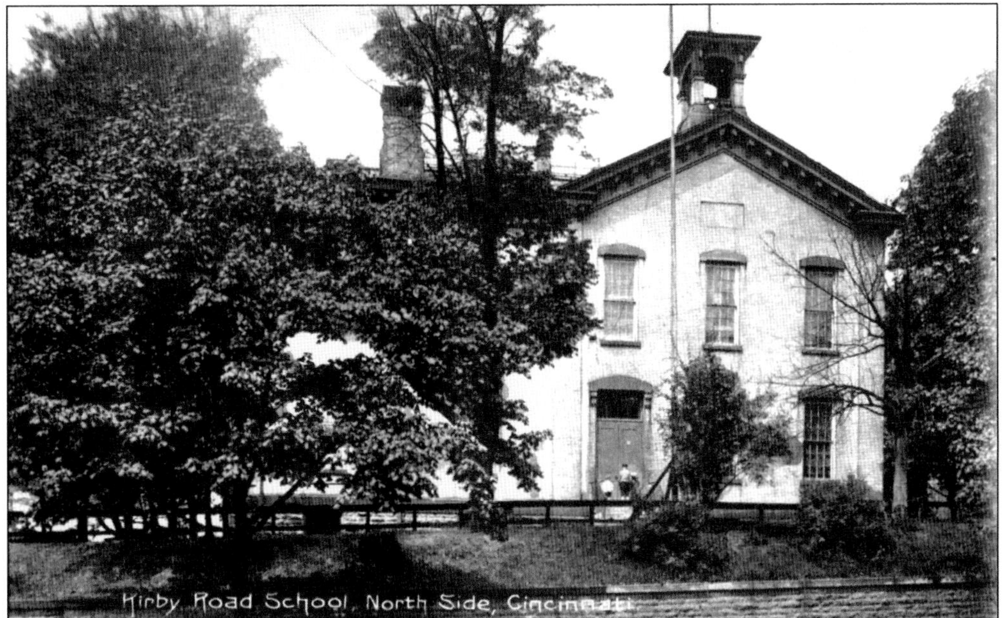

The first Kirby Road School was built in 1869 on a knoll at Kirby Way, just below the present Chase Avenue, for a total of $11,526. The neighborhood continued to grow, and the building was vacated in 1910, when the current Kirby Road School was built. The first Kirby Road School was demolished in 1912 for residences. (From the Collection of the Public Library of Cincinnati and Hamilton County.)

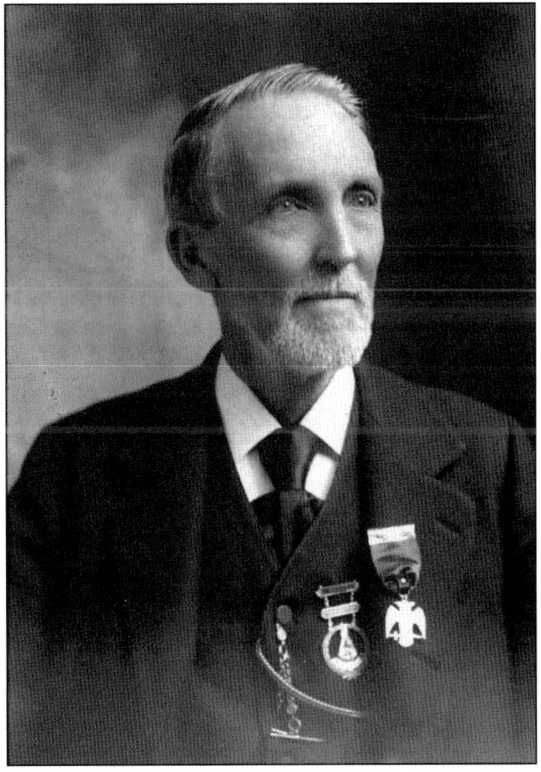

Merrill S. Turrill (1831–1918), shown in this 1898 photograph, could be called the father of education in Northside. A graduate of the Farmer's College in College Hill, Turrill was the principal from 1853 to 1885 of the Union Graded School, shaping the curriculum for Northside primary learning. Turrill was a founding member of the Hoffner Masonic Lodge and a member of the North Presbyterian Church. (Courtesy of the Northside Presbyterian Church Archives.)

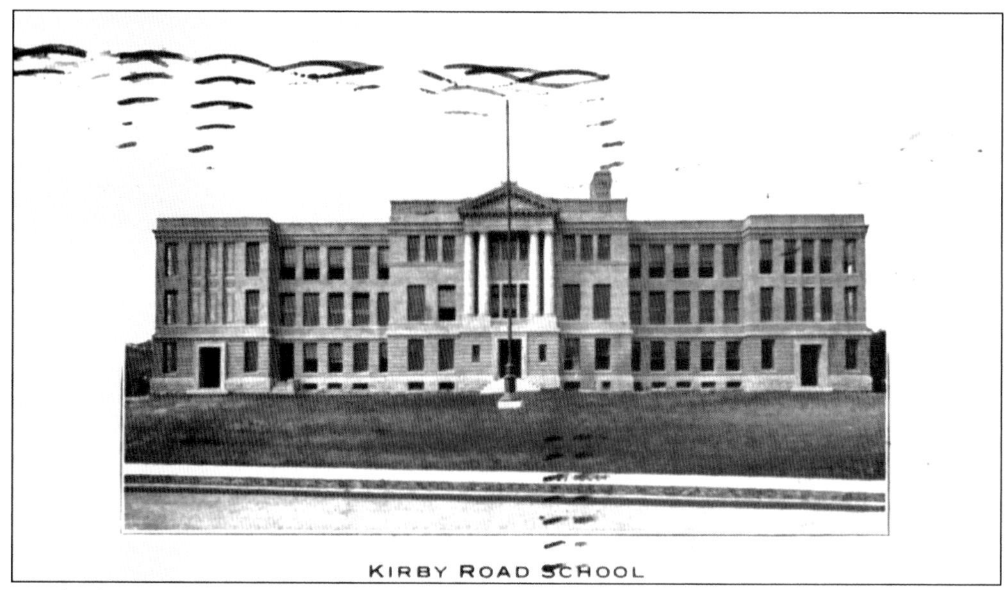

Northside continued to grow as streetcar lines extended up Hamilton Avenue, and in 1905, residents called for a larger and higher-quality school. As a result, in 1910, Kirby Road Primary School at 1710 Bruce Avenue and Kirby Road was built. Cincinnati architects Elzner and Anderson designed the sweeping neoclassical building on the highest point in Northside. (From the Collection of the Public Library of Cincinnati and Hamilton County.)

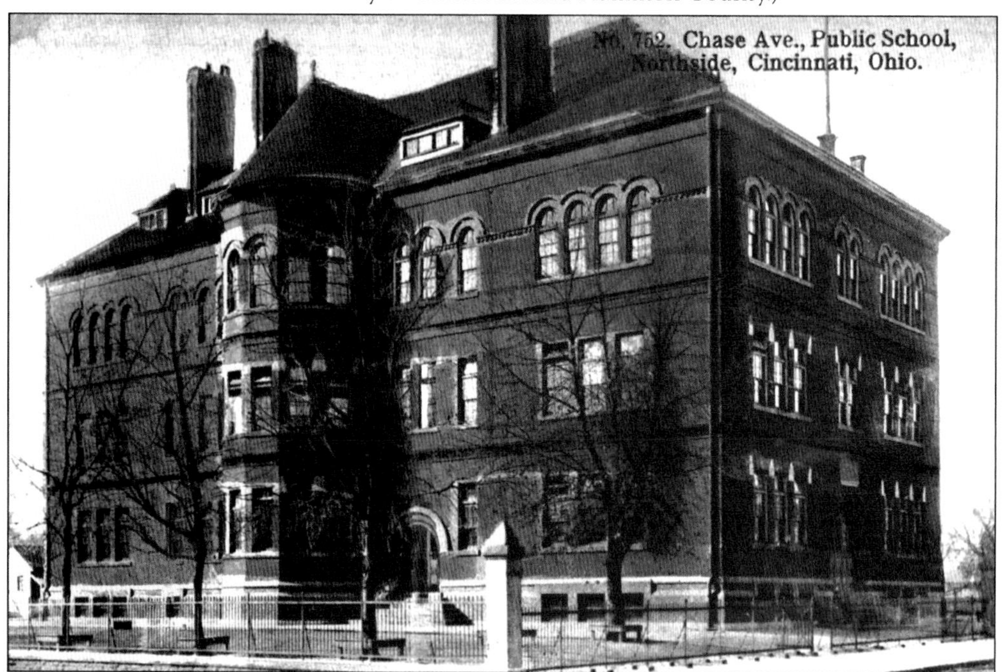

This postcard shows Salmon P. Chase Elementary School, which opened in 1888 as Northside's fourth public school. Chase had no lunchroom, so children either walked home or ate their lunch on benches in the central hallway. A 1962 tax levy provided funds for the building of Chase-McKie Intermediate School. Chase was vacated in 1979 and now houses condominiums. (From the Collection of the Public Library of Cincinnati and Hamilton County.)

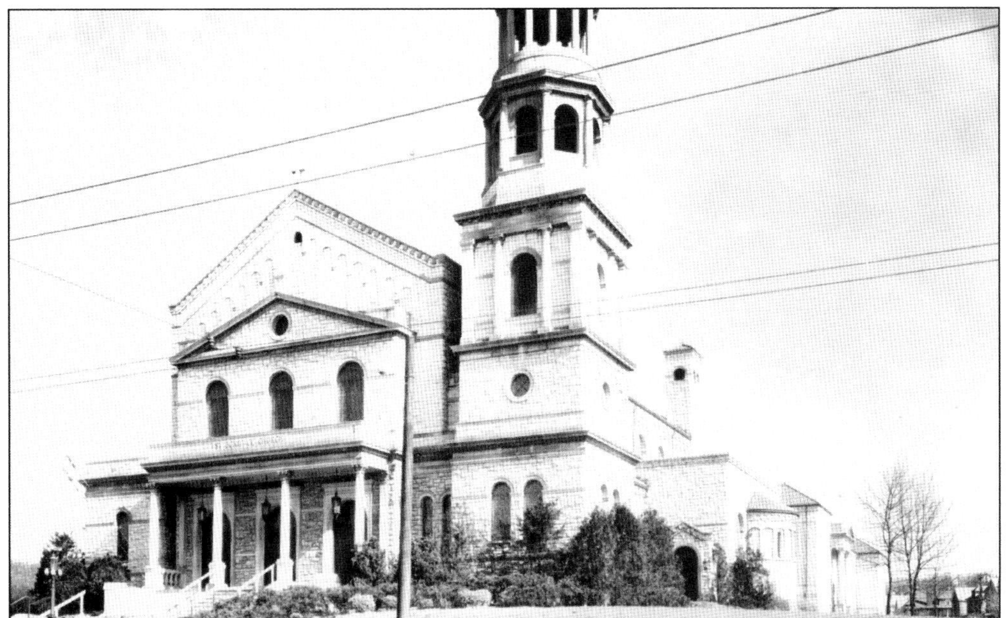

St. Boniface's parish was created when Archbishop John Baptist Purcell (1800–1883) gave the German Catholics of Northside permission to break with St. Aloysius Parish and start their own church. By 1910, the congregation had grown so large that two sister parishes were born—St. Clare's in College Hill and St. Pius in South Cumminsville. Under the guidance of Fr. George Schmidt, this sprawling Romanesque church based on the Basilica of St. Paul's Outside the Walls in Rome was built in 1927. (Courtesy of the Cincinnati Sisters of Charity Archives.)

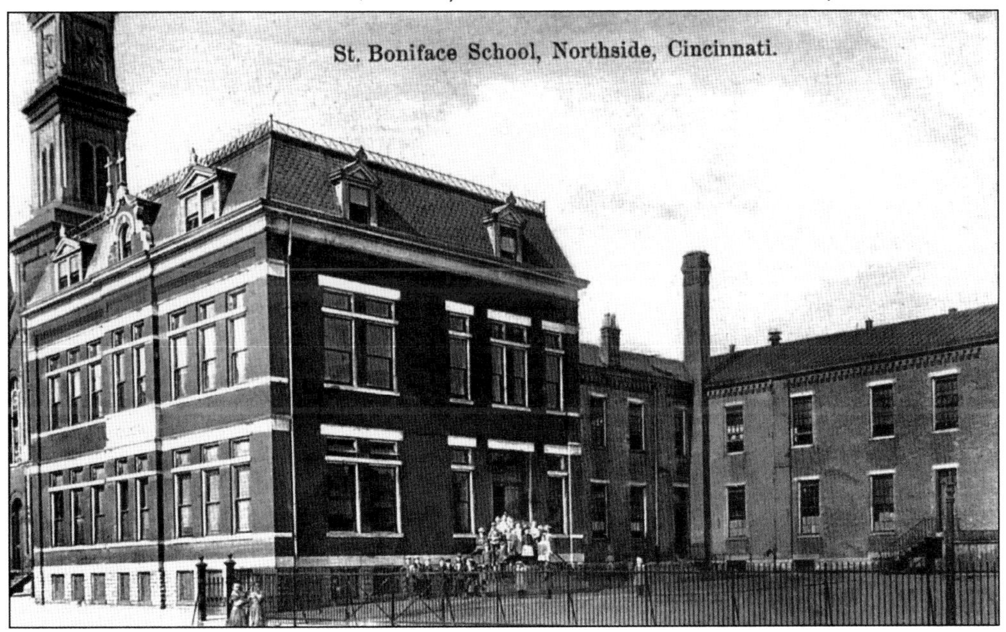

Old St. Boniface School was built adjoining the first church in 1870 at Blue Rock Street for a cost of $7,800 for the German Catholic community of Northside. Fr. Boniface Godfrey Topmoeller was pastor of the parish at the time and served until his death in 1887. (From the Collection of the Public Library of Cincinnati and Hamilton County.)

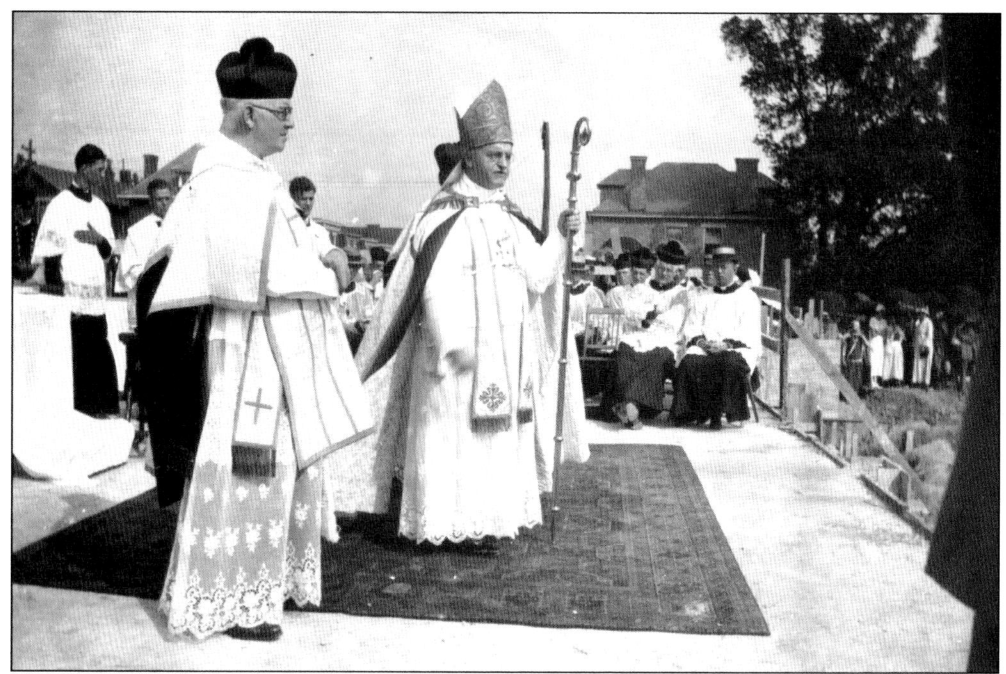

Archbishop John T. McNicholas (1877–1950) initiated the building of the new St. Boniface School at this 1932 blessing of the cornerstone ceremony on the new church campus on Delaney Avenue. In 1933, the school opened its doors. (Courtesy of the Cincinnati Sisters of Charity Archives.)

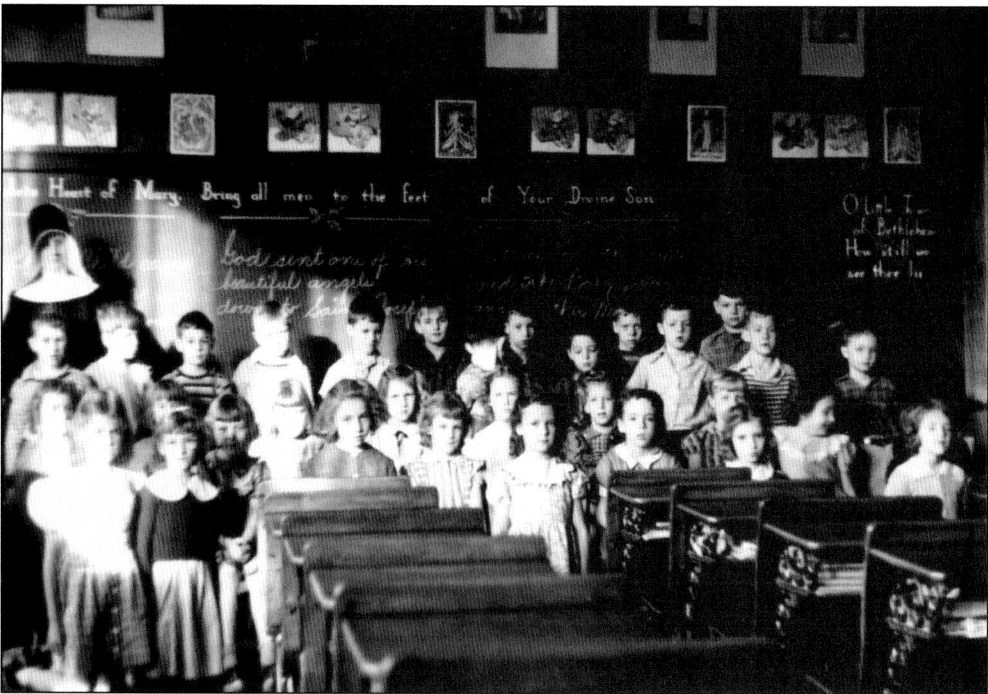

This photograph shows Sr. Ludmilla with her children at St. Boniface School. The favorite children's song "O Little Town of Bethlehem" is written on the chalkboard behind the students (Courtesy of the Cincinnati Sisters of Charity Archives.)

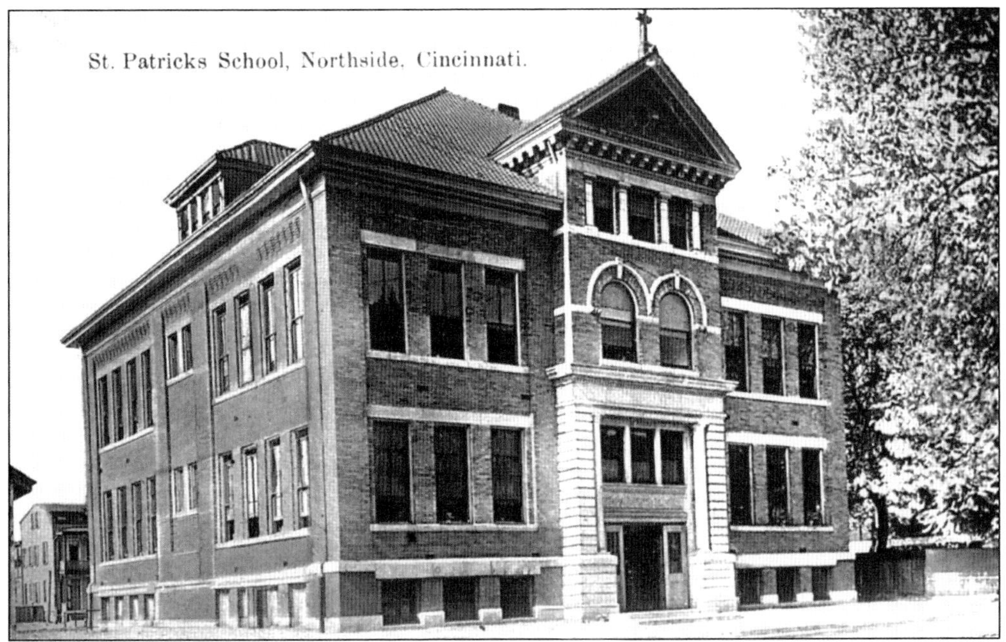

St. Patrick's School, shown here in the early 1900s, was served by the Sisters of Charity, but unlike the Sisters of Charity who served the German St. Boniface parish, they did not have their own motherhouse and lived at St. Joseph's Orphanage. When St. Patrick's School was closed in 1969, the students were sent to St. Boniface, ending the sports rivalry between the two schools. (From the Collection of the Public Library of Cincinnati and Hamilton County.)

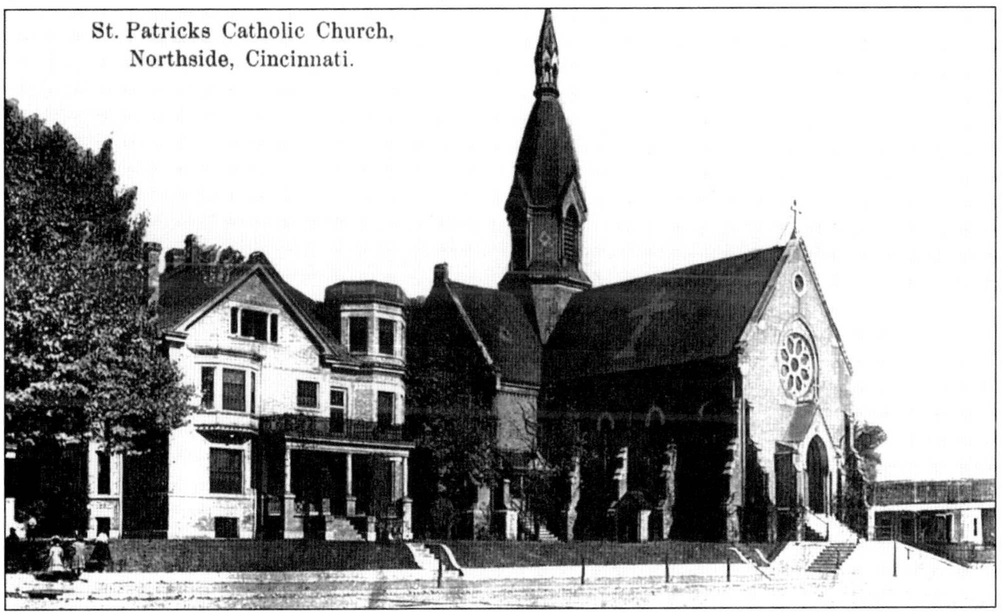

This early-1900s photograph shows St. Patrick's Church at 1663 Blue Rock Street. It was the Irish parish resulting from the 1861 division of St. Aloysius. Fr. David Walker, a civil engineer by schooling, started building the church in 1870, but his successor, Fr. David Crowley, completed it in 1873. The church closed in 1969 and was added to the National Register of Historic Places in 1980. (From the Collection of the Public Library of Cincinnati and Hamilton County.)

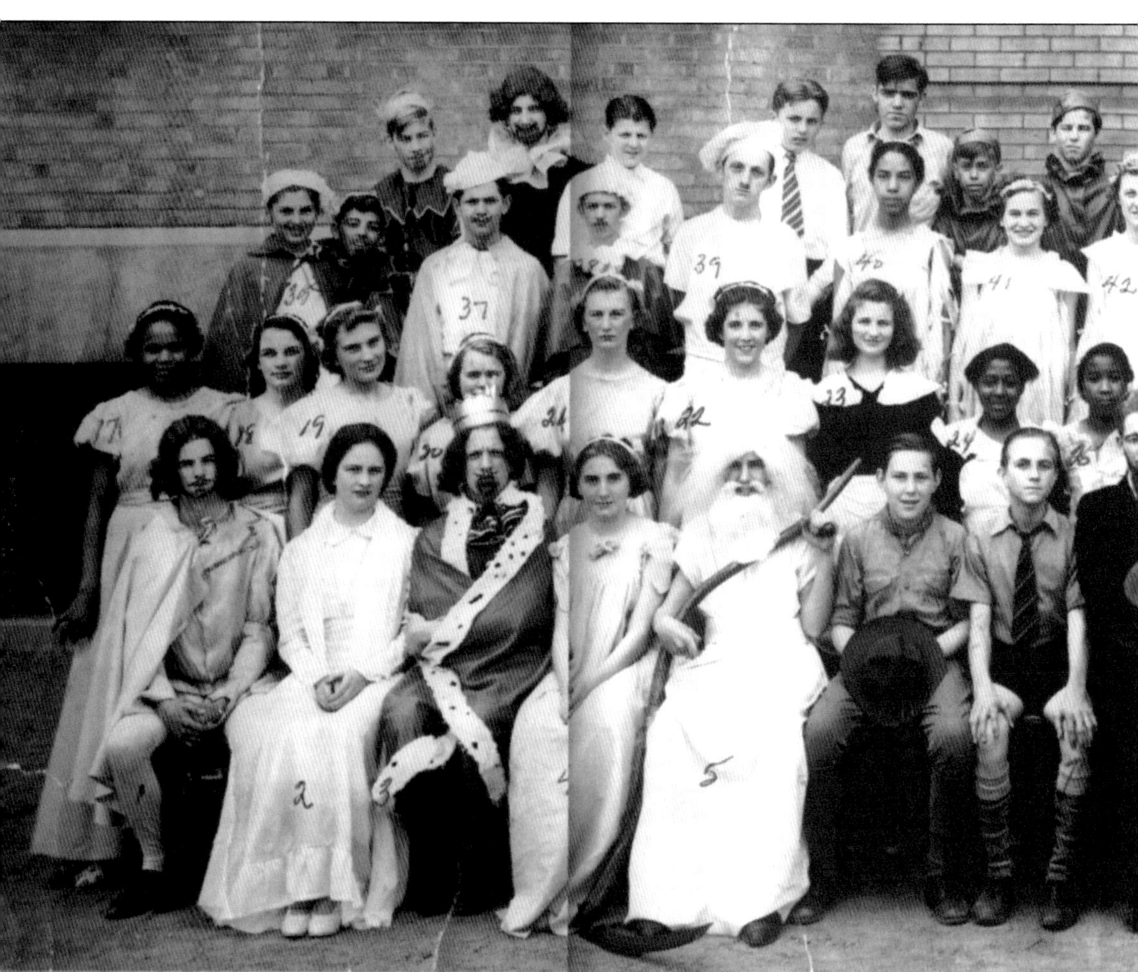

Garfield School produced a stage drama every year, requiring participation from every student. Those identified in the cast of characters from this 1938 production are Carl Siefried (1), Jean Sibethaler (2), Ray Hamilton (3) (who became the owner of the current Ray Hamilton Movers) Viola Voltmer (4), Robert Butler (7), Martin Harp (8), Ralph Lorenz (9), Hazel Griffin (10), Eleanor Greely (11), Ruth Lawrence (13), Kathleen Guenther (14), Claire Heath (16), Frances Johnson (17), Edna Roy (18), Mae Bierman (19), Laura Kahle (20), Margie Prussie (21), Dorothy

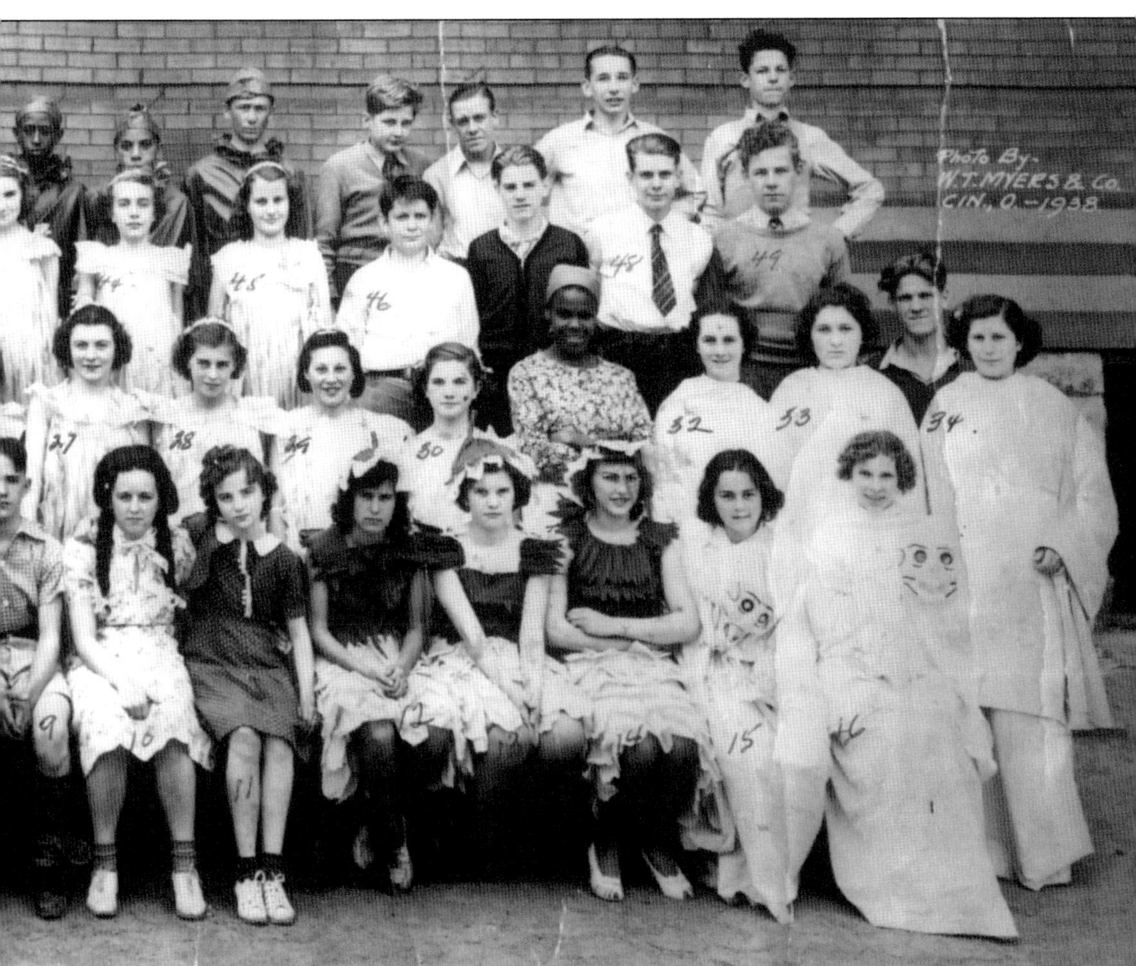

Fitz (22), Cora Wright (23), Ruth Riley (24), Bessie Wolf (25), Melox Naegle (27), Wilma Wolf (28), Esther Thomas (29), Ruth Smlag (30), Alice Martha Bun Fletcher (31), Helen Hienman (32), Rosalyn Weber (33), George Spence (36), George Engle (38), Frank Hildakraut (39), Carrie Craig (40), Fern (41), Eileen Roth (42), Robert Steinhew (46), and Robert Farber (48). (Courtesy of Alice Martha Bun Fletcher.)

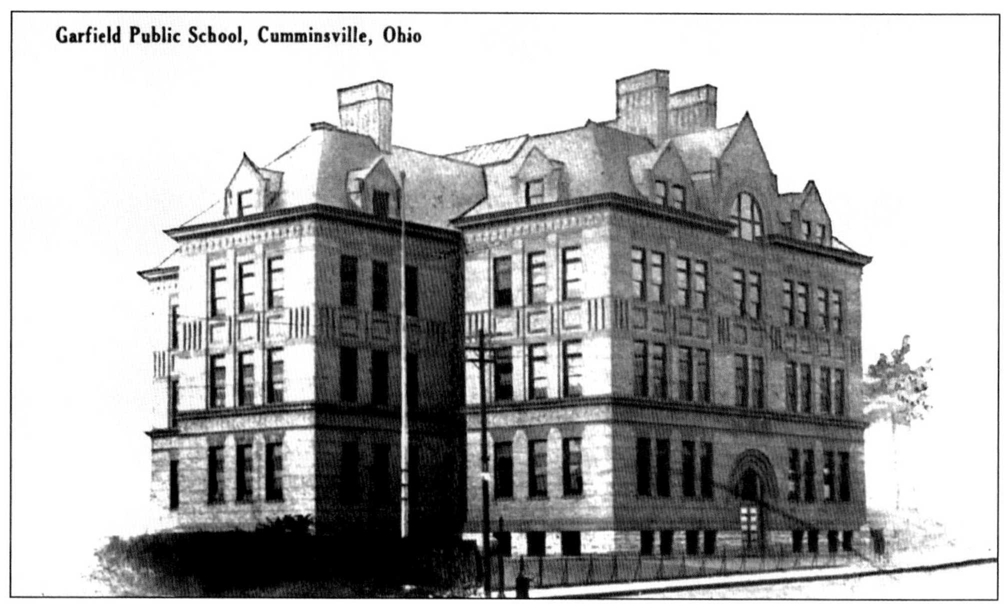

This 1908 postcard shows the James A. Garfield Public School at 1905 Elmore Street. Built in 1896 for $62,897 by architect Henry E. Siter (1851–1913), it housed 1,008 pupils. The original principal was John H. Locke, but it was principal Chester M. Miller who created "Garfield City" and ran it with a mayor and vice mayor. It closed in 1979 due to low enrollment. (From the Collection of the Public Library of Cincinnati and Hamilton County.)

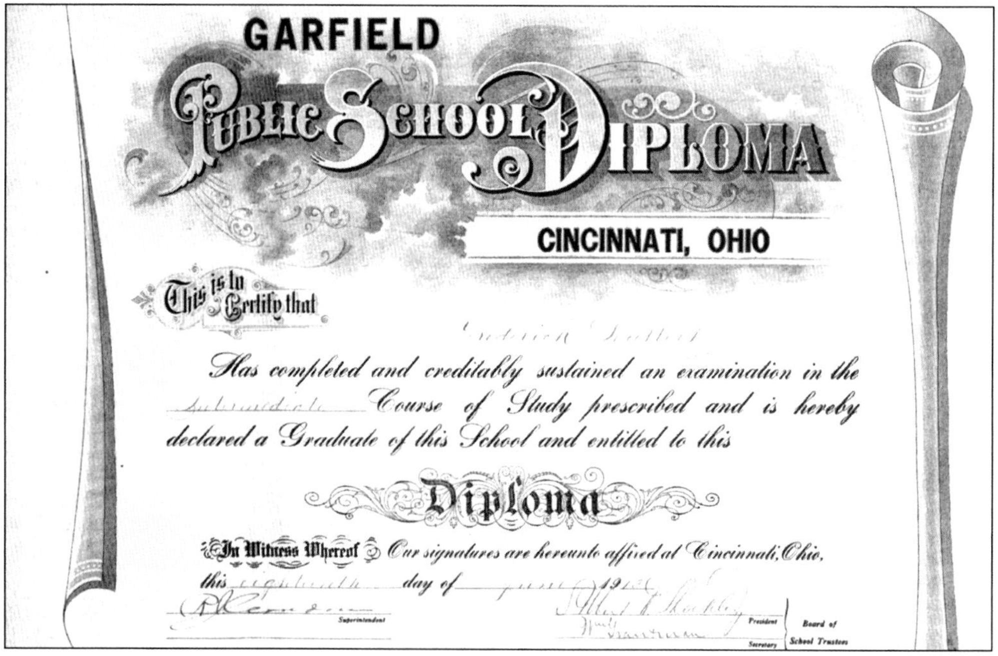
GARFIELD

PUBLIC SCHOOL DIPLOMA

CINCINNATI, OHIO

This is to Certify that

Has completed and creditably sustained an examination in the ____ Course of Study prescribed and is hereby declared a Graduate of this School and entitled to this

Diploma

In Witness Whereof Our signatures are hereunto affixed at Cincinnati, Ohio, this ____ day of ____ 1913

Superintendent

President

Secretary

Board of School Trustees

This is Fredrick W. Woellert's diploma dated June 18, 1913, from Garfield School. It is signed by Albert Shockley, president; William Grautman, secretary; and Richard Cerndon, superintendant. Instead of attending Hughes High School in Clifton, Woellert began working as a machinist at Cincinnati Milling Machine Company in Oakley. Shockley, signer of this diploma, owned a candy store across the street from Garfield school, catering to a grade-schooler's sweet tooth.

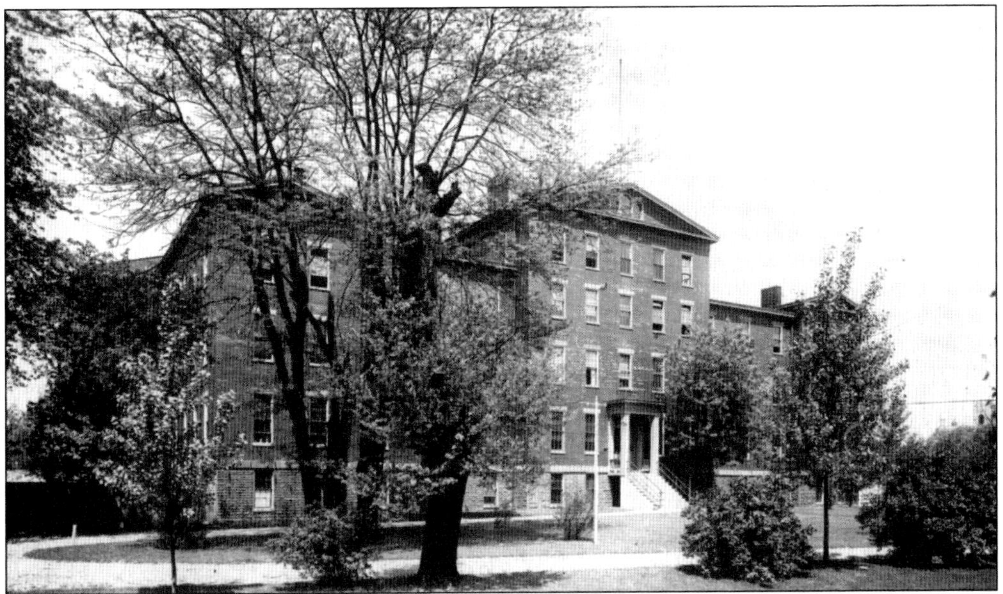

This 1924 photograph shows St. Joseph's Orphanage, at Blue Rock and Cherry Streets, now home to the McKie Recreation Center. Archbishop John Baptist Purcell purchased the 11-acre site from Jacob Hoffner in 1852 for half price for use as an orphanage. In 1854, Mother Superior Sr. Anthony O'Connell, moved 100 boys via rail from the old orphanage downtown to Northside. (Courtesy of the Cincinnati Sisters of Charity Archives.)

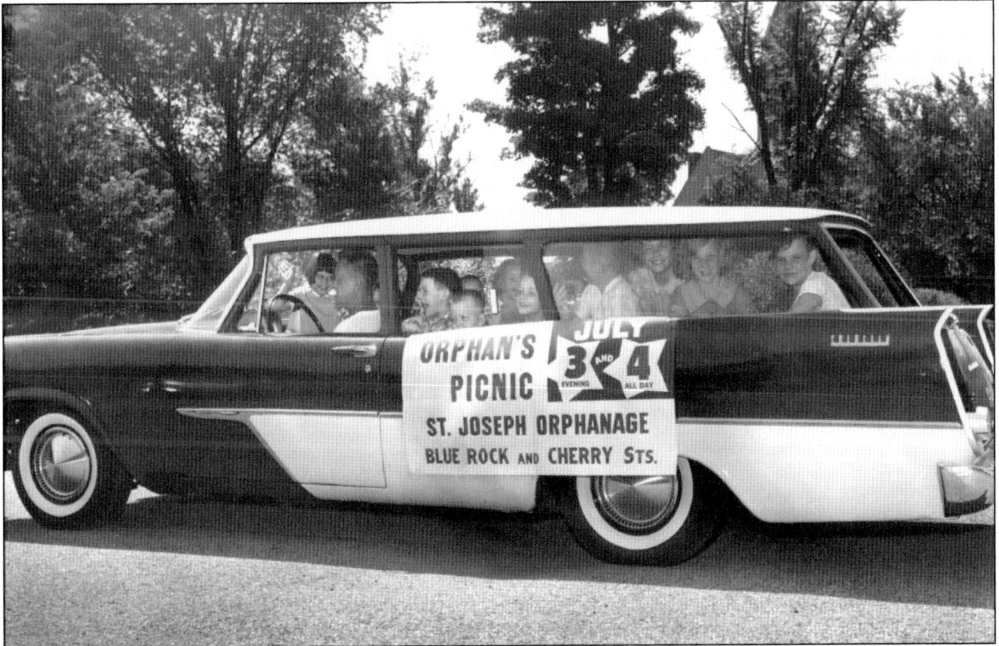

This photograph shows the parade car for the last St. Joseph's Orphanage Festival on Sunday and Monday, July 3 and 4, 1960. A longtime institution in Northside, the first parade in 1854 was a three-and-a-half-hour march from St. Peter in Chains Cathedral in downtown Cincinnati to Northside, led by grand marshal Capt. Robert Moore. (Courtesy of the Cincinnati Sisters of Charity Archives.)

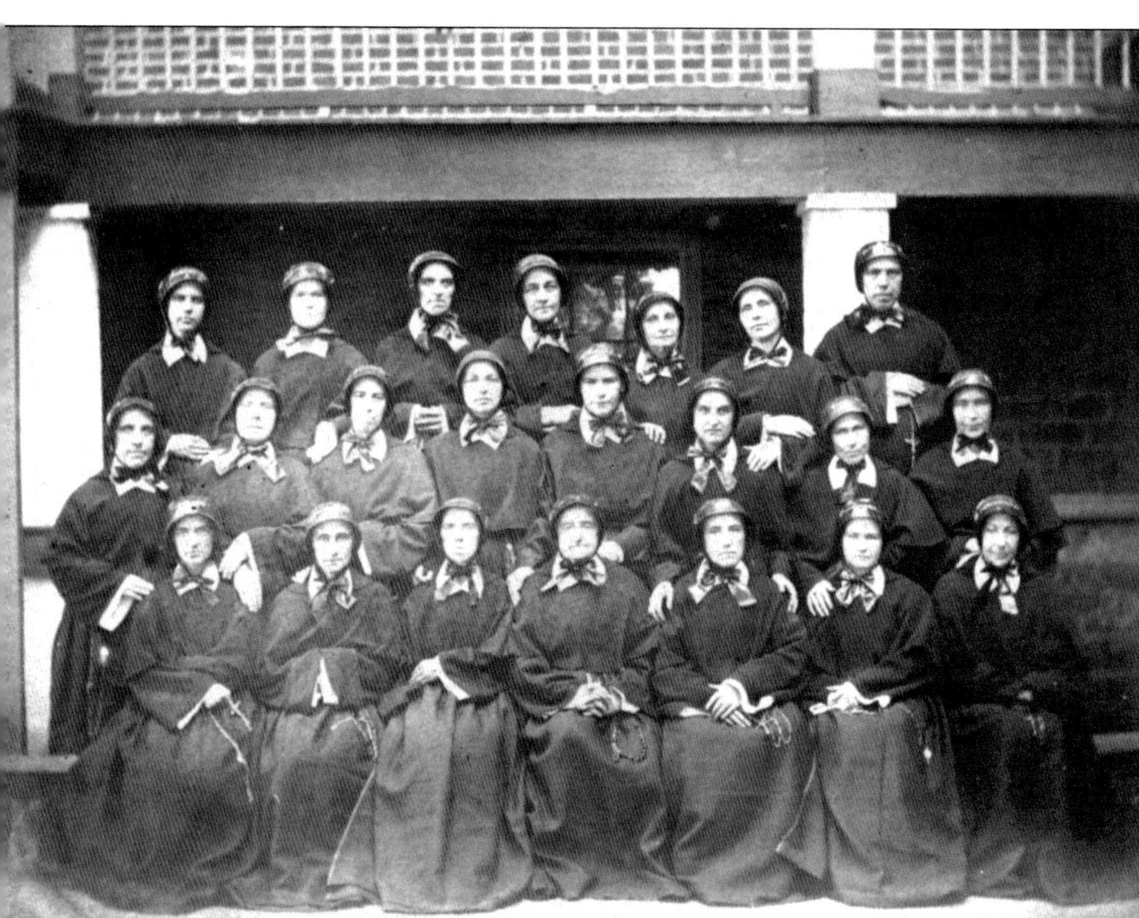

This 1870 photograph of the staff of St. Joseph's Orphanage shows an intimidating group of nuns with a predominance of Irish names. The Sisters of Charity shown in this photograph are, from left to right, (first row) Sr. Lucilla Connell, Sr. Ann Aloysia Bannon, Sr. Ligouri Kelly, Sr. Mary Lucy Feighn, Sr. Etienne Bonner, Sr. Romana Brenna, and Sr. Seraphine O'Meara; (second row) Sr. Felicula Fay, Sr. Anna Bernard McBride, Sr. Sebastian Shea, Sr. Mary Joseph Sullivan, Sr. Cleophas Cummins, Sr. Augusta Jacobs, Sr. Clara Haller, and Sr. Anna Francis O'Brien; (third row) Sr. Anna Maria McNamara, Sr. Gabriella Crow, Sr. Cephas Bray, Sr. Monica Bremen, Sr. Benedicta Cain, Sr. Xavier Maddock, and Sr. Francesca O'Brien. (Courtesy of the Cincinnati Sisters of Charity Archives.)

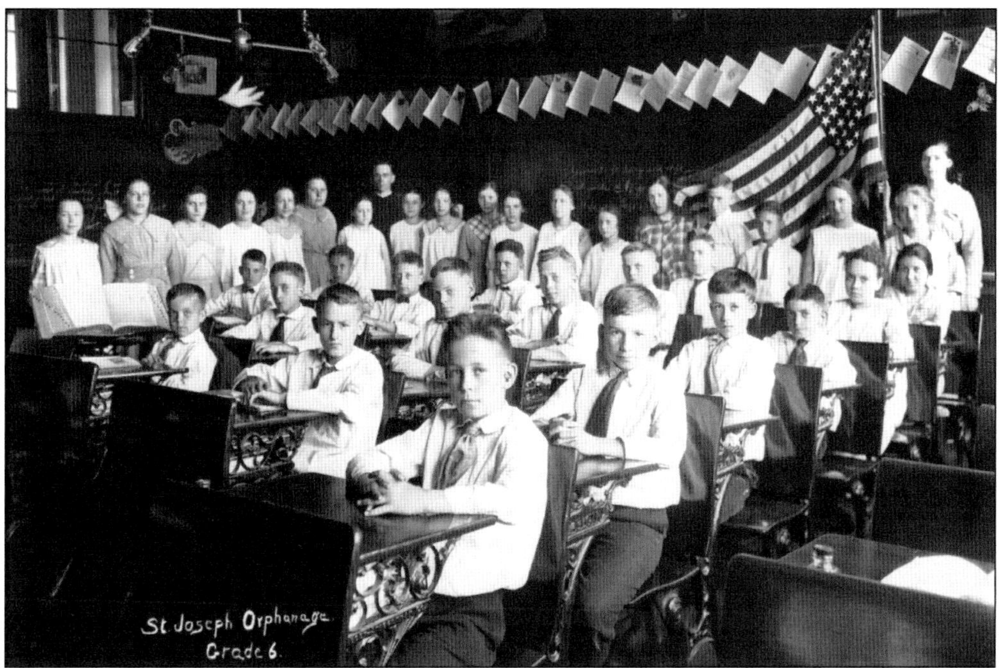

A sixth-grade St. Joseph's Orphanage class poses for a photograph in May 1922. By 1902, the orphanage was caring for over 500 children and educating them from kindergarten through high school. (Courtesy of the Cincinnati Sisters of Charity Archives.)

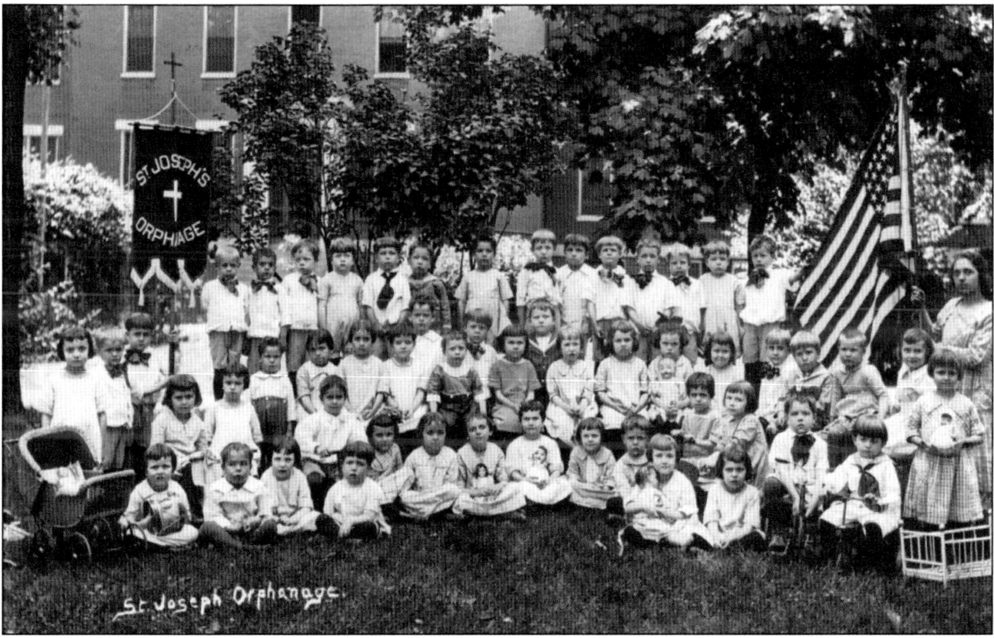

A kindergarten group at St. Joseph's Orphanage in 1922 shows the variety of dolls, hobbyhorses, and toys that the children were allowed. The Sisters of Charity seem to have cared well for the orphans. In the entire 106-year history of the orphanage, there is only one tragic death. On June 30, 1955, Michael Coyne, a baby boy, was killed in a fall from the infirmary window. (Courtesy of the Cincinnati Sisters of Charity Archives.)

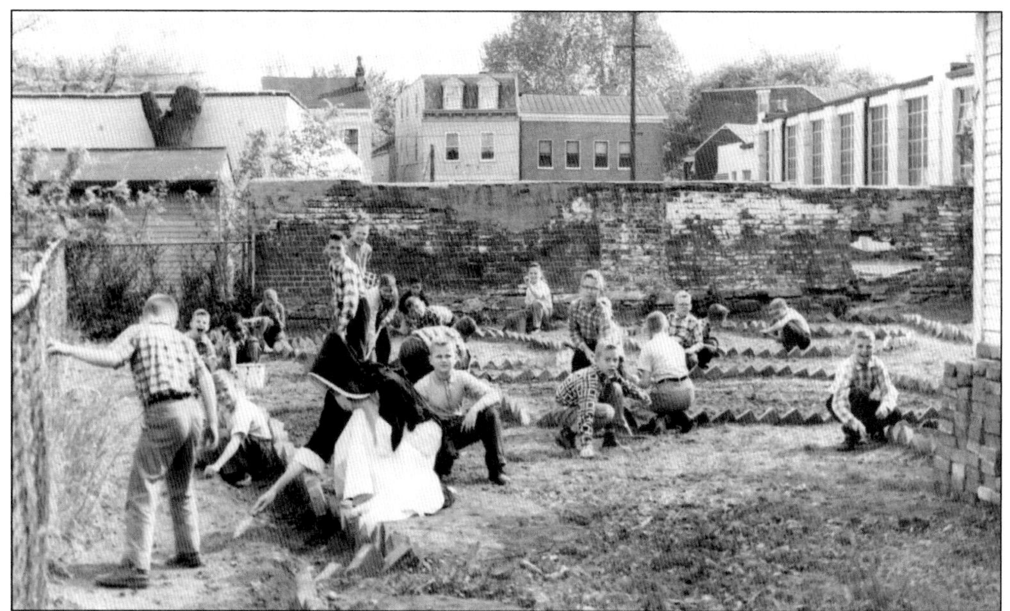

This photograph shows the junior boys class from St. Joseph's Orphanage planting a garden in 1961 with their housemother Sr. Thomas Patrice. The orphanage sponsored a variety of leisure activities including football and baseball teams, a band, and girls' chorales. (Courtesy of the Cincinnati Sisters of Charity Archives.)

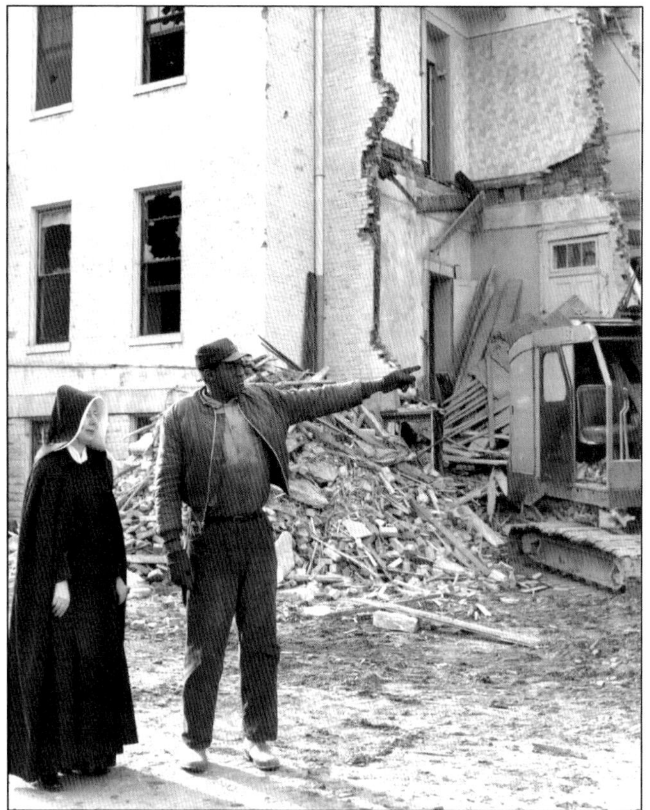

When the sad day came to raze the historic orphanage property in 1964, Sr. Mary Owen Downing was there to supervise. The Sisters of Charity cared for an estimated 10,000 children during the 106-year history in Northside. Many of the sisters devoted their entire career to the orphanage. (Courtesy of the Cincinnati Sisters of Charity Archive.)

Five

A GROWING SUBURB

The 1850s brought many German and Irish immigrants to Northside to help build and run the Cincinnati, Hamilton and Dayton Railroad. This was what motivated the wealthy landowners in Northside to subdivide their property and create the area's first subdivisions.

Ephraim Knowlton was the first to subdivide his land around Knowlton's Corner in 1845, which became largely inhabited by German immigrants. Jacob Hoffner was next, who in 1850 subdivided a large part of land between Hoffner Street, Hamilton Avenue, Blue Rock Street, and Delany Street. The heirs of Charles Williams in 1852 platted land south of the Knowlton subdivision including everything between Elmore, Miller, and Dreman Streets and Mill Creek, encompassing what is now South Cumminsville. Timothy Kirby followed them in 1852, dividing the area lying northeast of Colerain between Hoffner and Gordon Streets. Janet Langlands cut some of her land in the north into lots, and James C. Ludlow executors cut up some of the land near their mansion on the east side of Hamilton avenue north of Spring Grove Avenue. The Jo Williams subdivision west of Hamilton and east of Colerain by Wesleyan Cemetery was carved out in 1852. The Gary Owen subdivision at Blue Rock, Jo Williams, Cherry, and Lower Lakeman Streets was created in the 1860s.

From 1880 to 1900, Northside experienced its major period of growth and developed into two distinct communities, South Cumminsville and Northside. This was when the explosive home building boom came to Northside and created the gingerbread-trimmed Queen Anne–Victorian houses that are so characteristic of the area. For many years, today's South Cumminsville was the southern portion of the larger settlement of Cumminsville. In the 1890s, merchants north of Cumminsville's Knowlton's Corner began calling that area Northside, while the area south and west of Knowlton's Corner bordering Camp Washington, kept its identity as South Cumminsville. As early as the 1890s, working-class African American families began moving to the area around Follett and Dreman Avenues.

The growth brought in supporting infrastructure like the six loan and building companies, three first-run movie theaters, two telephone exchanges, and a variety of saloons, groceries, and eateries.

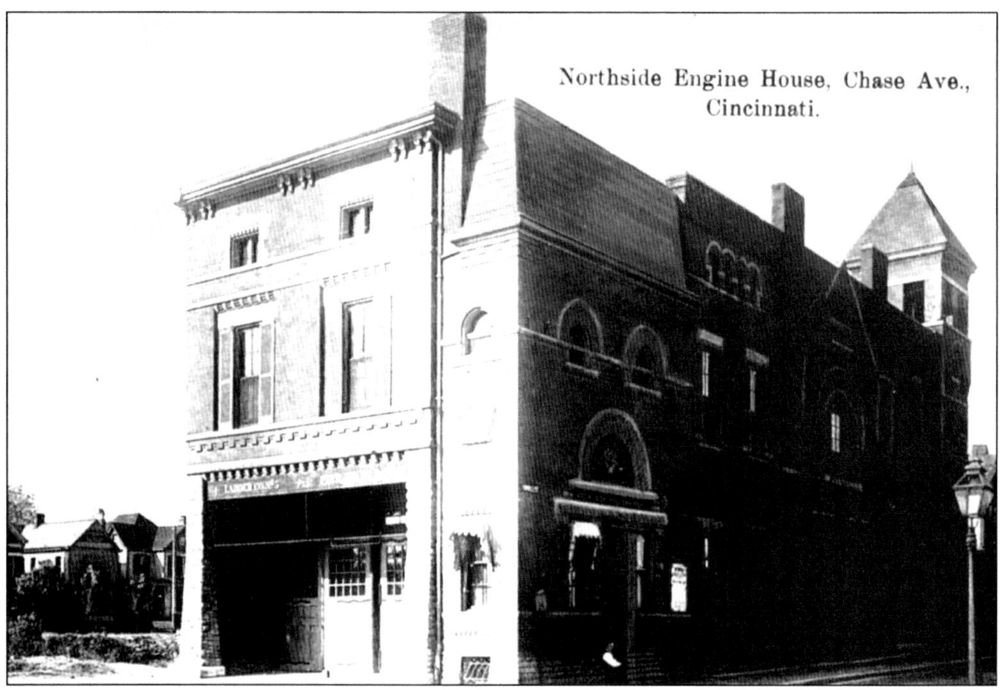

Fire Engine Company No. 20 was built in 1890 by architect Charles Fox at 1636 Chase Street when a growing community needed better emergency support. A plaque on the building commemorates the men responsible for its 1888 Ohio legislature funding. The property was vacated in 1982 for the new station at 1668 Blue Rock Street. (From the Collection of the Public Library of Cincinnati and Hamilton County.)

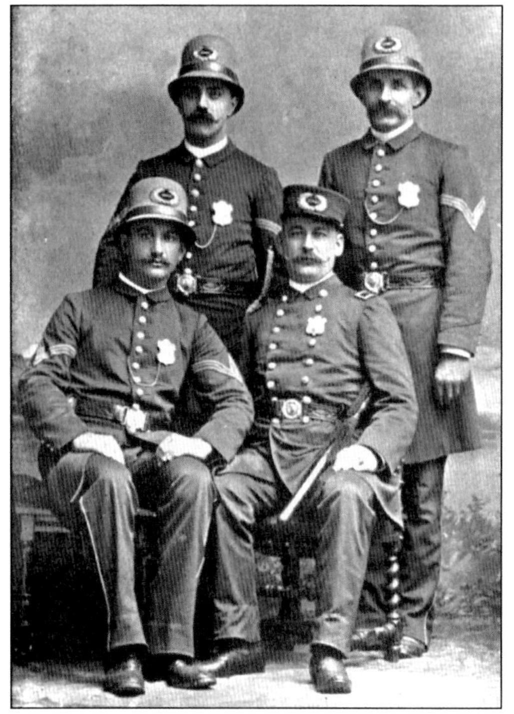

This 1890s photograph shows the Northside District 10 police force. Seen here from left to right are (first row) Sgt. William Krumpe and Lt. William Heheman; (second row) Sgt. Michael Rigney and Sgt. John Winters. The original police station stood on east Spring Grove Avenue, south of the Ludlow Avenue Viaduct. It housed a two-cell basement jail, and in 1872, it served as the Cumminsville mayor's office for Mayor Gabriel Dirr.

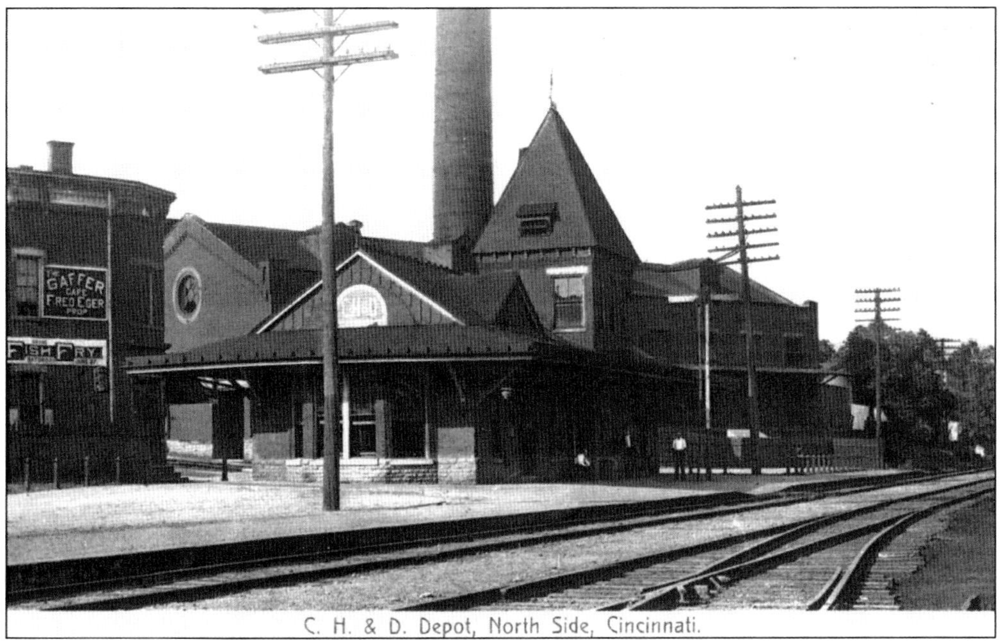

C. H. & D. Depot, North Side, Cincinnati.

This 1908 postcard shows the passenger depot of the Cincinnati, Hamilton and Dayton Railroad at the corner of Apple Street and Vandalia Avenue. Its opening in 1851 made Northside Cincinnati's first commuter suburb. The railroad was purchased by the Baltimore and Ohio Company in 1917. In 1966, the track crossing at Hamilton Avenue and Hoffner Street were removed, eliminating the dusty "Five O'Clock Special" crossings. (From the Collection of the Public Library of Cincinnati and Hamilton County.)

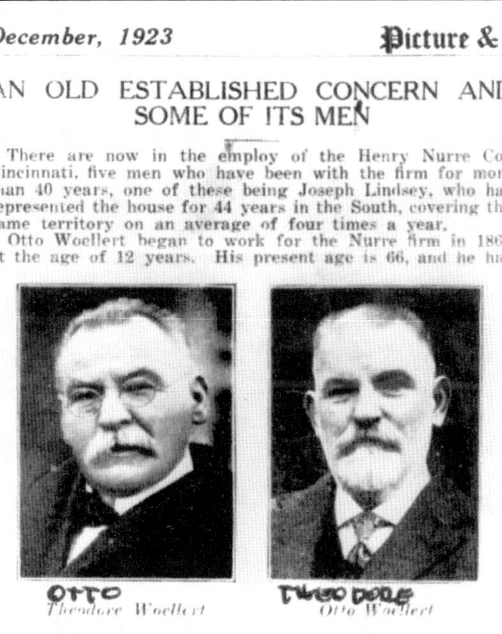

December, 1923 **Picture &**

AN OLD ESTABLISHED CONCERN AND SOME OF ITS MEN

There are now in the employ of the Henry Nurre Co., Cincinnati, five men who have been with the firm for more than 40 years, one of these being Joseph Lindsey, who has represented the house for 44 years in the South, covering the same territory on an average of four times a year.

Otto Woellert began to work for the Nurre firm in 1869 at the age of 12 years. His present age is 66, and he has

OTTO
Theodore Woellert

THEODORE
Otto Woellert

been with the firm 54 years. Theodore Woellert began at the same age as his brother, Otto, on November 15, 1873, and has been with the firm just 50 years. His present age is 62 years. Both have been working together at the same bench and doing the same kind of work, namely cutting and

This article from the 1923 *Cincinnati Picture and Gazette* honors Otto Carl (1856–1935) and Theodore Ernst Woellert (1860–1929) for their over 40 years of service to the Nurre Picture Frame Company in downtown Cincinnati. Along with their German immigrant father, Theodore Sr. (1829–1901), they commuted daily to downtown Cincinnati on the Cincinnati, Hamilton and Dayton Railroad, like many other Northsiders.

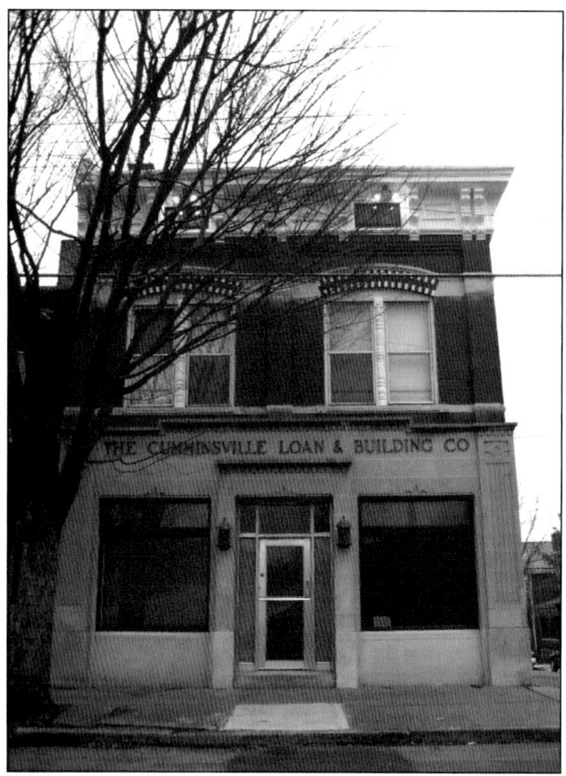

The Cumminsville Loan and Building Company played a vital role in the growth of residential housing along Chase Avenue. Built in 1896 when the company incorporated, its second-story window trim resembles a piano keyboard, with alternating black and white stones. This popular style can be seen in several other Northside commercial buildings. The Cumminsville Loan and Building was merged with Brentwood Savings in April 1981.

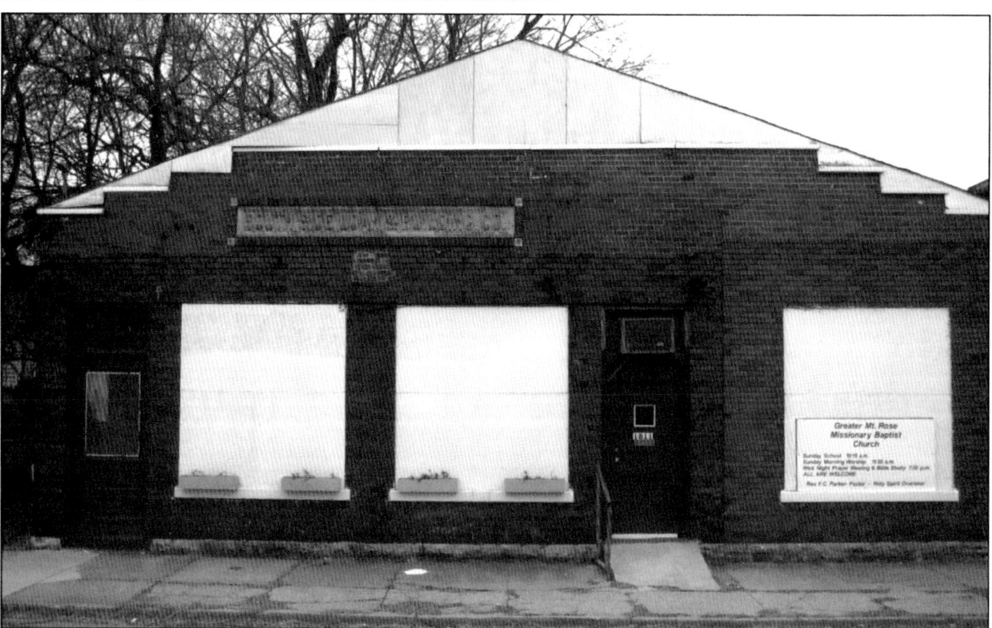

The Southside Loan and Building Company at 1805 Powers Street, shown here, incorporated in 1890. It financed many of the houses in South Cumminsville in the 1890s. Southside merged with Evanston Loan and Building and then became Midwest Savings. It was one of six other Northside loan and building associations, formed to help the hardworking middle class build their own homes. It now houses Greater Mount Rose Missionary Baptist Church.

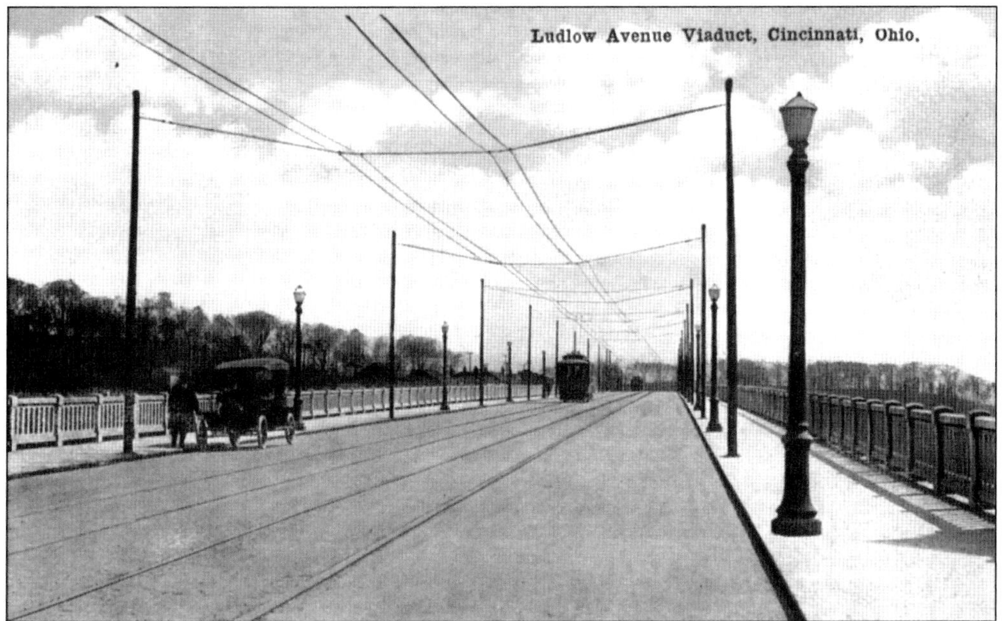

Engineer Frank L. Raschig designed the Ludlow Avenue Viaduct. Completed in 1913, its 1,750-foot span held two trolley tracks in the center, flanked by two lanes for automobile traffic and pedestrian walks on either side. Its opening linked Northside more directly to the city and made Knowlton's Corner one of the busiest shopping districts in Cincinnati. (From the Collection of the Public Library of Cincinnati and Hamilton County.)

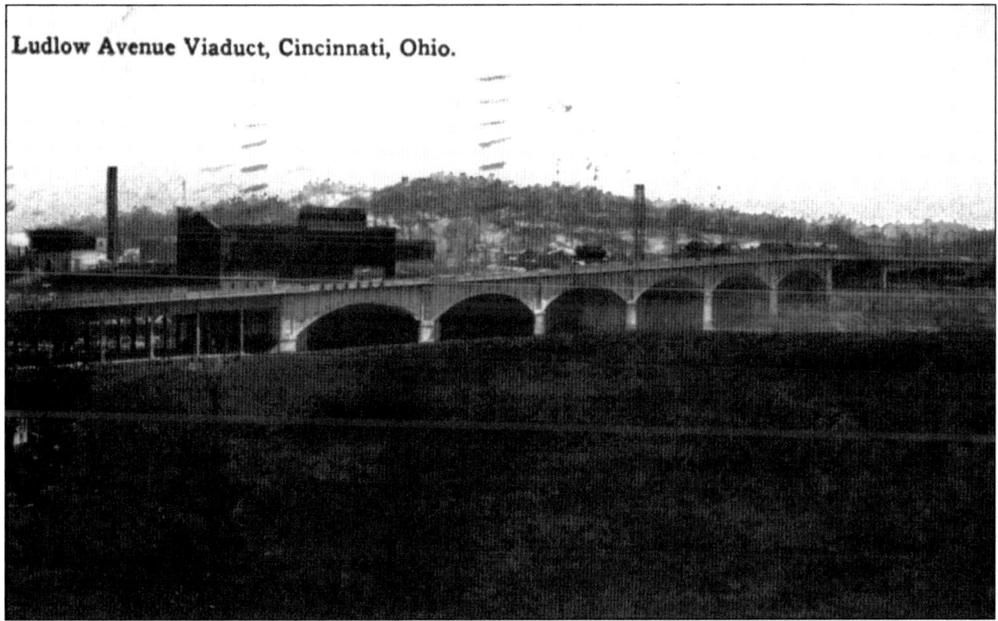

This photograph shows the Ludlow Avenue Viaduct span at completion in 1913. Underneath the original viaduct was a park where the Northside Business Association hosted a carnival from July 22 to 31, 1915. Events included speakers from around the country, band concerts, a public marriage at Knowlton's Corner, and the crowning of Helen Volz as "Queen of the Carnival." (From the Collection of the Public Library of Cincinnati and Hamilton County.)

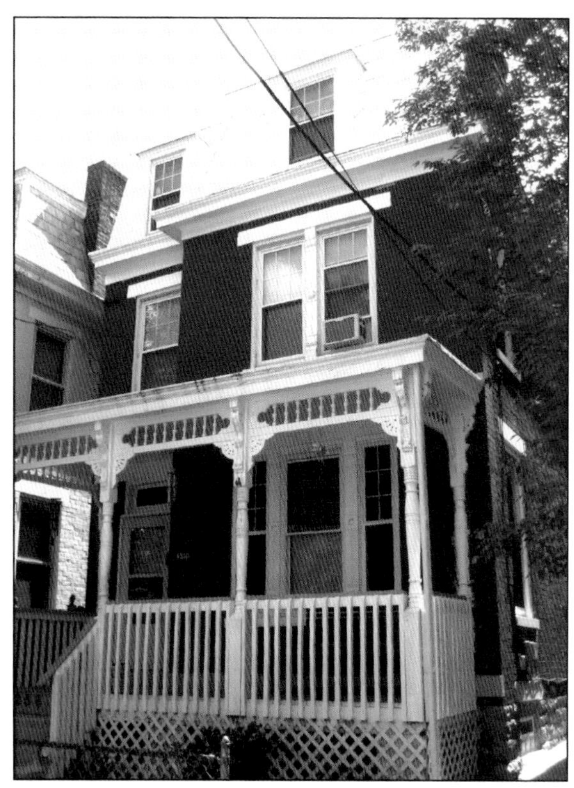

This home built for Otto and Elizabeth Dhonau Woellert (1859–1945), at 4256 Langland Avenue, typifies Northside's Victorian-era housing. Otto was a foreman at the Nurre Picture Frame Company in downtown Cincinnati, and his wife was daughter of Fred Dhonau, Northside's carriage maker. Abraham Bell developed two small subdivisions on the east side of Langland Avenue in 1888 that became homes to dressmakers and skilled craftsmen such as machinists, plumbers, painters, pressmen, and carvers.

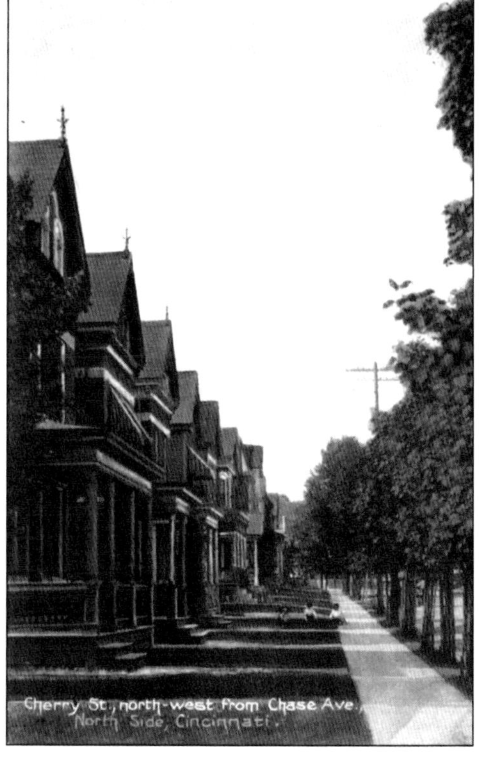

This 1908 postcard shows the brick, two-and-a-half-story, Queen Anne–style homes on Cherry Street west from Chase Avenue, built for the growing middle class during the housing boom in Northside. Most of the homes had large front porches and no driveways. (From the Collection of the Public Library of Cincinnati and Hamilton County.)

This 1908 photograph shows the stone castle of soap baron Andrew Jergens (1852–1929) that graced the corner of Hamilton and Bruce Avenues. The family willed the lot for a park, and it was demolished in 1968. Jergens Park was dedicated on April 26, 1970. The Cincinnati Art Museum received an entire room of the house, the Damascus Room, brought back as a souvenir from Syria by the Jergenses. (From the Collection of the Public Library of Cincinnati and Hamilton County.)

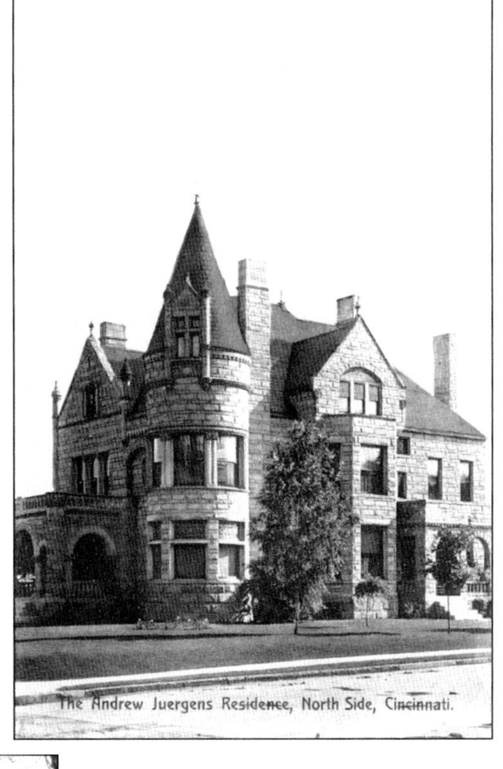

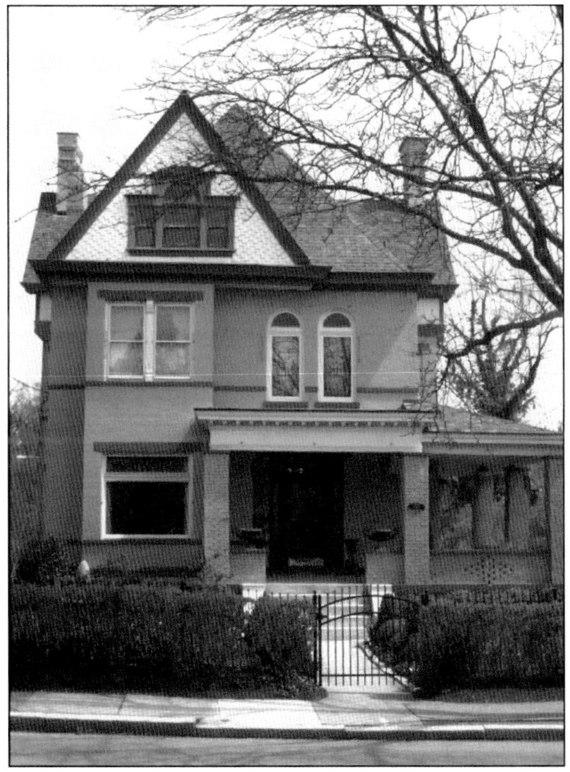

Although smaller and less grandiose than his brother's castle, Herman Jergens's (1857–1946) house at the southeast corner of Hamilton and Bruce Avenues, built in 1895, says more with less. It showcases stick, shingle, and craftsman styles and, unlike his brother's house, still stands today with its carriage house intact. Herman and his wife, Catherine Bletter (1860–1907), raised their only child, Olive Jergens Bolles (1890–1964), here in the 1890s.

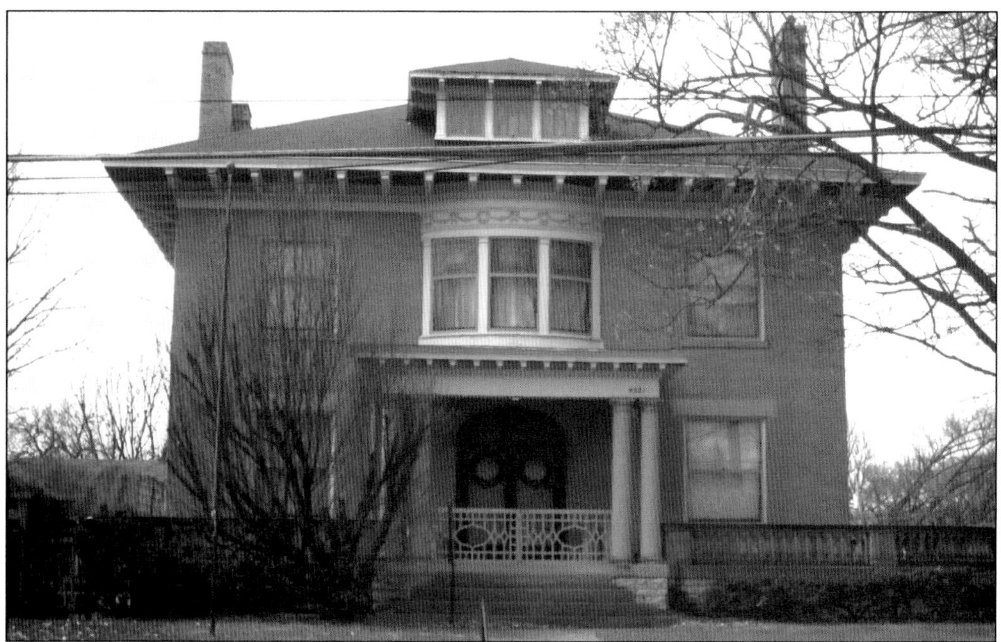

The Bullerdick house was designed by architect William Franklin (1848–1918) and built in 1907. Fred (1863–1926) and Kathryn Bonin Bullerdick (1869–1944) owned a mattress factory on Spring Grove Avenue and raised six children here. The house contains murals by Francis Pedretti (1829–1891), an Italian muralist employed by wealthy Cincinnatians. The property was listed on the National Register of Historic Places in 2007.

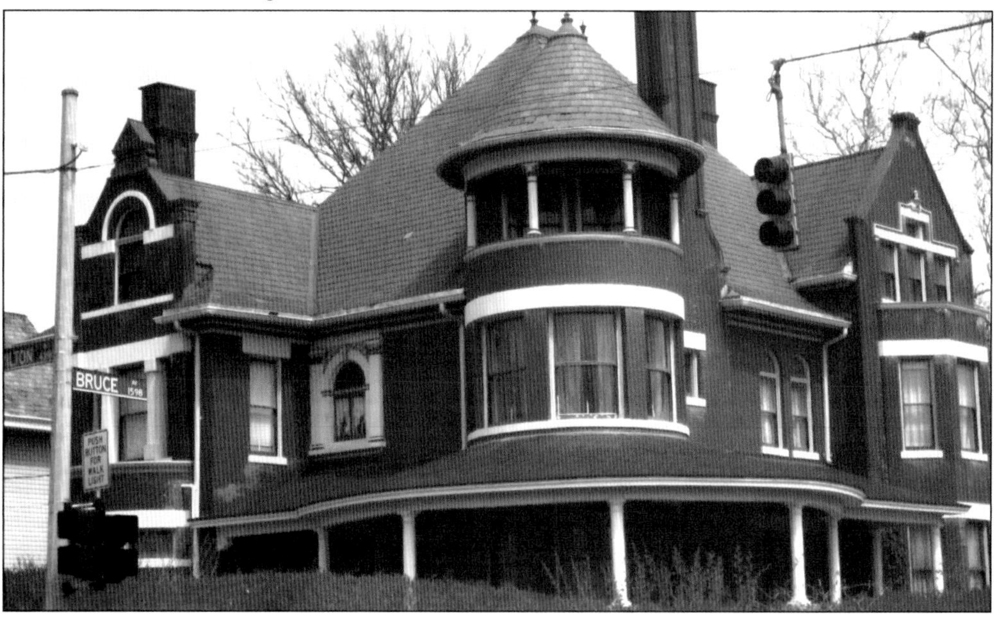

This photograph shows the Geiffus house at Millionaires Corner, at the northwest corner of Hamilton and Bruce Avenues in Northside. Built in 1898 for the third officer of the Andrew Jergens Company, Charles Geiffus, this 15-room, Queen Anne–Victorian house has retained its handsome woodwork, eight fireplaces, and 20 stained and leaded glass windows. Its elaborate carriage house behind the house still remains.

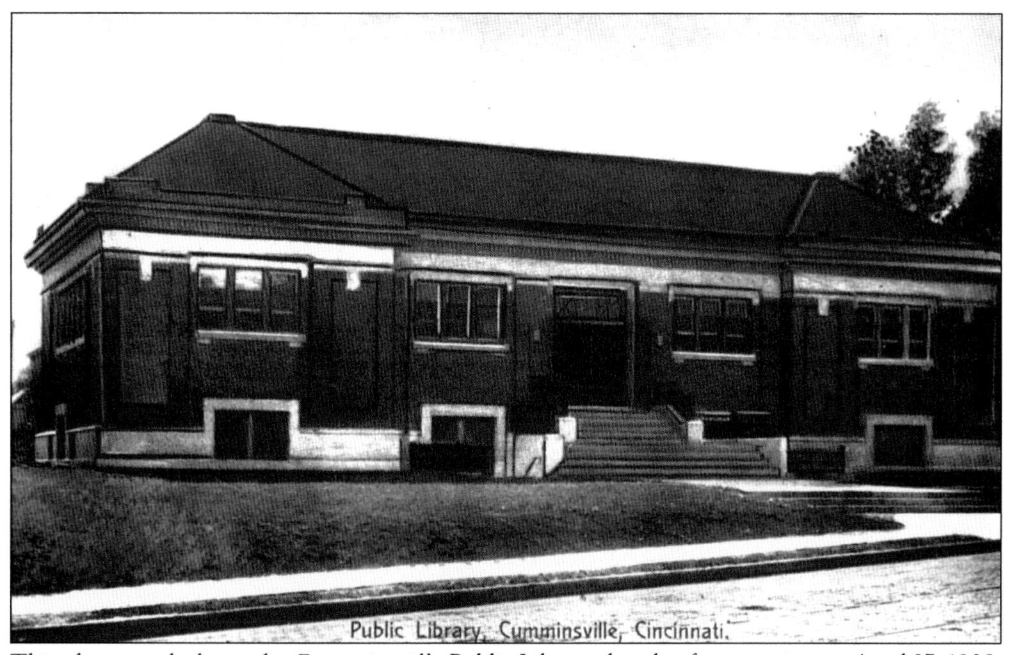

This photograph shows the Cumminsville Public Library shortly after opening on April 27, 1908. It is one of nine Cincinnati libraries funded by the Andrew Carnegie Foundation. Designed by architects Tietig and Lee in the French Renaissance style, its high windows maximize natural light and once had a 149-seat auditorium. It operates today as the Northside Branch Library. (From the Collection of the Public Library of Cincinnati and Hamilton County.)

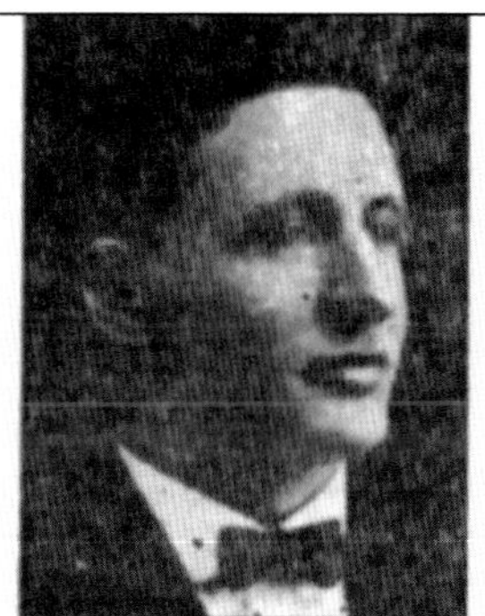

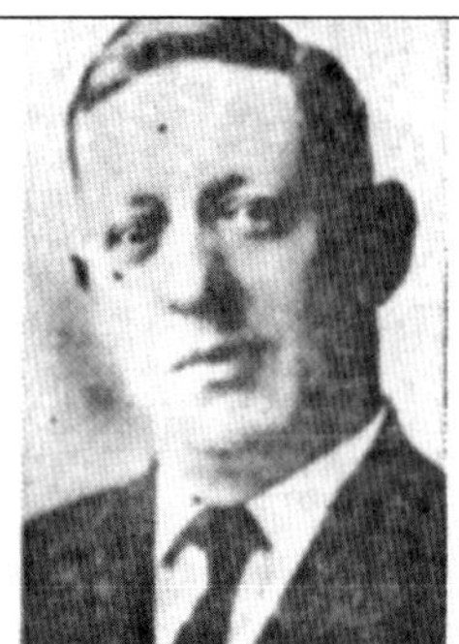

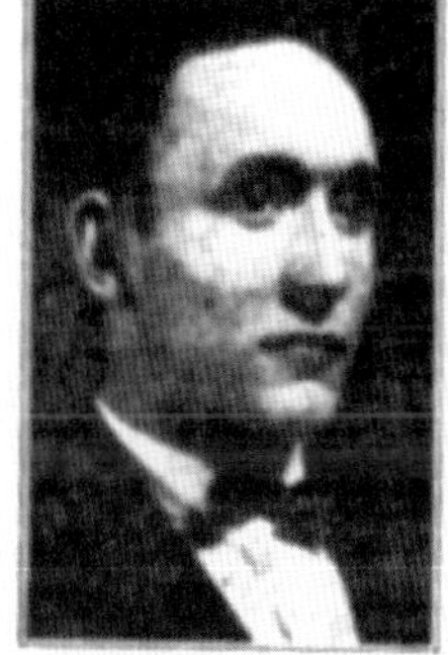

Ray Hamilton
V.-Pres. & General Manager

Frank Hamilton
President

Lee Hamilton
Director & Ass't. Manager

FRANK HAMILTON, Inc.

Expert Furniture, Piano, Hotel and Office Movers

Phones Park 1189-1792 3830 SPRING GROVE AVENUE

This 1925 advertisement shows a long-standing Northside family business, Hamilton Movers. Frank Hamilton (1875–1931) started his moving business with one wagon in 1893 and operated at 3830 Spring Grove Avenue. Frank's sons Ray and Lee Hamilton helped to manage the business, but Ray took over after his father's death. Although no Hamilton family member is connected to the business today, it still provides large-scale office moves to Cincinnati businesses.

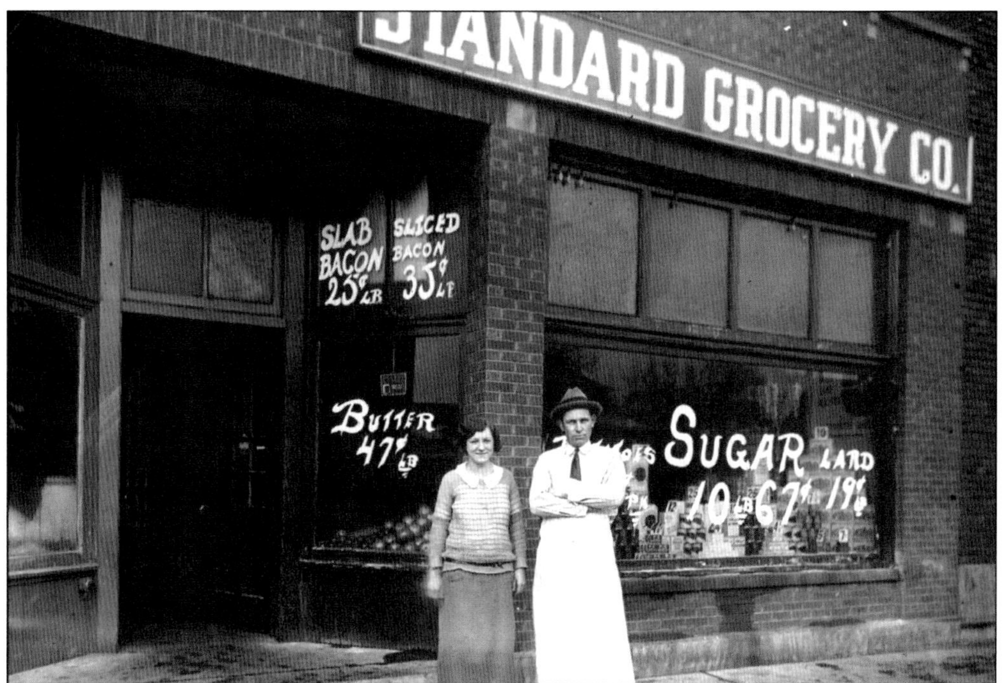

In Northside, there was a bar, grocery store, or bakery on nearly every corner. Standard Grocery, shown here in the 1920s, was one of the many family-owned grocers supplying the hungry people of Northside. In a 1925 souvenir program published by the Northside Business Association, there were 33 grocers advertising in Northside. (Courtesy of Don Beimesche.)

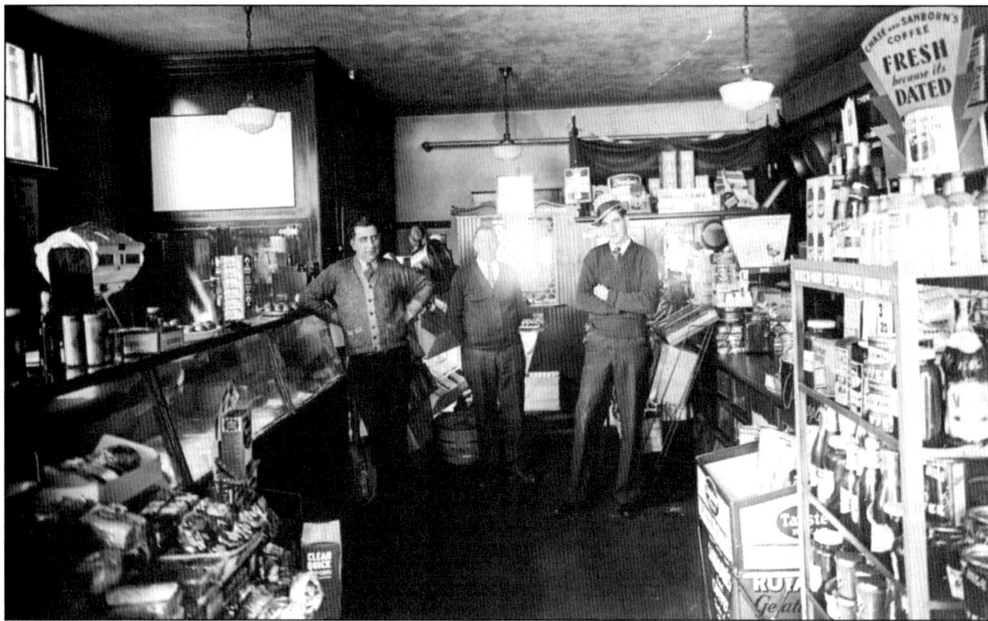

Schilling's Grocery operated in a building no longer standing on Elmore Street, at Miller Street, in what is now South Cumminsville. This late-1940s photograph by Tom Finley, shows Bill Bocklet on the right with hat, and his father-in-law Fred Schilling, the butcher in the center. While Bocklet served in World War II, his wife, Edith, became butcher until he returned. (Courtesy of Al Bocklet.)

Charles H. Dhonau (1861–1944) built this funeral parlor at Hoffner Street in 1913. In a time when funerals were home affairs, this was a modern showplace to house a large public or a small private funeral. Charles was a son of Fred Dhonau, Northside's carriage maker. Charles's son, Charles O. Dhonau (1886–1971), was president of the Cincinnati College of Embalming and influenced modern funeral practices. They vacated the Northside location in 1967.

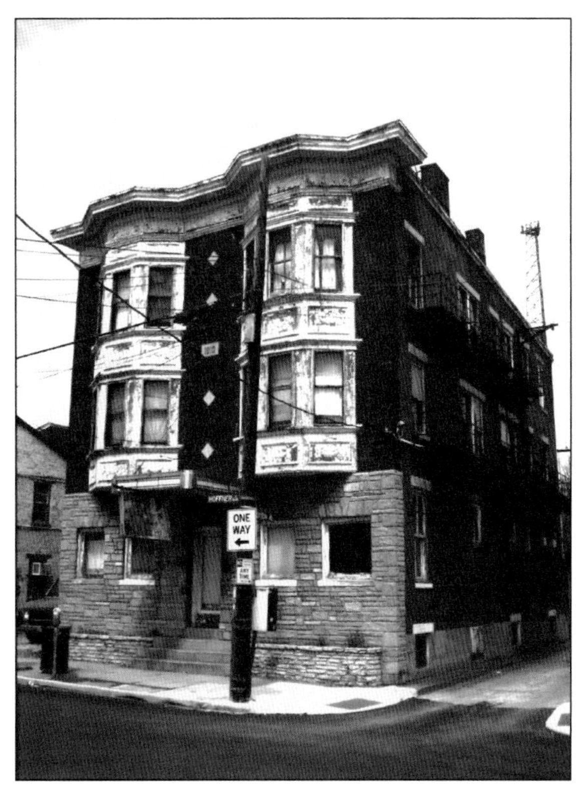

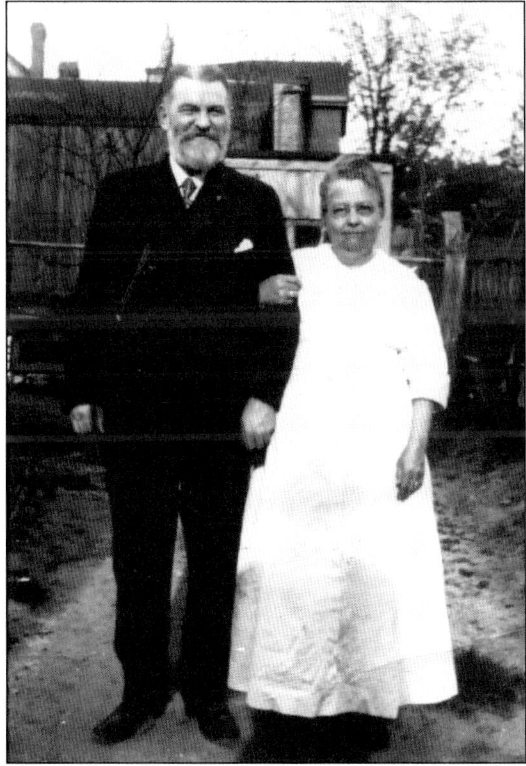

Theodore Woellert (1860–1929) and Carrie Henke Woellert (1859–1926) pose in a 1923 photograph that could be called "Cumminsville Gothic" in the backyard of their home at 3906 Beekman Street that they built in 1895. Visible behind them is the large henhouse where, like many Northsiders, they raised chickens. The meat and eggs were used for their own family and to supply the many local grocers for extra income.

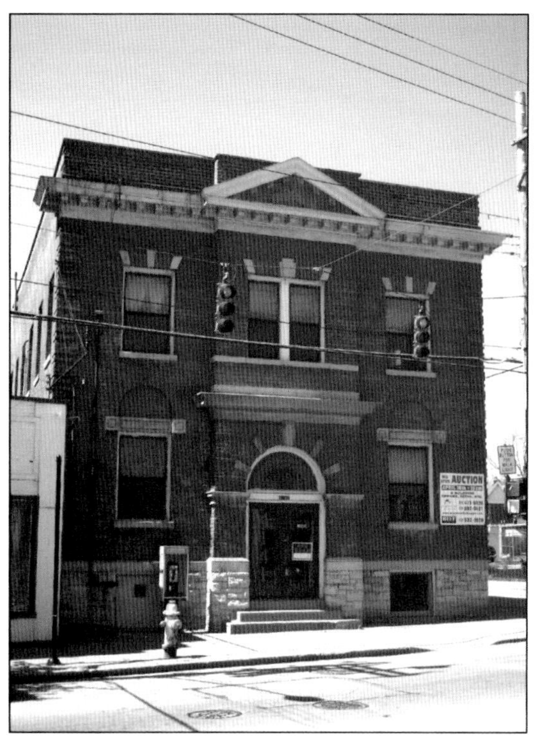

The Park Telephone Exchange, with a ghostly past, opened in 1903 when telephone service was a luxury. On the night of November 2, 1904, Alma Steingeweg, an exchange operator here, left work and became one of five victims of the "Cumminsville Ripper," who terrorized Northside from 1904 to 1910. The victims were found mutilated near the streetcar tracks by Spring Grove Cemetery. Despite the national buzz, the Cumminsville Ripper was never found.

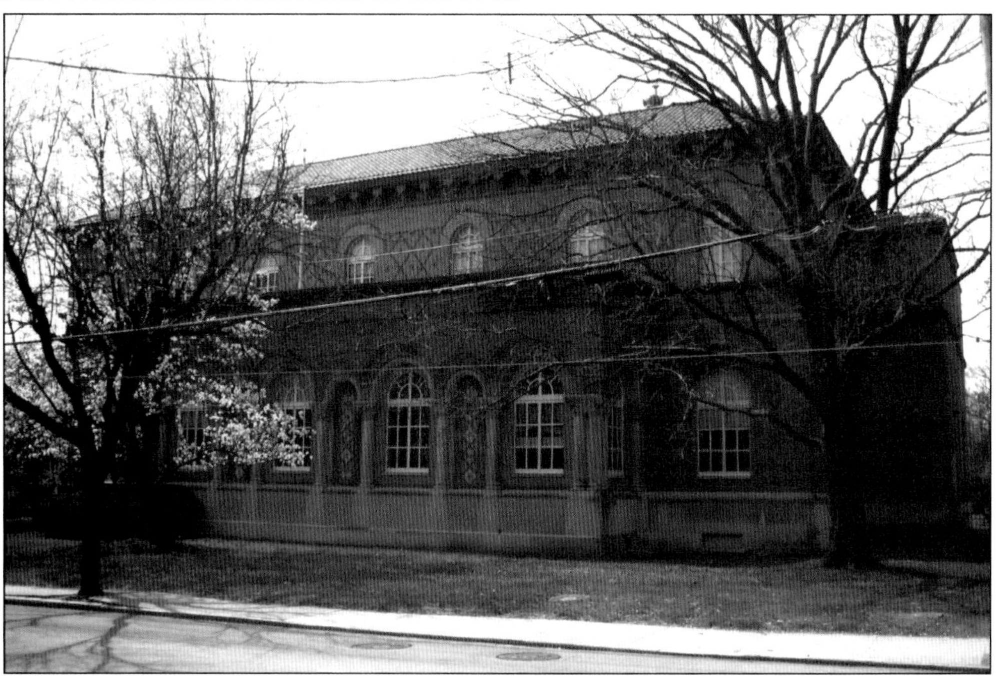

The explosive growth in population and wealth caused Northside to outgrow the Park Telephone Exchange. In 1925, the Renaissance Revival building at Hamilton and Bruce Avenues was built as the Kirby Telephone Exchange. Architect Harry Hake (1871–1955) designed it like he did the Cincinnati Bell Telephone building downtown—with a tall first floor to house the large exchange equipment used at the time and with florid art deco carved details.

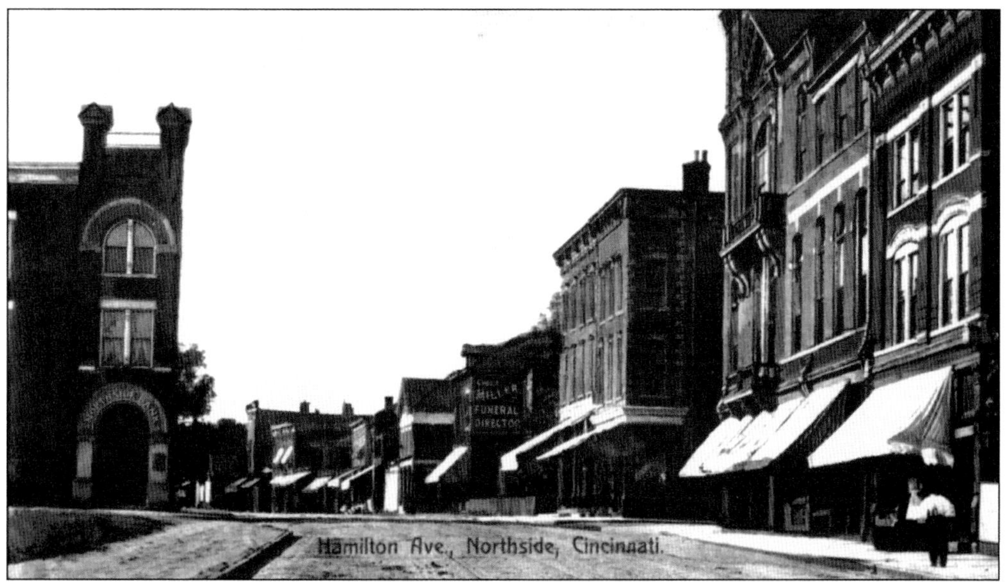

The Northside Bank, the neighborhood's oldest and largest, was established by George L. Thomson and Walter S. Titus in February 1888. Their cashiers were first in the Hoffner Lodge, and then growth motivated them to build the bank on the northwest corner of Hamilton and Palm Avenues. For over 100 years, the Northside Bank has funded Northside businesses. (From the Collection of the Public Library of Cincinnati and Hamilton County.)

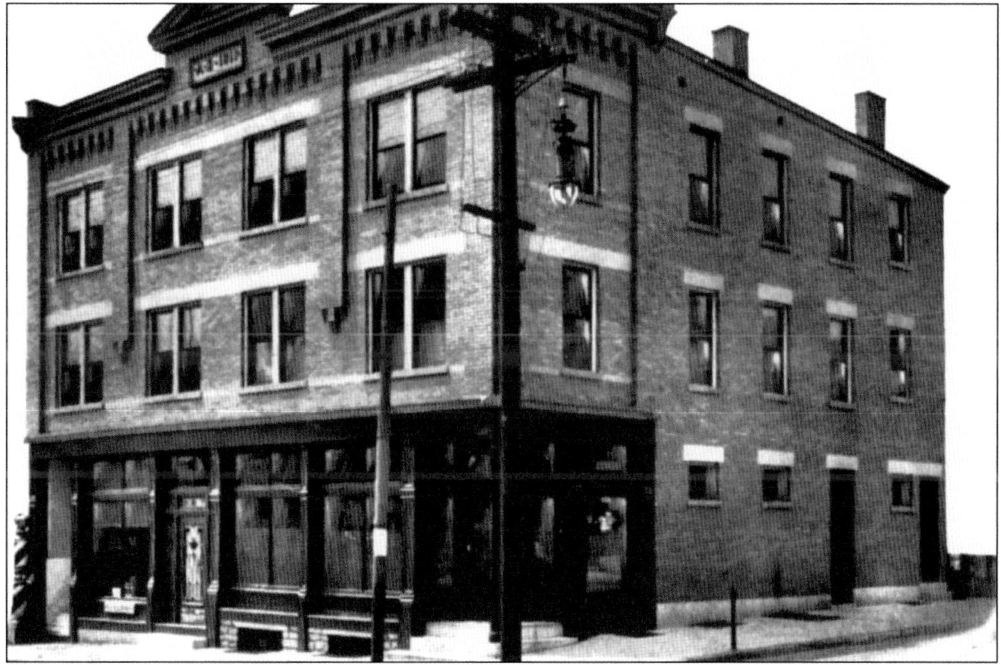

This 1914 photograph shows the Dillman Café in the Palm Building. Henry Dillman (1863–1938) built the Palm in 1905 on land bought from the Hoffner Estate. He operated the café with his sons Clifford (1886–1957) and Wheeler Dillman, renting rooms above. It was sold in the 1940s to Reds catcher Eugene "Bubbles" Hargrave, who operated it as Bubbles Hargrave's Bar and Grille. Today it houses the Gay and Lesbian Community Center of Cincinnati.

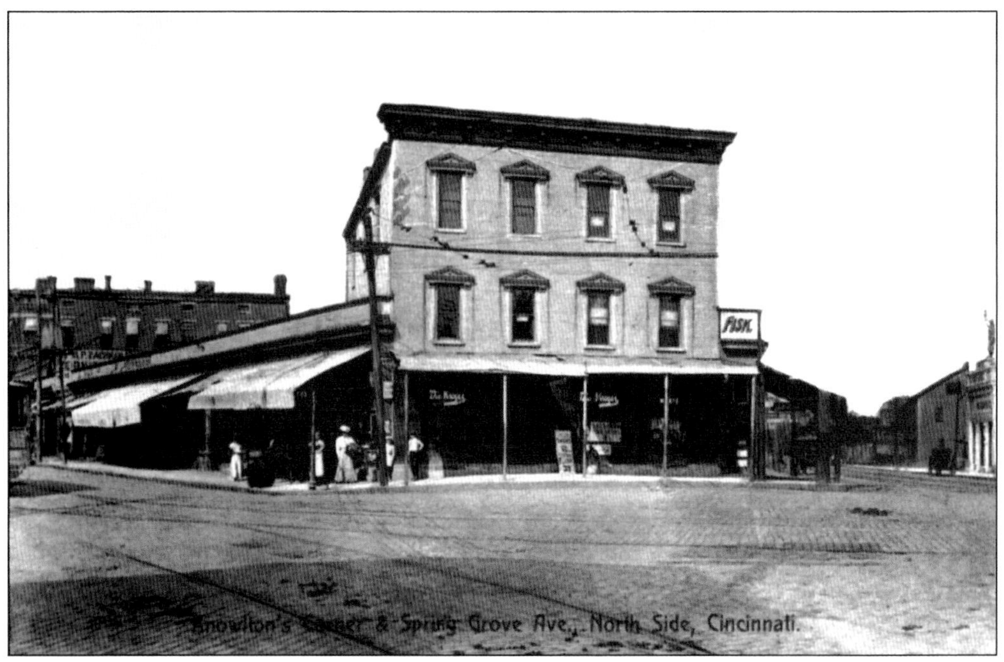

A 1908 postcard shows the Kroger Grocery Knowton's Blockhouse and the open air markets behind. To the right is the Fisk Monument Company and the office of Judge William Howard Taft, dean of the University of Cincinnati College of Law. A woman sports the popular wide-brimmed Gainsborough chapeau hat, probably made at Jennie McGuire's Millinery on Hamilton Avenue. (From the Collection of the Public Library of Cincinnati and Hamilton County.)

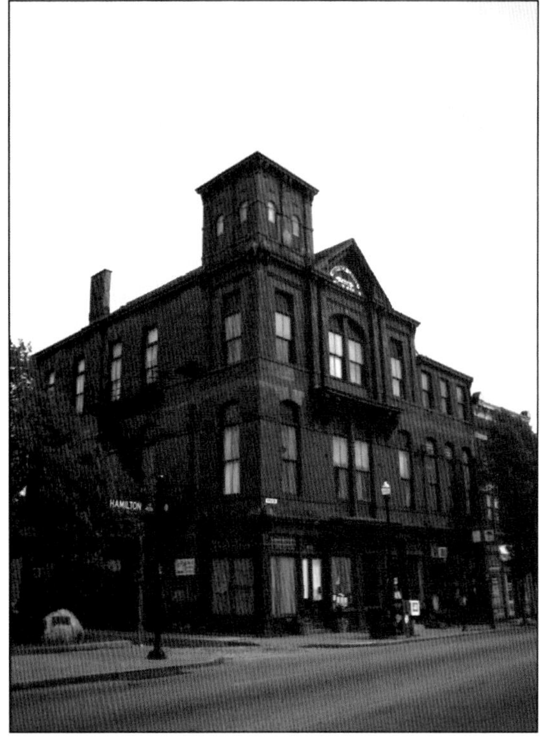

This photograph shows the Hoffner Masonic Lodge No. 254, designed by Samuel Hannaford and completed in 1884, or in Masonic dating, 4884 Anna Lucius. Jacob Hoffner, who had joined the first Masonic order in Cincinnati in 1824, donated the land. A bell, dismantled when the lodge moved out in the 1960s, rung during every member initiation ceremony.

This wooden frame building is the oldest surviving Italianate building on Hamilton Avenue. It was financed for $462 in 1871 for Mecklenburg immigrants Theodore and Fredaricka Burchard Woellert (1835–1894) by the Cumminsville German Building and Savings. The Woellerts operated a framing and notions store there for over 30 years, while raising four children—Theodore Jr., Otto, Maria (1869–1894), and Magdalena (1871–1944)—above the store. Since 2005, it has housed Honey restaurant.

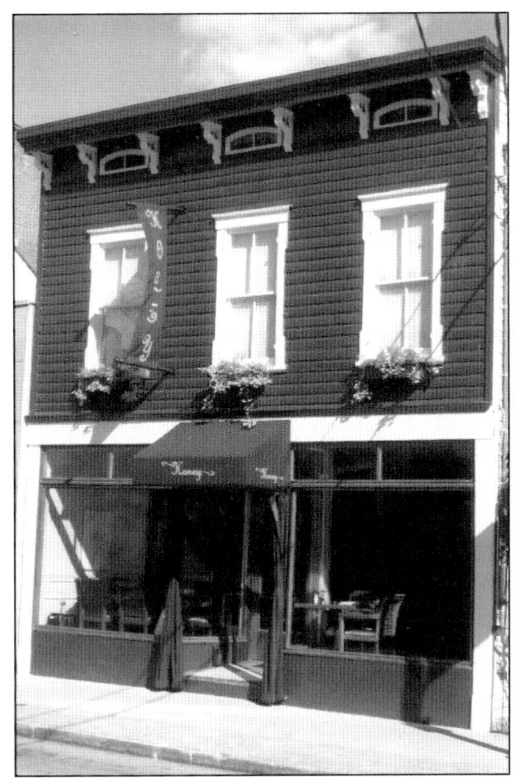

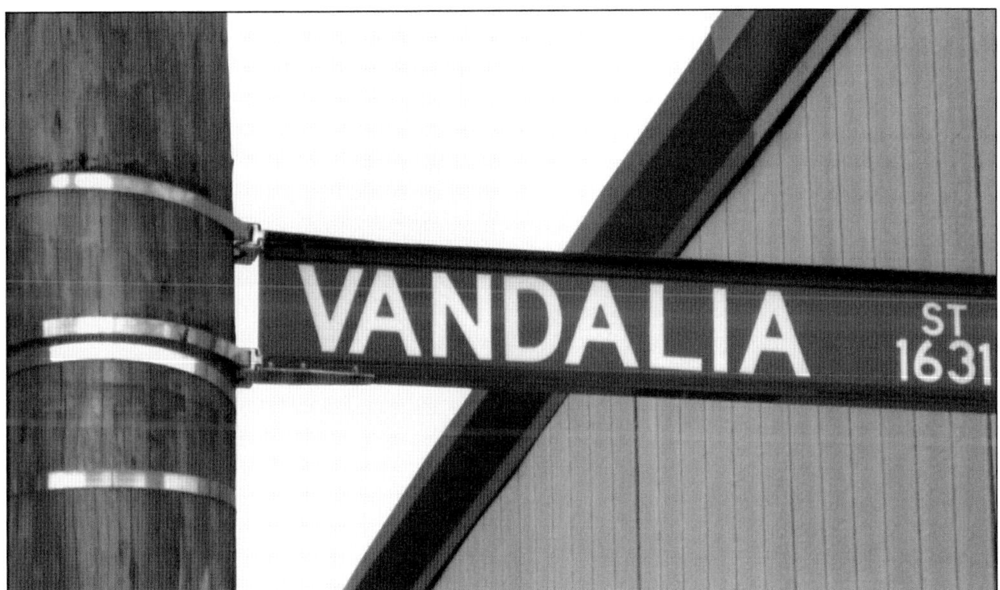

Vandalia is an old nickname for Mecklenburg in northern Germany. Vandalia Street in Northside is named for the group of Mecklenburg immigrants who lived in the blocks bounded by Hamilton Avenue and Vandalia, Gulow, and Hoffner Streets. Six families came in a chain migration from the village of Penzlin from 1855 to 1871. They were Theodore and Fredaricka Burchard Woellert, Carl and Berna Burchard Sonnenburg, Carl and Therese Burchard Dankert, Fred Dankert, August Gulow, and Johann and Lizette Mentzel Woeller.

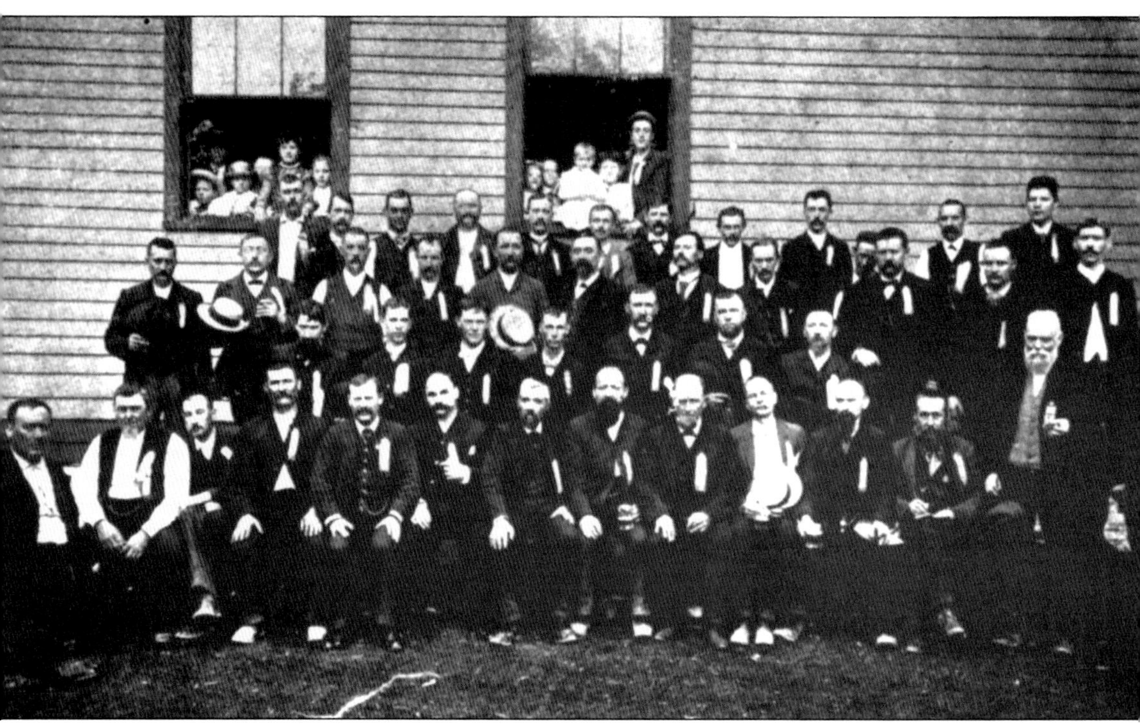

The Cumminsville Turnverein of 1889 are seen standing in front of their Hoffner Street hall. Leader August Ernst Gulow (1837–1901), after whom Gulow Street is named, led the group that year in the Cincinnati National Turnfest downtown. The Cumminsville Turners, a German sport and social club, were founded on August 6, 1870, by Wilhelm Sanders and originally met in Streng's Hall in Cumminsville. The founding members were Phillip Lorenz, John C. Bruckman, Ed Herberg, August Ernst Gulow, Andreas Spaeth, Otto Woellert, Christian Schamberger, Joe Eiselein, Franz Freitag, Reuben Leun, Mathias Pfeffer, Cassius Tschus, Herman Krumpe, Adam Kraus, and others. In 1889, there were 126 members, 20 of whom were gymnasts. The group had a German-language school with 86 boys and girls, some shown peeking through the windows behind the group, who were instructed by Oscar Sputh. A woman's auxiliary was founded in 1881, and the wives made a beautiful flag that flew above their *Turnerplatz*, or hall. In addition to hosting parties and *sangerfests*, the Cumminsville Turnerplatz on Hoffner Street was home to the Cumminsville Raucher Casino. The group disbanded and meshed into the Cincinnati Central Turners in 1895.

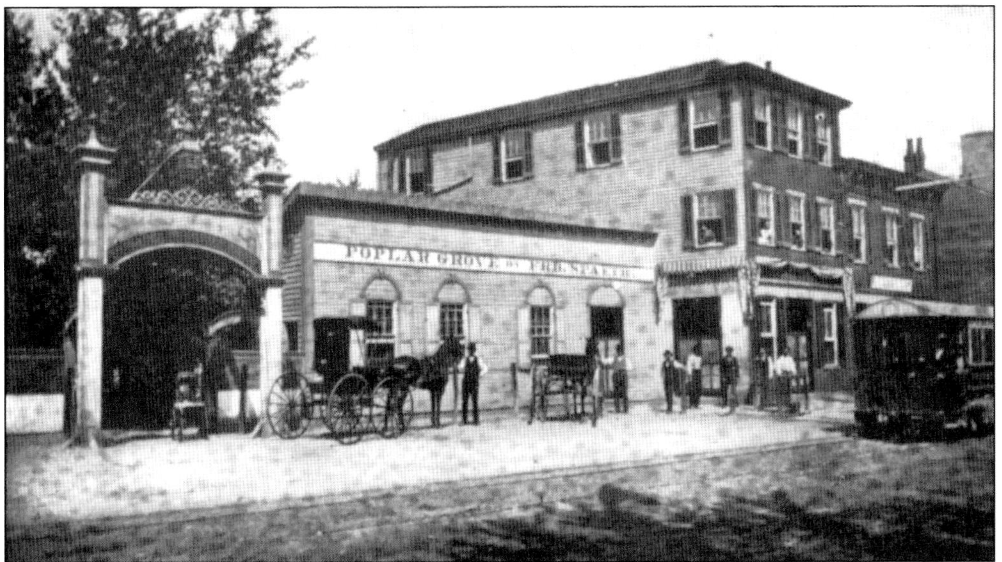

Poplar Grove, a German beer garden at 3733 Spring Grove Avenue, was founded in the 1860s by Fredrick Spaeth (1824–1871), a German immigrant. It was purchased in 1912 from the estate of Fredrick Spaeth Jr. (1860–1912) by Theodore Hoelscher, an immigrant from the Rhineland in Germany, who remodeled the dining room to serve dinners for large family gatherings. In the summers, Hoelscher hosted cabaret shows and twice-monthly band concerts.

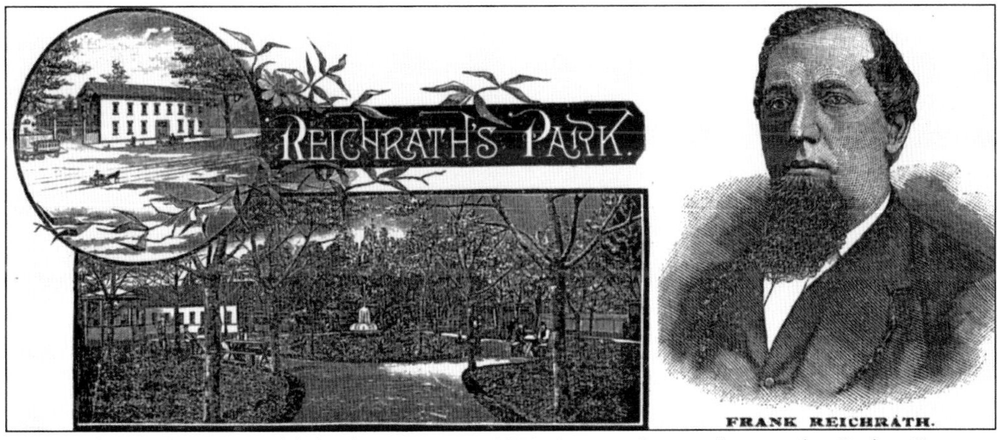

Reichrath's Park was established in 1862 at 3720 Spring Grove Avenue by Baden-German immigrant Frank Reichrath (1840–1903). This was the popular pleasure resort for German Cincinnatians. The business survived the 1884 flood, and it passed to his son Frank Jr. after his death in 1903. Frank Jr. operated the business into the 1920s. A 1915 advertisement in German touts Reichrath's as the biggest and best picnic area for German clubs, housing two big dance halls for summer and winter celebrations.

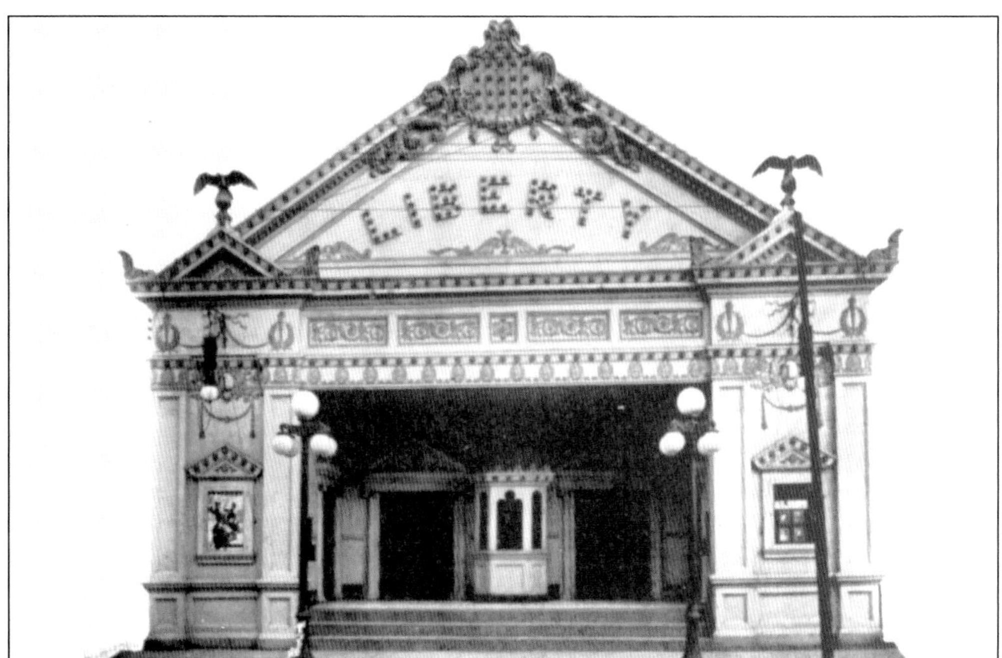

The Liberty Theatre at 3938 Spring Grove Avenue was built in 1909 for Henry Levy. Blazing with red, white, and blue lights spelling "Liberty" on its pediment, it featured silent pictures with a live piano accompaniment by William H. Schmitt and a vaudeville show on Friday nights. Closing in 1929, it became the Liberty Chili Parlour. Kays Restaurant took over in 1954, and it was added to the National Register of Historic Places in 1982.

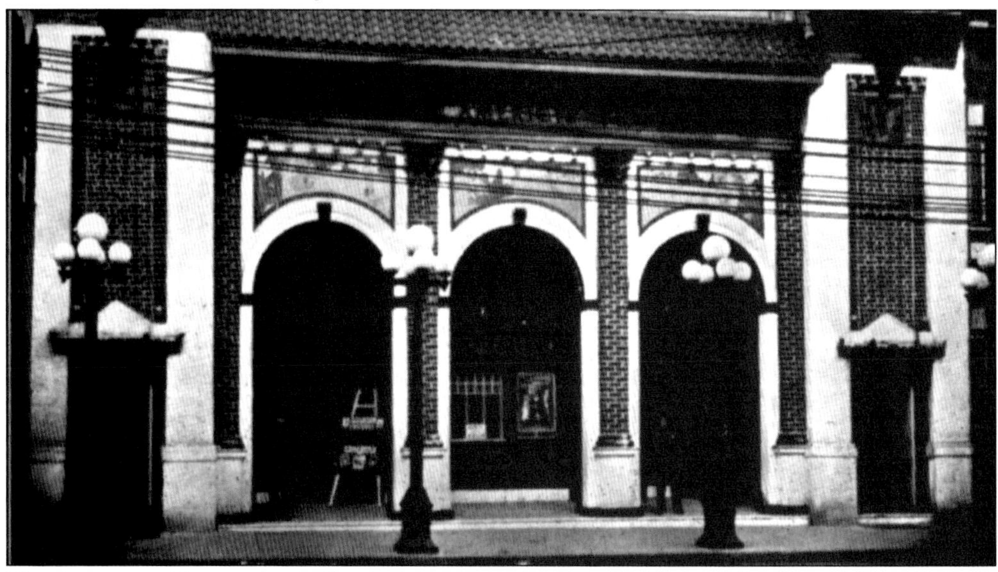

The Americus Theatre was built in 1911 at Hamilton Avenue by Northside bricklayer William Erd for the Queen City Amusement Company. It showed first-run motion pictures, and minstrel shows performed by the Northside Business Association. The theater was purchased by the Northside Business Association under association president Elizabeth Permut in the early 1950s and demolished to make the current Northside parking lot. She owned Permut's Pharmacy at 4009 Hamilton Avenue.

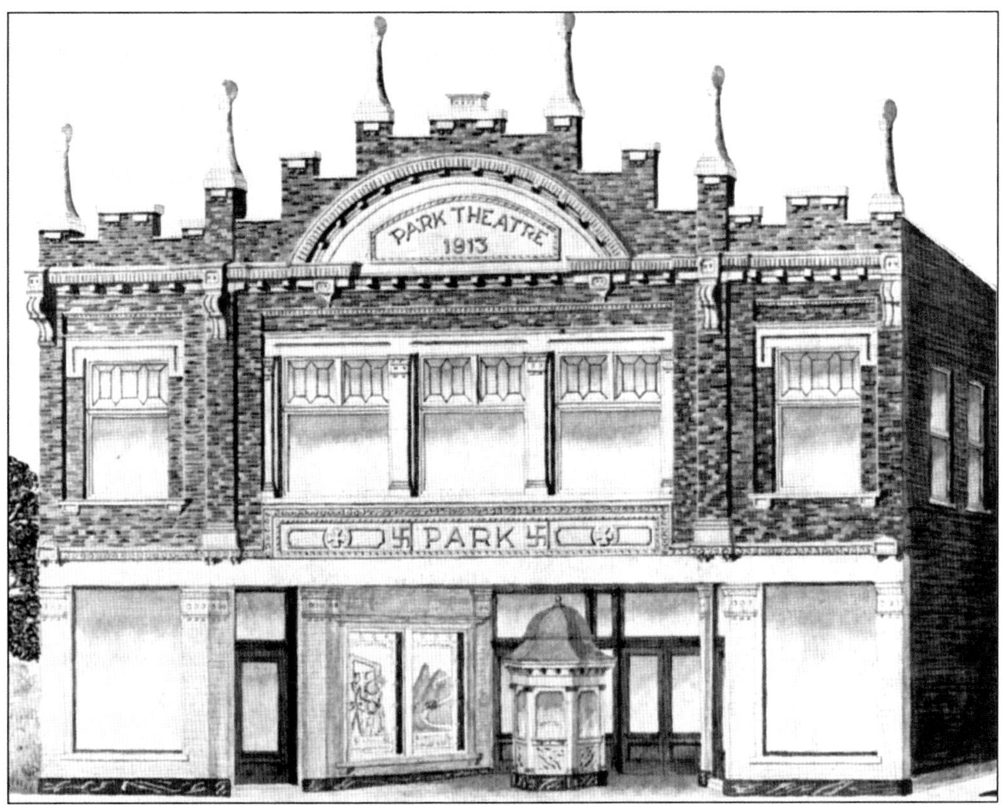

The Park Theatre at 4161 Hamilton Avenue was built in 1913. It housed a barbershop and a billiard room and had air conditioning vents for each seat. In the 1940s, the second floor housed the Southern Ohio Business College under the leadership of Harold Nagel. It ran in the 1970s as the Alpha VI Theater, showing X-rated films. In 1983, it was sold to the Grote Bakery business.

PARK Northside's Foremost Theatre The Newest and Best Photoplays Daily: 7:00—8:45. Sundays and Holidays Continuous 2:00 to 11:00 HEAR THE NEW ORGAN!	LIBERTY Always Your Money's Worth Vaudeville and Musical Revues With FEATURE PICTURES

These advertisements for the Park and Liberty Theatres from early in the second decade of the 20th century ask the reader to "hear the new organ," which at the time was played by organist William H. Schmitt. Albert Laile Sr. ran the Park Theatre, while his son Albert Laile Jr. (1908–1973) ran the Americus Theatre, ensuring neither's business competed with the other. In 1947, the Park Theatre had two shows nightly, double features Saturday, and matinees twice a week, all 45¢.

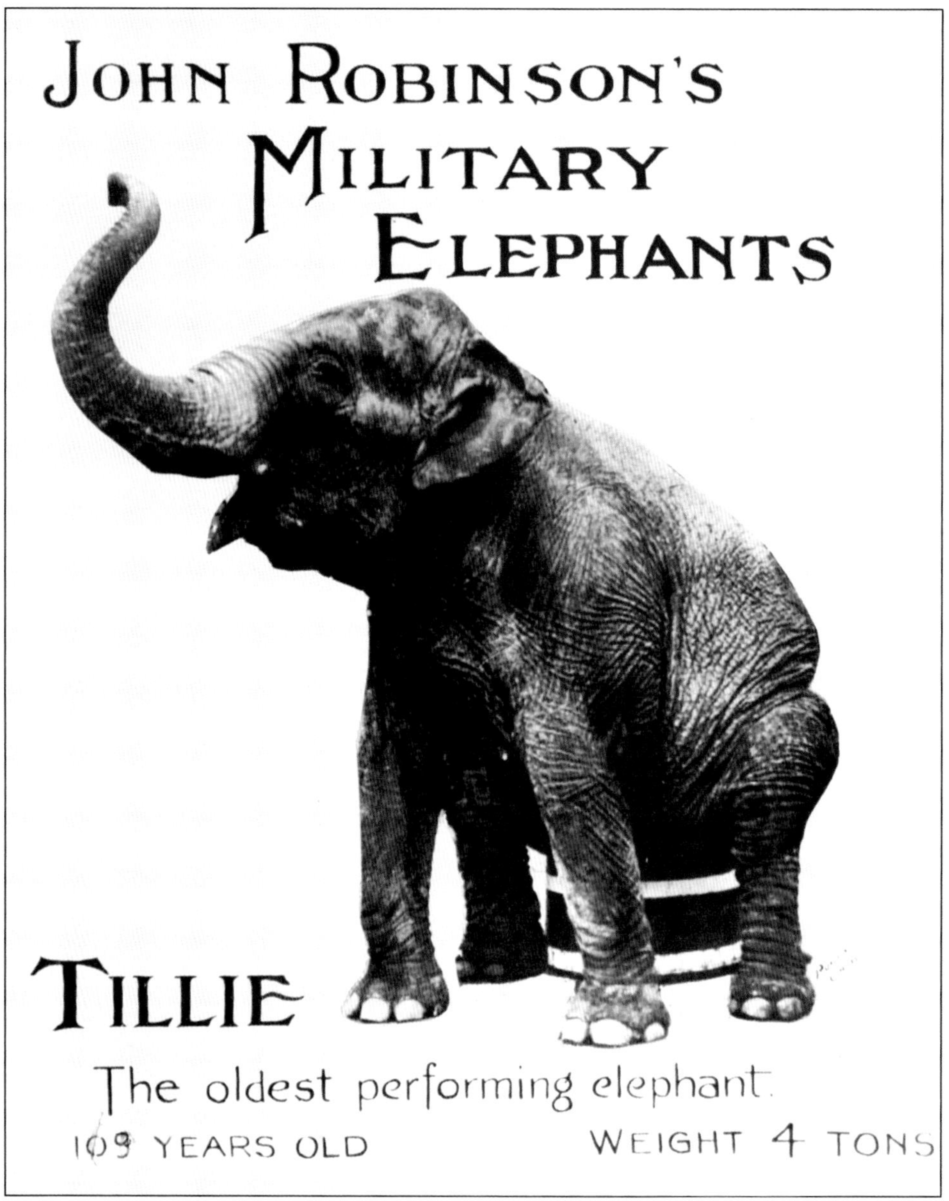

A 1921 advertisement promotes Tillie the elephant, the leader of the military elephant show of John Robinson's Circus. The John Robinson Circus, along with four other big circuses—namely Cole Brothers, Ringling Brothers, Barnum and Bailey, and Hagenback-Wallace—made annual trips from 1900 to the 1940s to Northside, pitching their big tops at Luckey's Field in South Cumminsville behind Dreman Street near the Ohio Knife Company. An annual circus parade started at the Cincinnati, Hamilton and Dayton Railroad spur at Hamilton Avenue and Blue Rock Street and a trail of exotic animals proceeded to the circus grounds. Tillie's trainer Henry Sheak, noted in his diary that Tillie was a temperamental leader and caused a stampede of the entire herd in the second decade of the 20th century at a show in Northside, without injuring anyone. She died in 1932 at the age of 120 years. Her owner John G. Robinson was a landowner in Northside and is the person for whom Robinson Circle in Northside is named. (Courtesy of the Cincinnati Museum Center–Cincinnati Historical Society Library.)

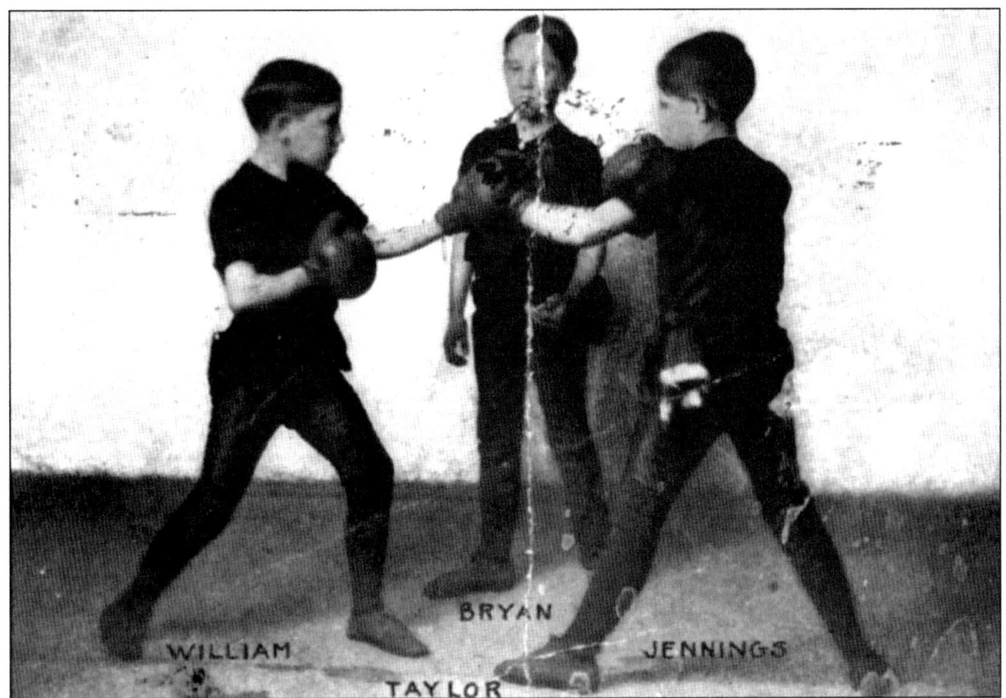

Triplets William, Jennings, and Bryan Taylor performed a boxing act for the Barnum and Bailey Circus in Northside on May 29, 1911. They were a favorite act of Northside boys, who could also watch boxing matches at Chester Park on Spring Grove Avenue, now the Cincinnati Waterworks. The triplets were named after presidential candidate William Jennings Bryant, who lost to William Howard Taft in 1908. (Courtesy of the Kevin Grace Collection.)

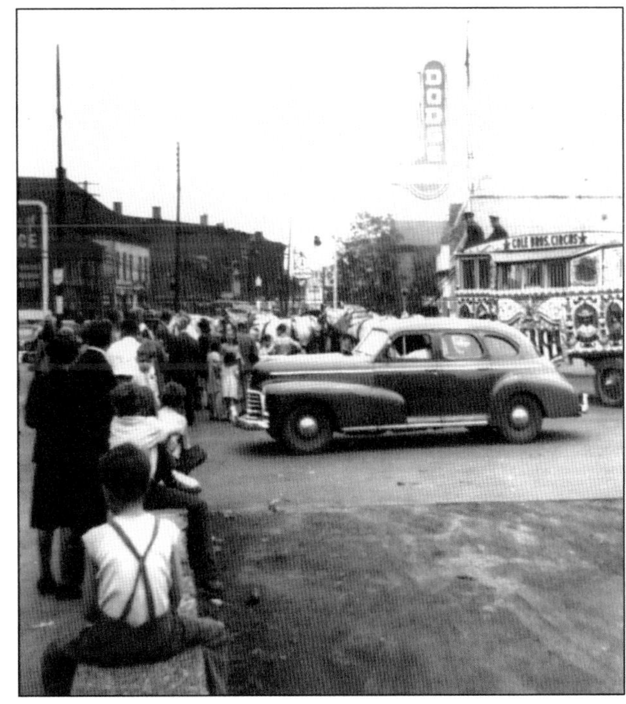

This May 1947 circus parade shows the Cole Brothers Circus horse-drawn calliope making its way down Spring Grove Avenue past the Dabney Thompson automobile agency to the circus grounds in Northside. (Courtesy of Roberta Lipka Landwehr Watson.)

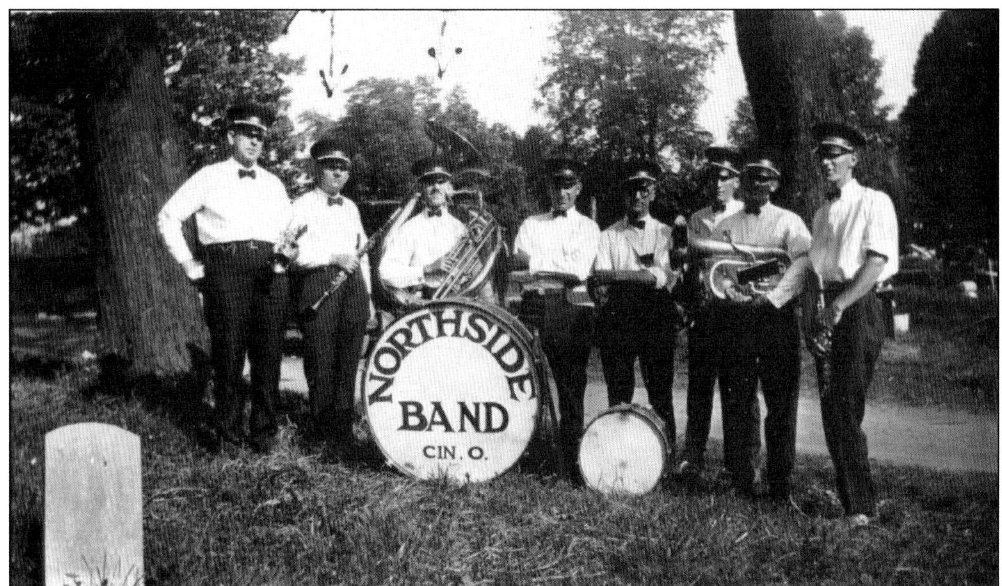

Northside had its own community band from the second decade of the 20th century into the 1940s. This 1920s photograph shows a smaller group of the Northside band. August Lipka is on clarinet, Oscar Lipka is on tuba, and Eugene Lipka is on sousaphone. (Courtesy of Roberta Lipka Landwehr Watson.)

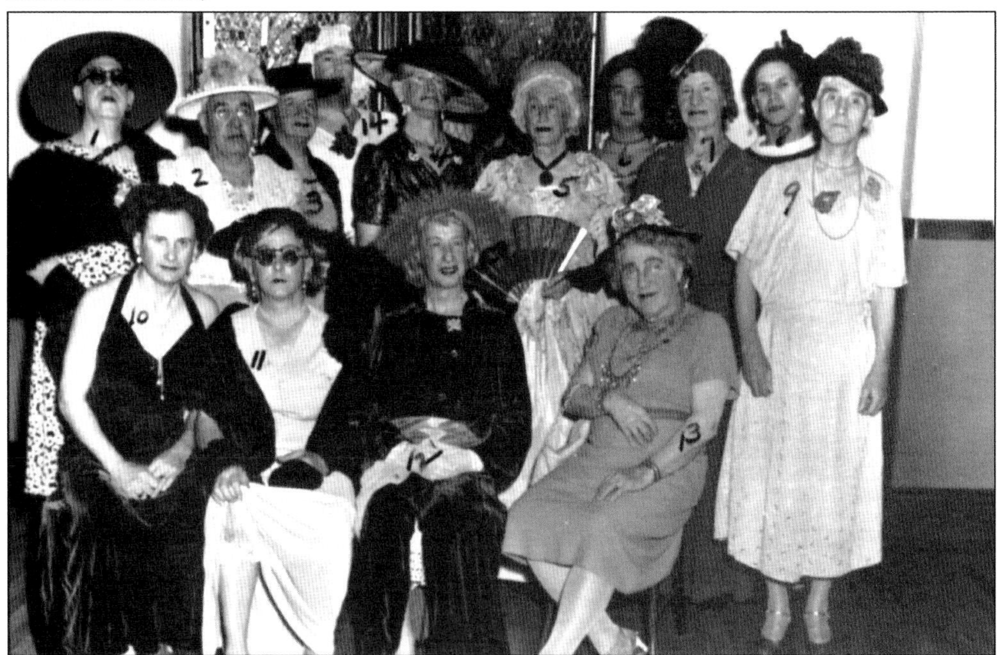

This motley crew starred in a fashion show fund-raiser in 1952 for the North Presbyterian Church. The men in drag are Herb Doll (1), Walter Rider (2), Mr. Usinger (3), Mr. Dools (4), Mr. Ragsdall (5), Don Young (6), Tom Fox (7), Dave Whers (8), Harry Alber (9), Larry Schmid (10), Walter Heinrich (11), Tony Wibben (12), Mr. Meithan (13), and Tom Schrimp (14). This was neither the first nor the last drag show in Northside. (Courtesy of the Northside Presbyterian Church Archives.)

Six

MILK AND BEER

The rolling hillsides in west Northside, along West Fork Road at the foot of Mount Airy and along Kirby Road, were home to a plethora of dairy farmers. These farmers supplied milk to one of several area dairies or had their own home-delivery service. Ammon Avenue, off of Colerain Avenue, is named for one of the earliest of these dairy farmers, Johann Georg Ammon (1818–1891), a Bavarian immigrant and blacksmith. Other Northside dairies were the Bosse Dairy, Henry Meyer Dairy, Blessing Dairy, and John T. Reuther Dairies. Many people today remember receiving milk home delivery and skimming the cream off the top before the homogenization process was standard. The Reuther Dairy, the longest lasting Northside dairy, operated into the 1950s and served customers outside of Northside, until they became victim of the dairy conglomeration of the later half of the 20th century.

On the east side of Northside, another favorite drink was being made at John C. Bruckmann's brewery. John C. Bruckmann (1829–1887) and his wife, Amelia Detert, came to Cincinnati in 1850 from Berka, Eisenau, Germany, purchasing 37 acres of farmland in Cumminsville, on the canal for easy access. They began brewing lager beer in the basement of their original house for their friends, who would visit on Sunday's by canalboat. The friends brought beer home, distributing to their friends in Cincinnati. In 1856, such a demand for the beer had been created that John incorporated the firm. For the first 15 years, the records were kept in German and had amusing entries recording the exchange of chickens and meat for beer kegs. "Good Ole Brucks" was one of the more popular brands in Cincinnati, advertised at Crosley Field, and the only one to stay open during Prohibition, manufacturing nonalcoholic cereal beverages and 2 percent alcohol malt tonic. The brewery distributed Brucks Beers in 17 states and sponsored out-of-state groups, like a West Virginia girls basketball team and various Boy Scout troops and events. William Bruckmann, third generation owner, was the last president of the brewery, before the board sold it to Herschel Condon in 1949.

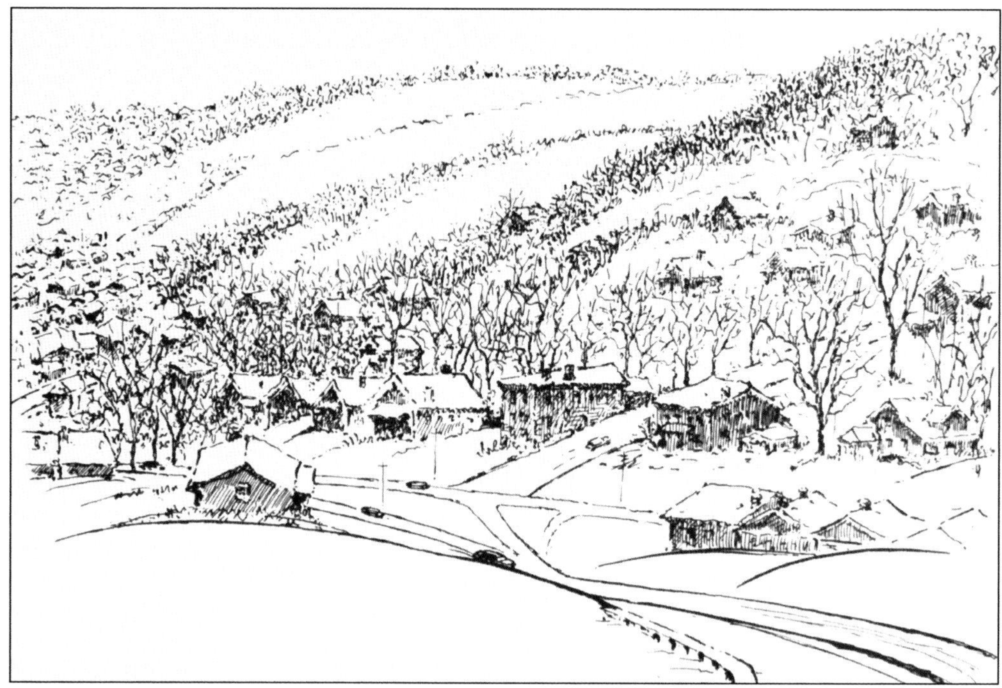

This illustration by Caroline Williams shows the snow-covered hills of the Kirby Avenue dairy farms in 1959, when Ashtree Drive was cut in from Hamilton Avenue.

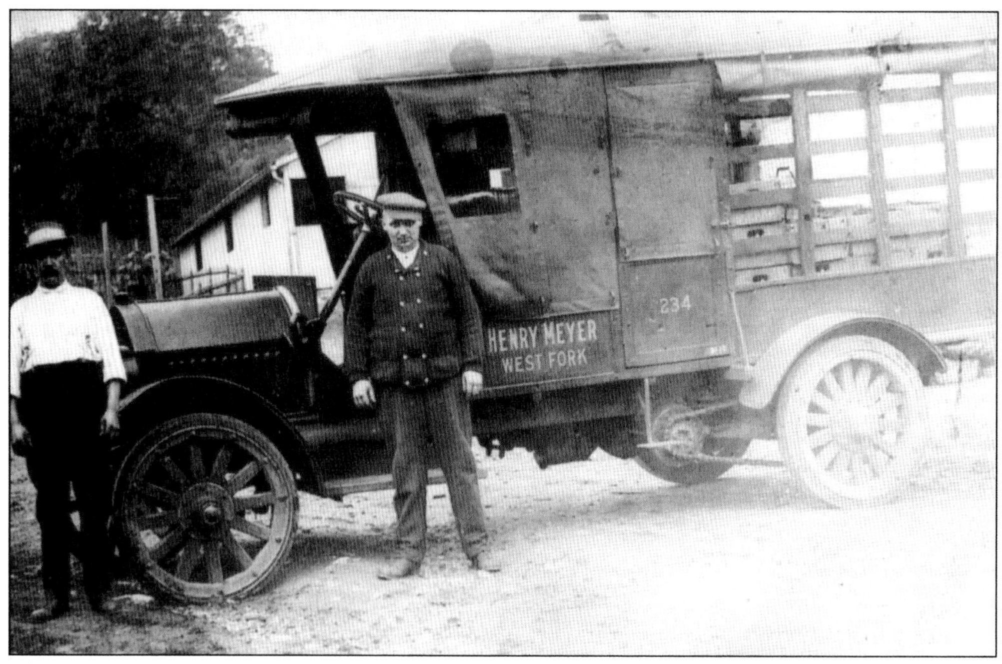

This 1915 photograph shows Prussian immigrants Henry Meyer (1882–1958) and his brother Gus Meyer (left) in front of their delivery truck. Henry started his milk delivery business in 1904 on West Fork Road and bought milk from those area farmers. He began to pasteurize the milk and bottled it with the imprint "Henry Meyer Dairy." In 1924, he sold the business to Townsend-West Dairy. (Courtesy of Robert Meyer.)

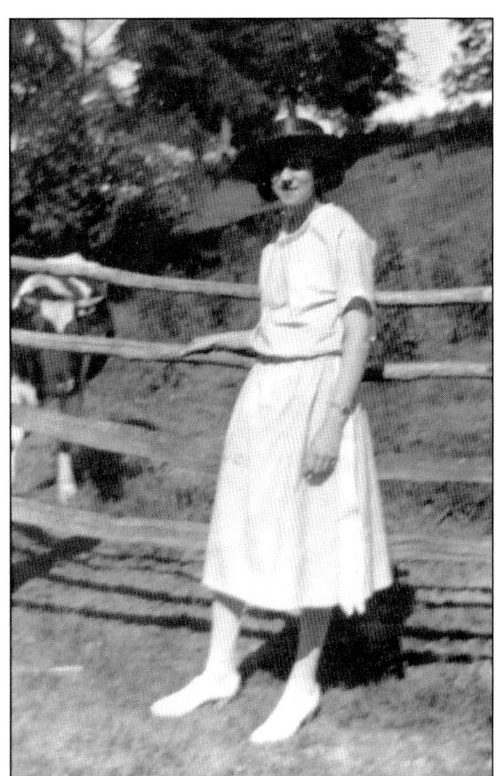

Fred (1898–1971) and Norma Schaeser Woellert (1901–1993) stand in front of dairy cows on West Fork Road in the early 1920s, on a romp through Mount Airy Forest in their Sunday best. Northside was known for its many dairy farms in two areas, West Fork Road between Colerain and Montana Avenues and Kirby Road from Colerain to as far away as Glenview.

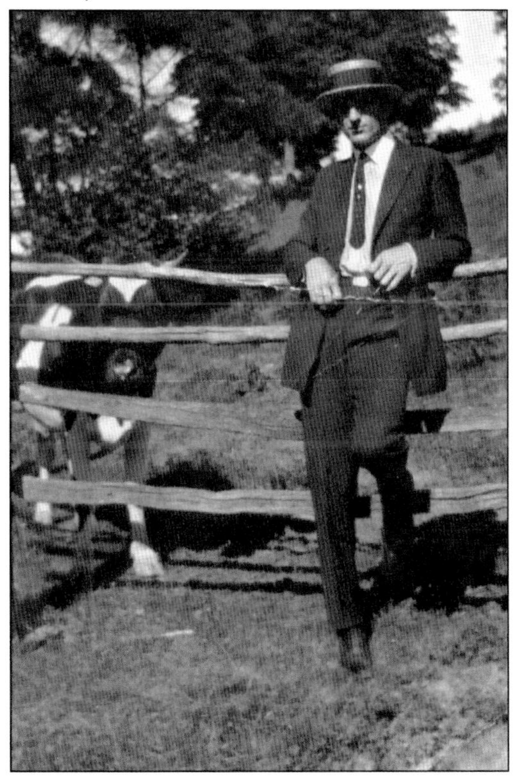

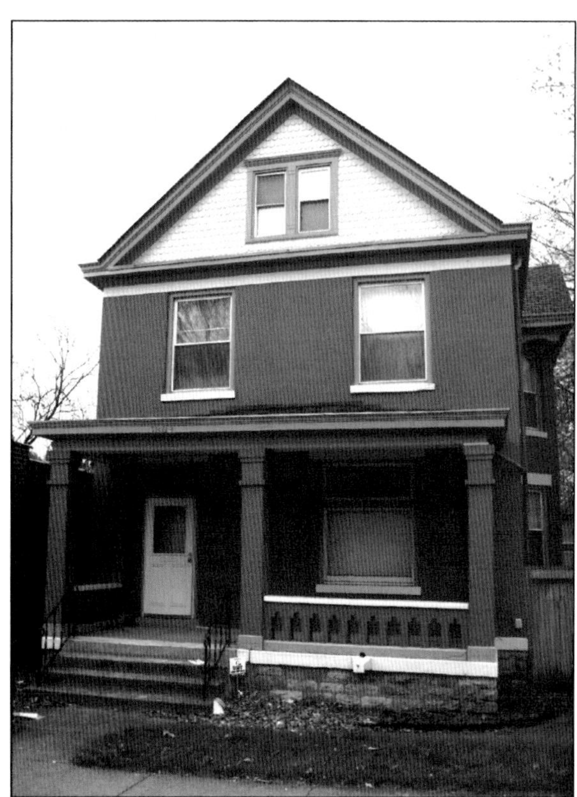

The Bosse family home stands at 1809 Hanfield Avenue. Joseph Bosse started a dairy in 1900 and built the family home in 1908. Their dairy ran two milk routes, delivering milk by the bucket as far as Brighton, until bottling came around in 1914. Joseph sold the dairy in 1920 to John Theodore Reuther, who also ran a dairy delivery business one street over on Dalton and whose wife was Katherine Bosse.

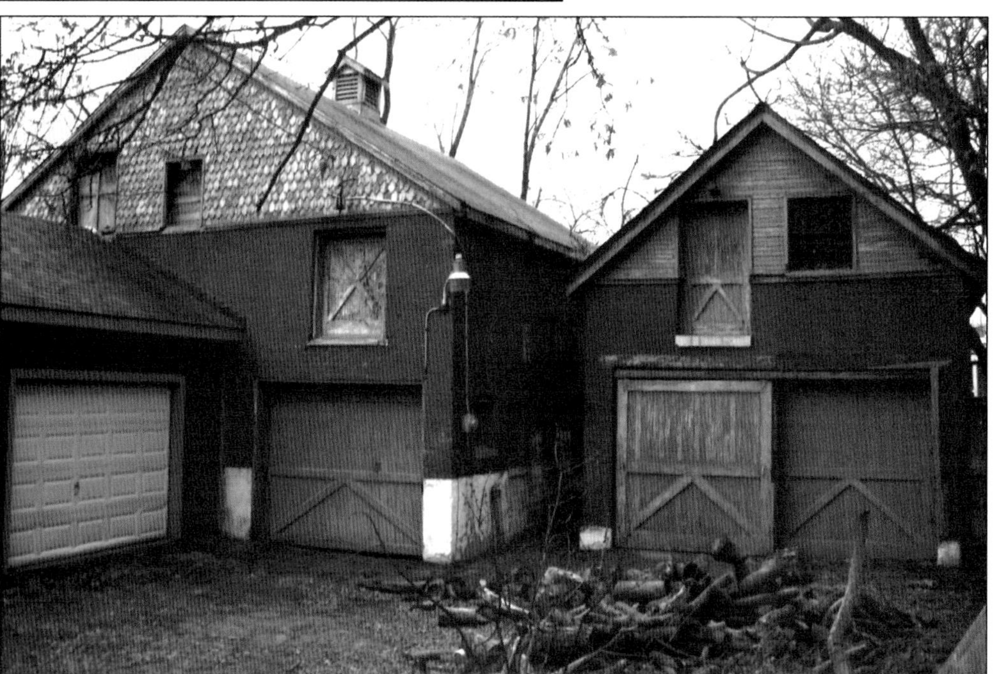

These redbrick dairy barns, built in 1932 by contractor Victor Beischel, still stand behind the Bosse home at Hanfield Avenue. Now used as garages, they once housed Joseph Bosse's herd of 48 dairy cows.

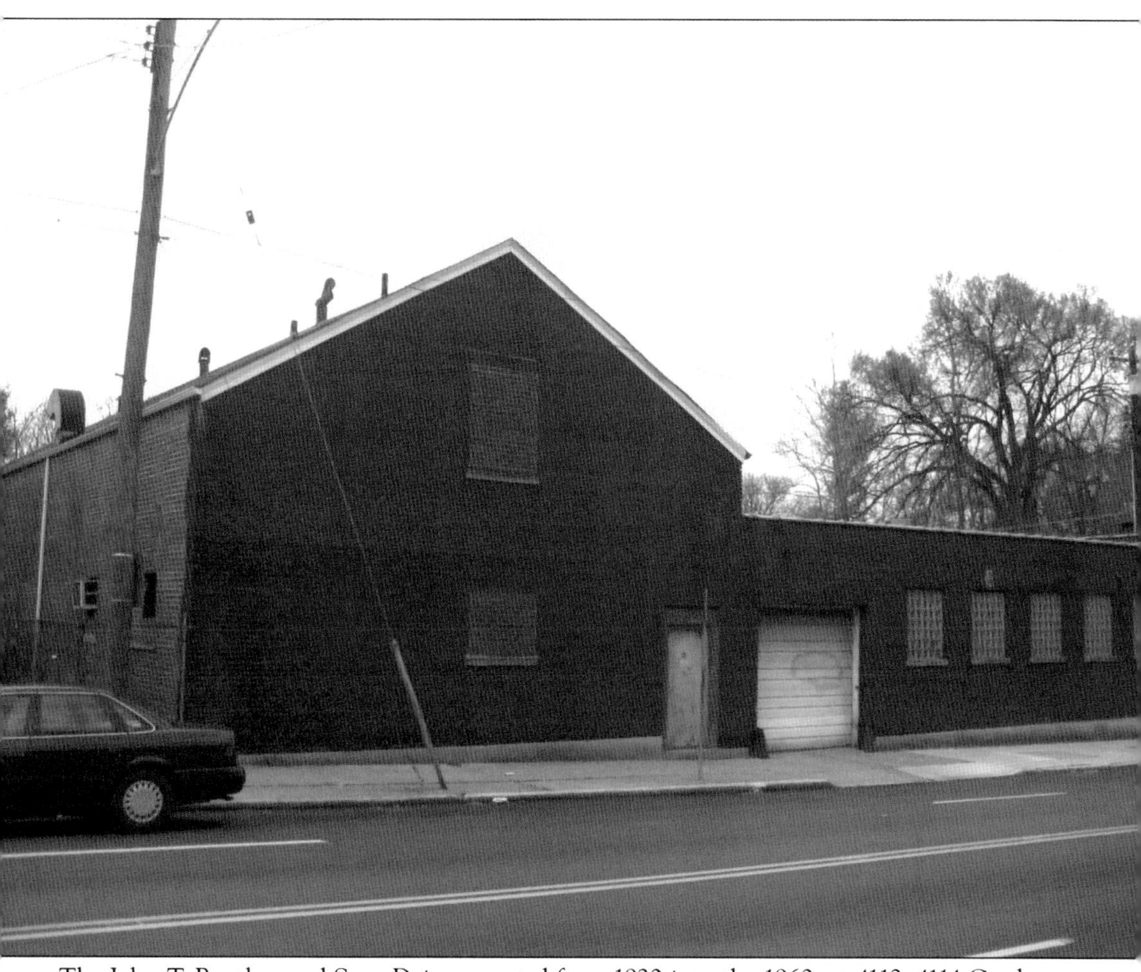

The John T. Reuther and Sons Dairy operated from 1920 into the 1960s at 4112–4114 Gordon Street in Northside, until they were bought by Coors Dairy, formerly on Gray Road in Winton Place. These garages for their delivery trucks are still on Colerain Avenue at Gordon Street. They sold pasteurized milk, special milk, single and double cream, buttermilk, cottage cheese, butter, eggs, and a chocolate milk product called Chocolishus.

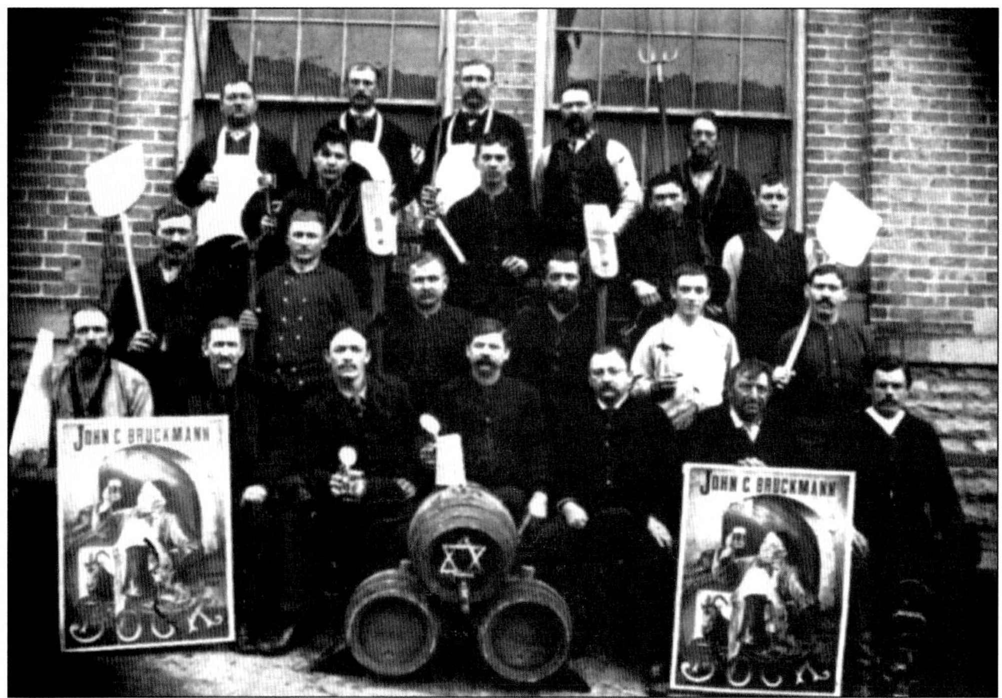

The tapping of the first kegs of Bock Beer was a great celebration at Bruckmann's brewery. This 1880s group photograph shows brewery employees with the tools of their trade—wort paddles, hygrometers, and pitch forks to haul barley and hops. The Star of David is marked in the center beer barrel, a reference to the Biblical David, considered the first brewer, and a symbol of beer purity. (Courtesy of Jim Bruckmann.)

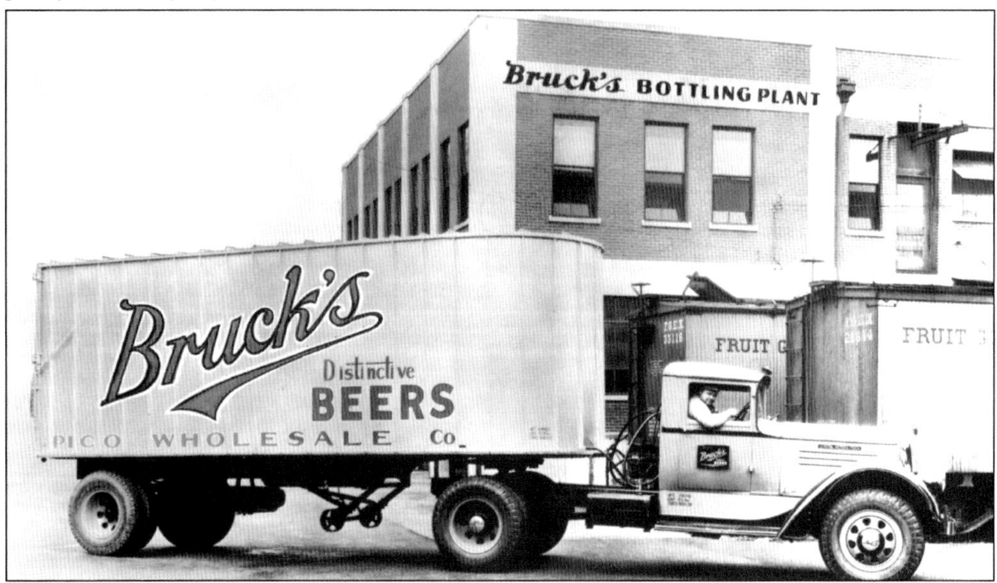

This shows a Bruckmann truck pulling into the bottling plant in the late 1930s to pick up its load of Brucks Beer. The bottling plant was added in the 1920s and was drawn out by John C. Bruckmann's grandson Ernst Bruckmann and his Hughes High School drafting class. (Courtesy of Jim Bruckmann.)

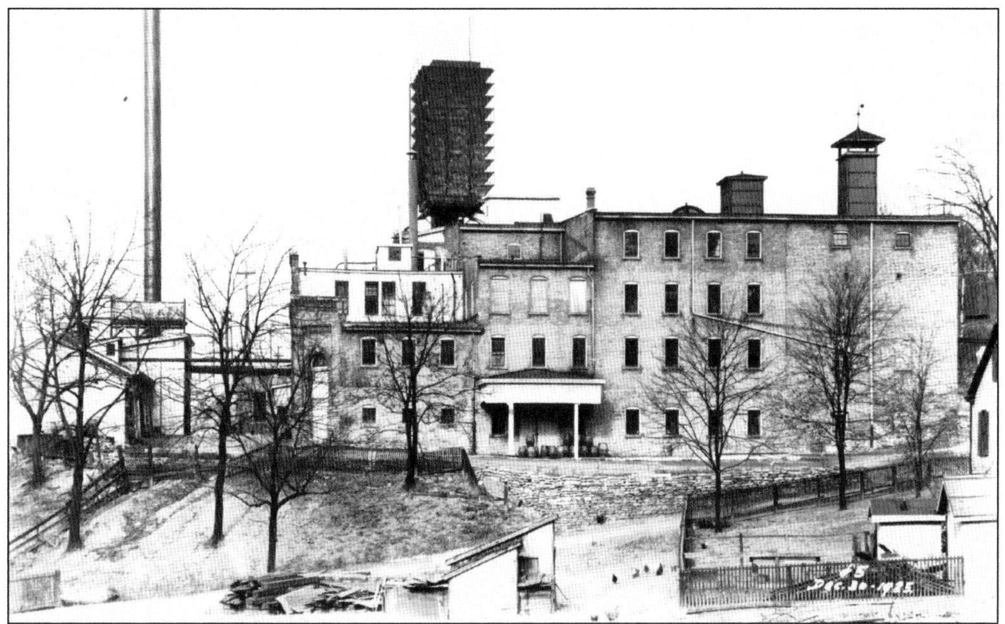

The brew house at plant No. 1, which opened in 1856 on Streng Street and Ludlow Avenue, is shown in this December 30, 1925, photograph. The Bruckmann executives still lived on the premises at that time, one of them raising chickens on the property. Bruckmann's was the only brewery in Cincinnati to have a railroad siding to deliver malt directly to the wort tanks. (Courtesy of Jim Bruckmann.)

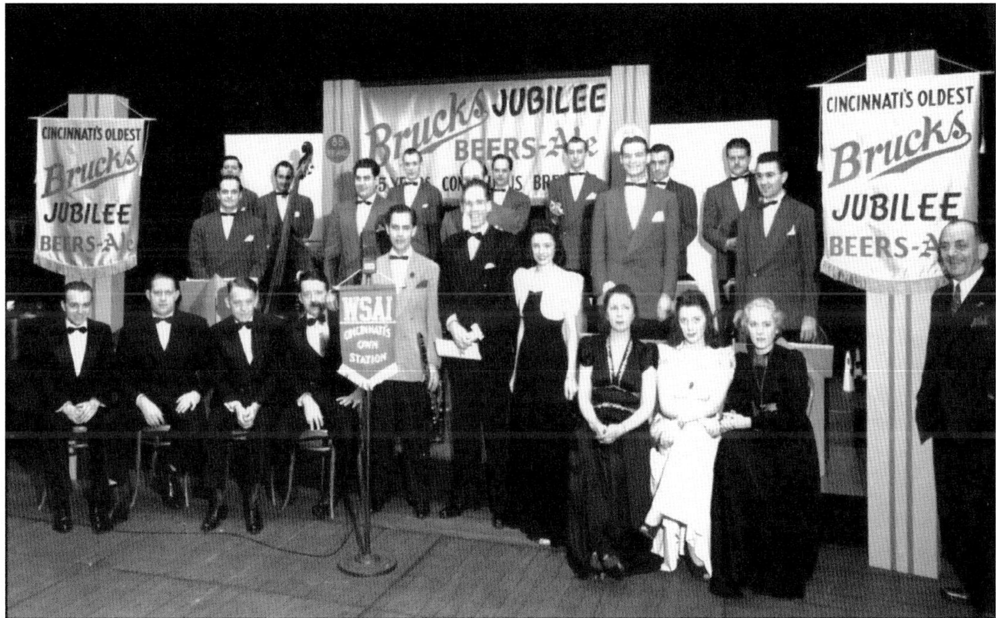

Bruckmann sponsored Cincinnati's own radio quiz show on WSAI in the 1940s called *One for the Money*. This photograph shows the March 3, 1941, Taft Theatre opening night cast of Mayor Stewart, Peter Grant, Nixson Denton, Dick Bray, Bob Maley, Layman Cameron, and the Jimmy James Orchestra. "Every Brucks show is clean and par excellence—worthy of highest commendation," was the show's tagline. (Courtesy of Jim Bruckmann.)

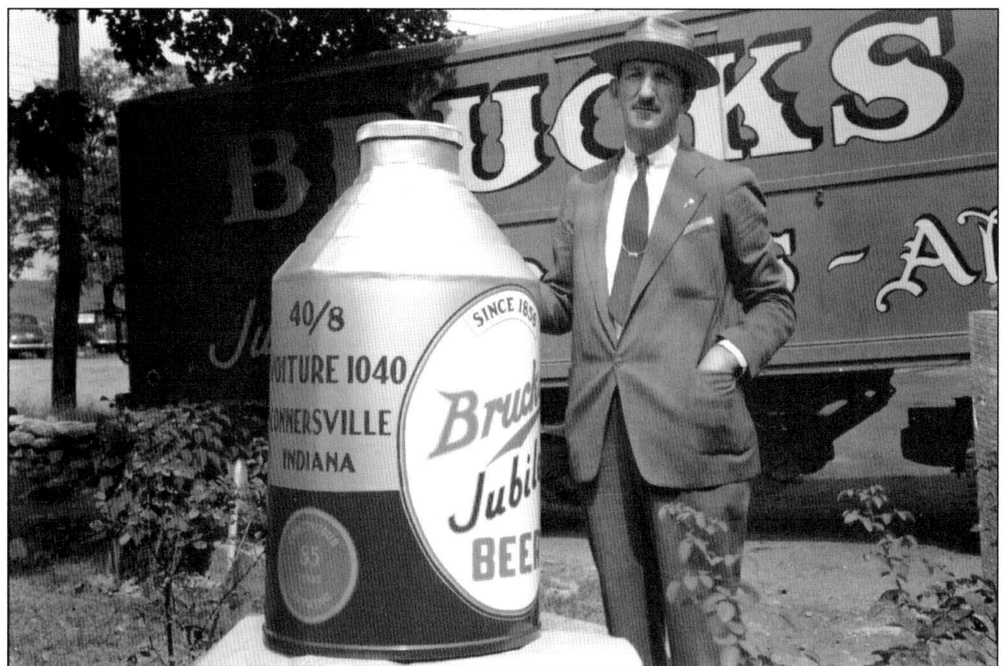

William Bruckmann (1893–1985), the last owner, is shown here in 1942. He poses alongside a giant replica of the Crowntainer used for Brucks 86th Year Jubilee Beer. During the 1937 flood, Cincinnati city water was undrinkable, so William delivered the purified brewery water to Cincinnati schools in beer barrels and would only allow comarketing with Pepsi products, because Coca-Cola had put money into lobbying for Prohibition. (Courtesy of Jim Bruckmann.)

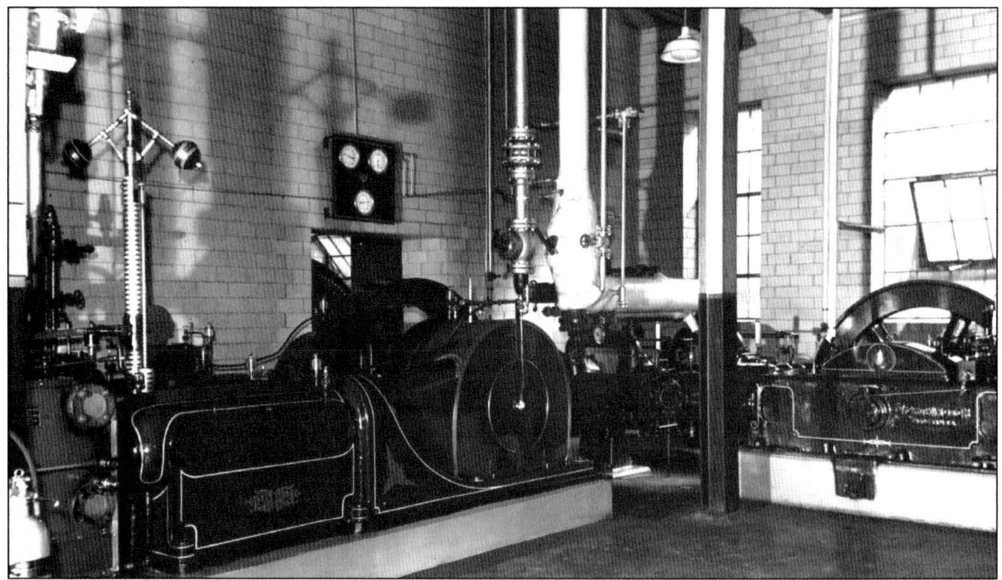

An interior shot of plant No. 1 at Ludlow Avenue and Streng Street in 1943 shows the massive chiller pumps used to refrigerate the beer-aging cellar. In 1917, 75 expensive Pfaudler glass–lined fermenters replaced old wooden tanks, allowing production of eight different brands of ales and lagers. Then in the 1920s and 1930s, the company invested in modern pasteurizing and bottling equipment, indicating high quality control. (Courtesy of Jim Bruckmann.)

Seven

NORTHSIDE INDUSTRY

The first industry in Northside was David Cummins's tannery at what is now Knowlton's Corner in 1817. The next industry of any size was the arrival of the Clifton Springs Distillery in 1848 on the Mill Creek, followed shortly in 1856 by the Bruckmann Brewery on Streng Street near the canal. The Cincinnati, Hamilton and Dayton Railroad opening in 1851 allowed other industries to locate near the railroad tracks to transport goods out of the neighborhood. Three of the largest industries before the 1920s were the Globe Folding Box Company, the Ohio Knife Company, and the Eagle Tool and Die Works, all of which were located within a block of the railroad or the canal. Most of the smaller industries were located near the Knowlton's Corner shopping area, like Davis and Siehl Ironworks, Bullerdick Mattress Factory, and the Dhonau Wagon Manufacturing plant. All could bring in moderately bulky raw material by railroad within a few blocks and acted as their own retailers.

The housing boom of the 1880s to the second decade of the 20th century brought in a variety of building contractors who serviced mainly the Northside neighborhood, as well as larger companies like Parks Woodworking, which supplied tools nationally. Several furniture companies, like Zachman and Herbert's, located near Knowlton's Corner to furnish the newly built middle-class houses as well as interior furnishings companies like William J. Todd. Three large shoe companies, Scheiffle, Helming-McKenzie, and Wilson's, located their factories in Northside because of its proximity to the Camp Washington stockyards and their cheap source of leather.

Northside's industry peaked right before World War I, with the exception of the largest factory, the American Can Company, built on the old Knowlton mansion in 1921. The Depression brought more decline in industry, which grew a bit to support the war effort during World War II. Automobile parts manufacturers had come into the area in the 1930s, like Spreen Automotive, Crosley's American Automobile Accessories Company, and Western Auto Parts. Most of the original industries like American Can, Fosdick and Holloway, and Eagle Tool and Die had moved out of Northside by the 1960s, and the community began looking for ways to redefine itself.

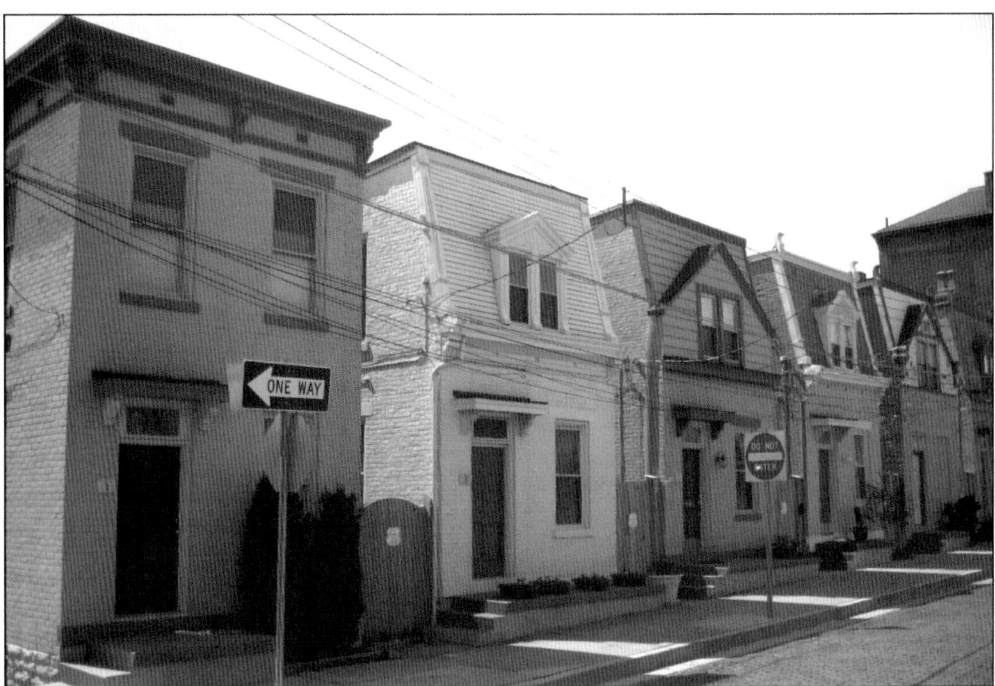

These six modest houses on Moline Court were built in 1894 by Charles R. Wild and Company, dealers in coal, lime, plaster, cement, and sewer pipe. They were built as employee housing for their proximity to his business. Moline Court was originally named Spring Street, after the many natural springs in the area. The houses are part of the Hoffner Historic District, added to the National Register of Historic Places in 1978.

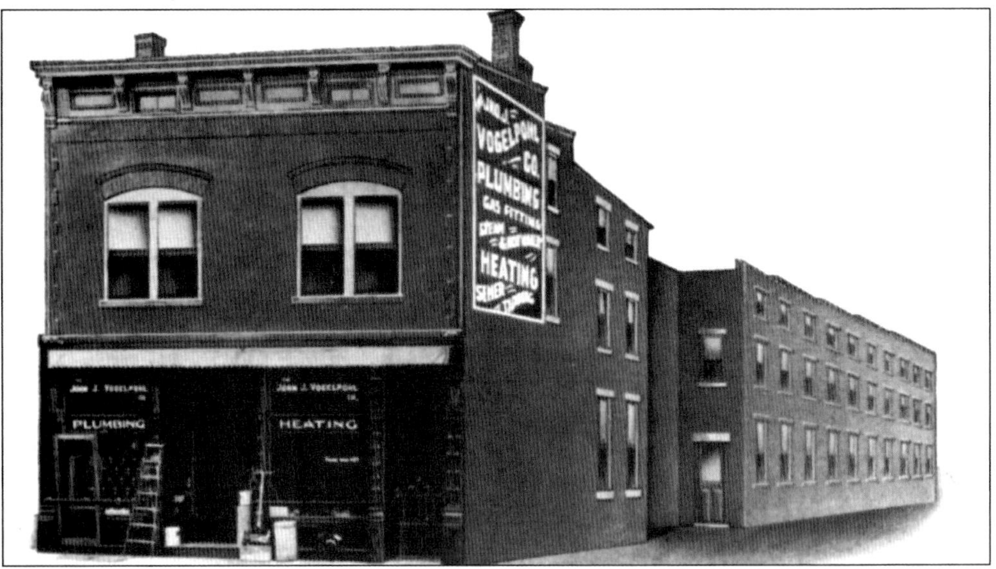

The Italianate building at 4156 Hamilton Avenue was originally home to the John J. Vogelpohl Plumbing and Heating business. He moved into the building in 1904, as one of many mechanical contractors in Northside. Vogelpohl was an active member of the Northside Business Association and served as director for St. Joseph's Orphanage. The building is now home to neighborhood anchor Shake It Records, owned by brothers Darren and Jim Blase.

William F. Armand, Northside's "Fashionable Tailor," started his tailoring business at this building at 4165 Hamilton Avenue in 1908. His slogan was "What a Difference Clothes Will Make," and although his business catered to younger businessmen, he also tailored clothes for older men, who "wished to retain their youthful appearance." The building now houses Melt Eclectic Deli, which was voted in 2009 "Top 3 Best of Cincinnati Restaurants."

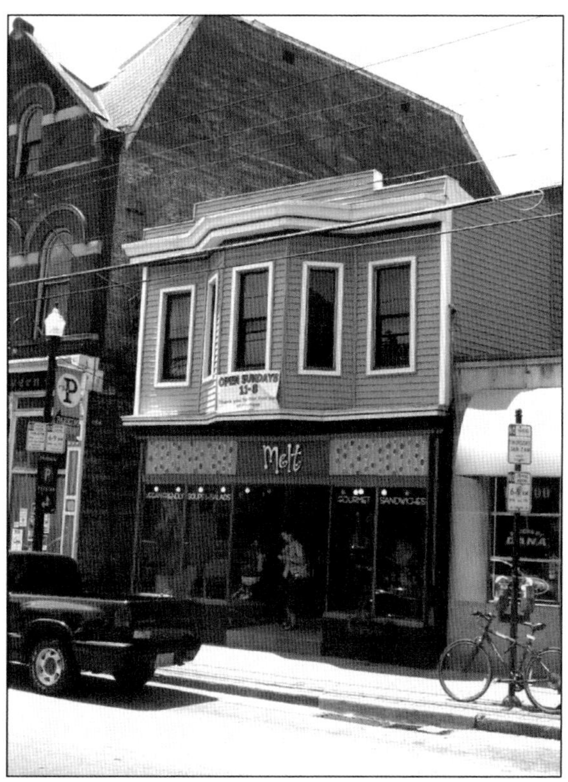

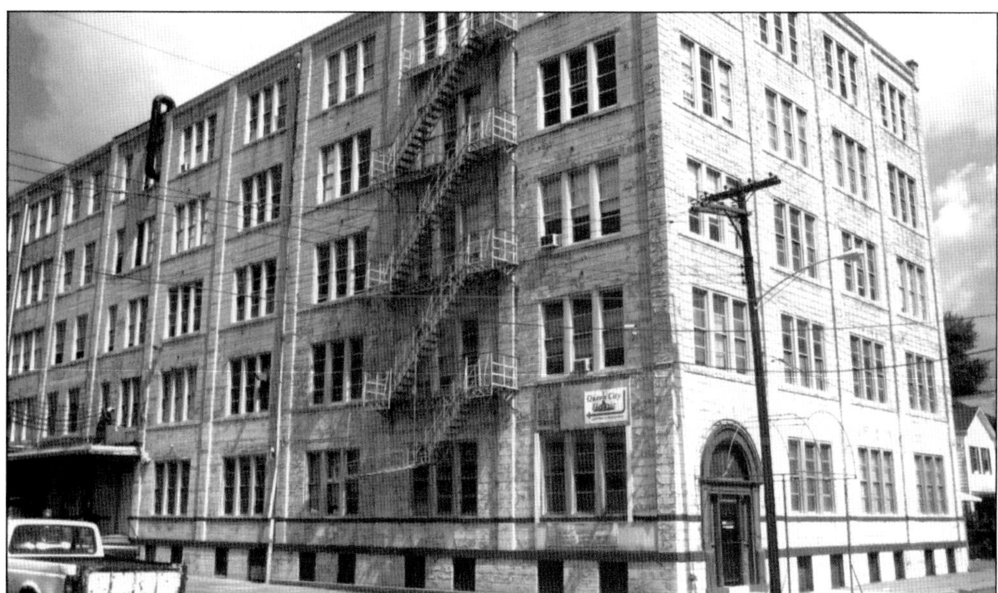

The Helming-McKenzie Shoe Company was organized in 1887 by John Helming Jr. and William S. McKenzie to manufacture ladies shoes. This photograph shows the warehouse at 4015–4019 Cherry Street, built in 1906, by Northside builders Fredrick and Anthony Weber. The proximity to the downtown slaughterhouses gave a cheap source of leather for the Northside shoe industry. Helming-McKenzie employed 500 shoe workers in 1914 and touted the "Swellest Line of Shoes in Cincinnati."

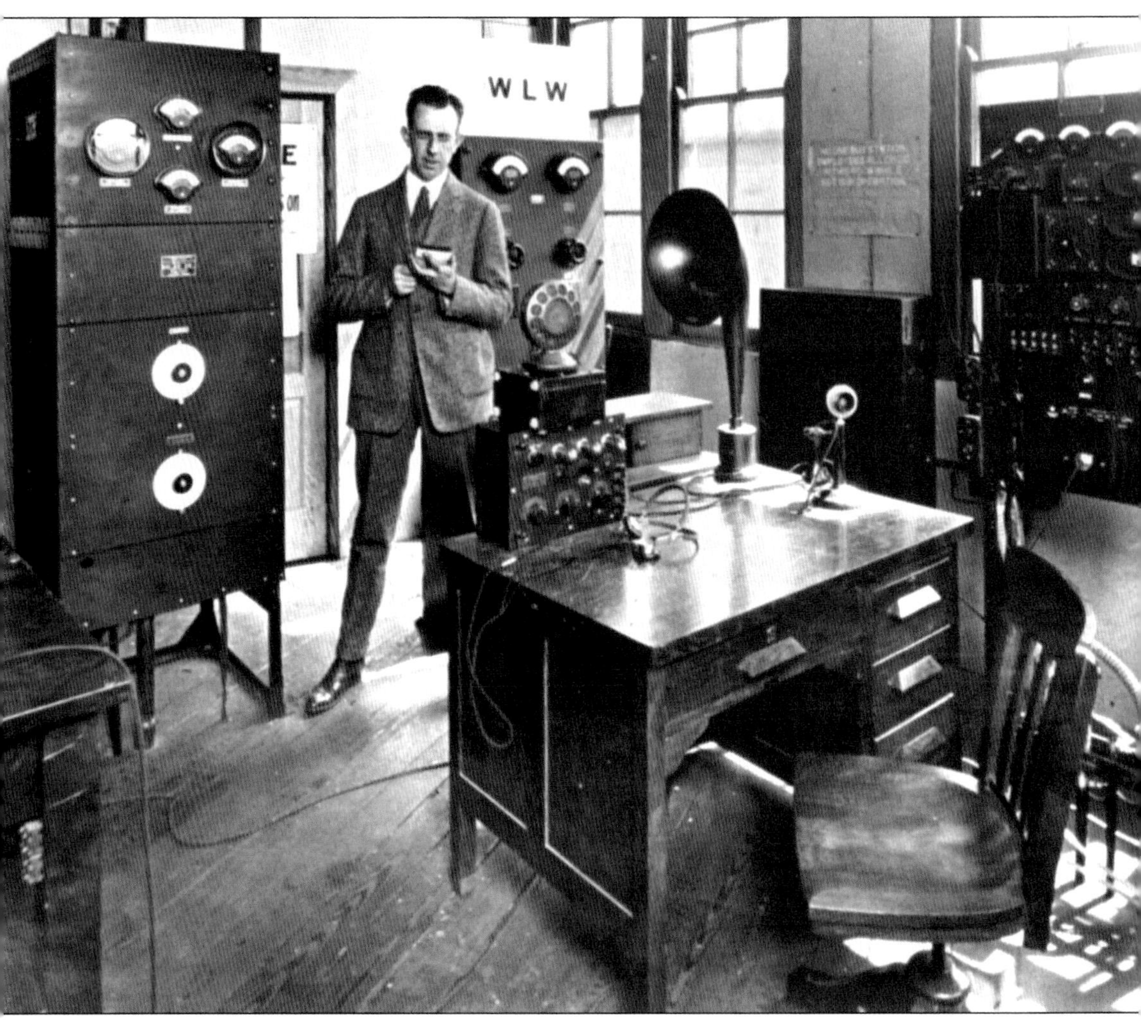

Powell Crosley Jr. is shown here in 1922 in his Northside WLW radio studio at 1601 Blue Rock Street. In 1921, Crosley experimented with a 20-watt radio transmitter, which he called 8CR. His first broadcast from his College Hill living room received such positive responses that he moved to 1601 Blue Rock Street, the site of his American Automobile Accessories Company. On March 22, 1922, Crosley received the license to broadcast his now 50-watt radio station with call letters WLW from this location. WLW started broadcasting live music from such groups as the Doherty Melody Boys at the Northside studios. With the studio next to the railroad, the train engineers liked adding the sounds of their whistles to the broadcasts at Crosley's requests. In 1924, Crosley moved WLW to a larger facility in Camp Washington. WLW went on from its humble Northside beginnings to became the "Nation's Station." In 1934, Pres. Dwight D. Eisenhower pushed the button from his White House desk to fire up the 500,000-watt station, the most powerful in the country. (Courtesy of the Clyde Haehnle/Ed Dooley Collection of Media Heritage.)

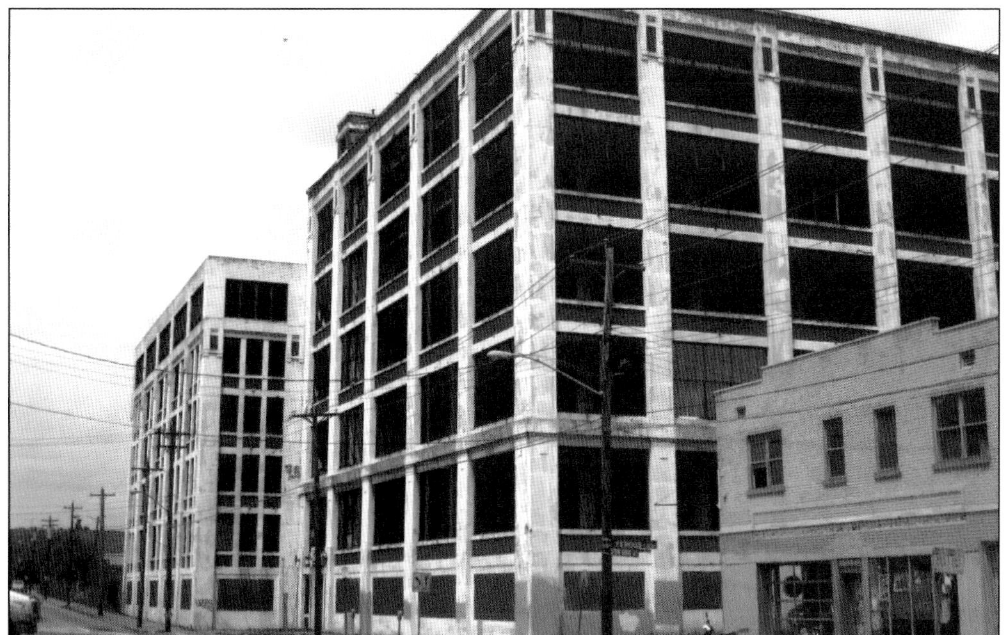

The American Can building at Spring Grove Avenue was built in 1921 by company engineer Carl G. Preis. The company invented machinery to make the sanitary can, flat and cone top beer cans, and high-speed vacuum packing of coffee. As Northside's largest factory, it made parts for the U.S. Navy and U.S. Air Force during World War II. After closing in the 1950s, the property was added to the National Register of Historic Places in 2007.

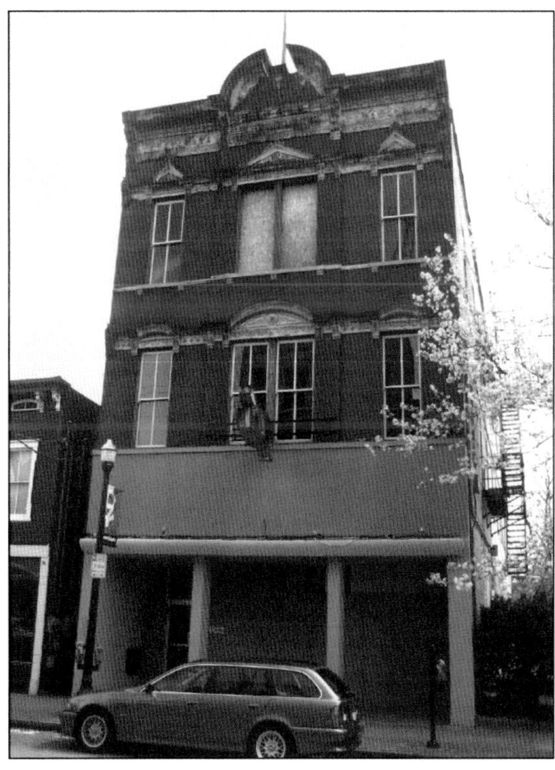

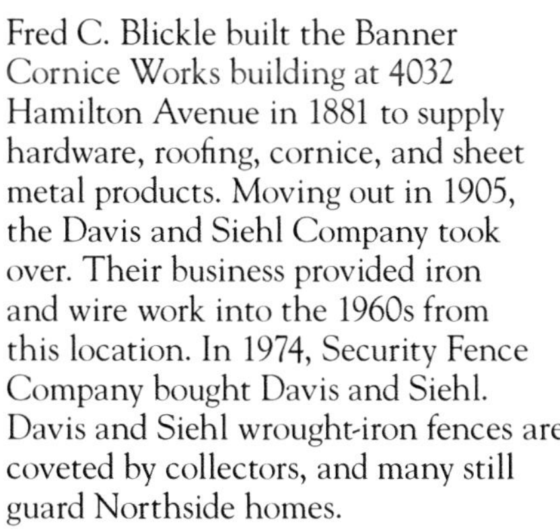

Fred C. Blickle built the Banner Cornice Works building at 4032 Hamilton Avenue in 1881 to supply hardware, roofing, cornice, and sheet metal products. Moving out in 1905, the Davis and Siehl Company took over. Their business provided iron and wire work into the 1960s from this location. In 1974, Security Fence Company bought Davis and Siehl. Davis and Siehl wrought-iron fences are coveted by collectors, and many still guard Northside homes.

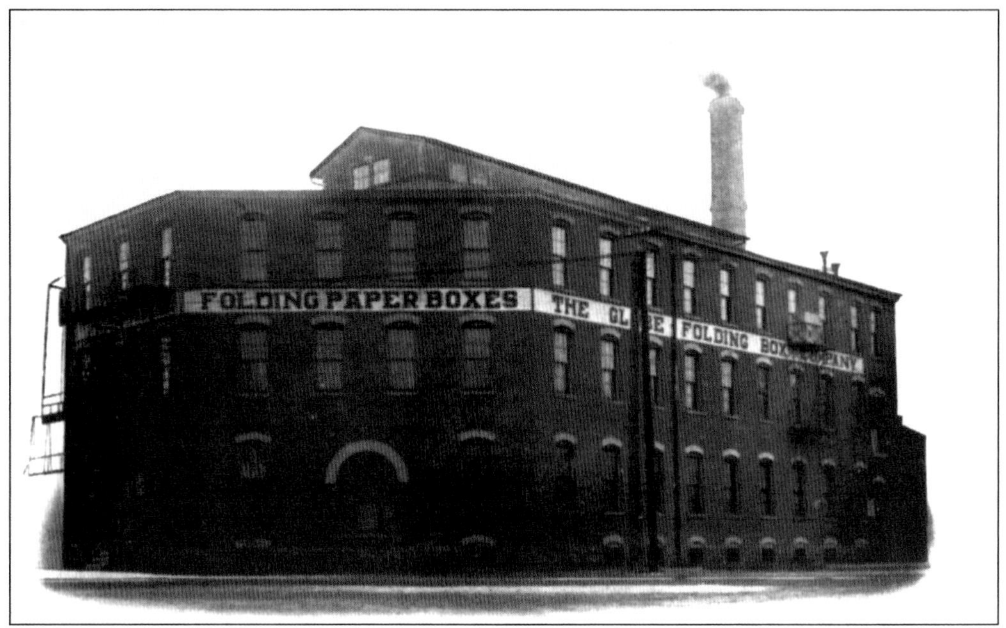

The Globe Folding Box Company at Hoffner and Cherry Streets was founded in 1909 and operated into the 1920s. It was founded by George Ault, the nephew of the ink baron Levi Ault, who founded Ault and Wiborg Company. Globe Folding Box Company employed 75–100 people and manufactured show cards, oyster and ice-cream pails, and suit and cake boxes with Ault and Wiborg inks. It now is home to Wooley Electric Supply.

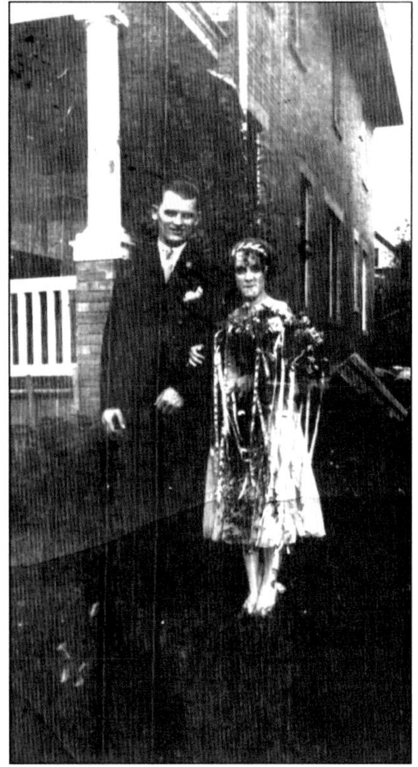

Many Northsiders met their partners while working at one of the large factories in the neighborhood. One example is German Lutheran Harry C. Woellert (1902–1928) and Irish Catholic Emily C. Maddock (1905–1979), who met at the Globe Folding Box Company while Harry was a stock boy and Emily was a secretary. They were married in 1926 as shown here at Harry's family's house at 3906 Beekman Street, demolished in the 1960s for Interstate 74.

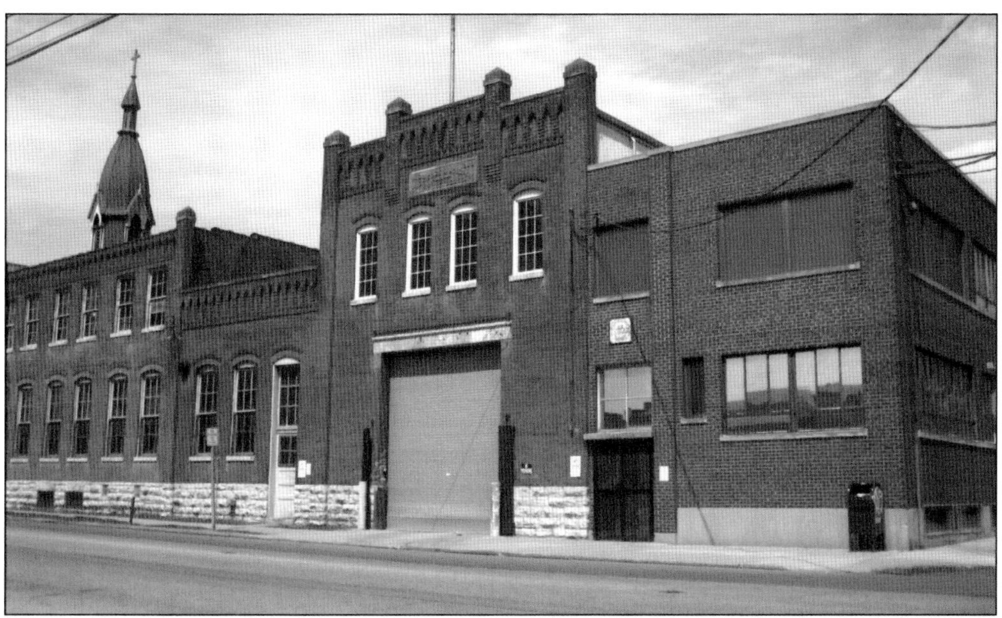

Phillip C. Fosdick (1858–1917) partnered in 1900 with John K. Holloway (1867–1905) and built the building shown here on Blue Rock Street, forming Fosdick and Holloway Company. They were famous for their jig borers and manufactured parts for the U.S. Army and U.S. Navy during World War II. In 1956, the company became a subsidiary of the Leblond Machine Tool Company and then in 1970 were folded into Leblond.

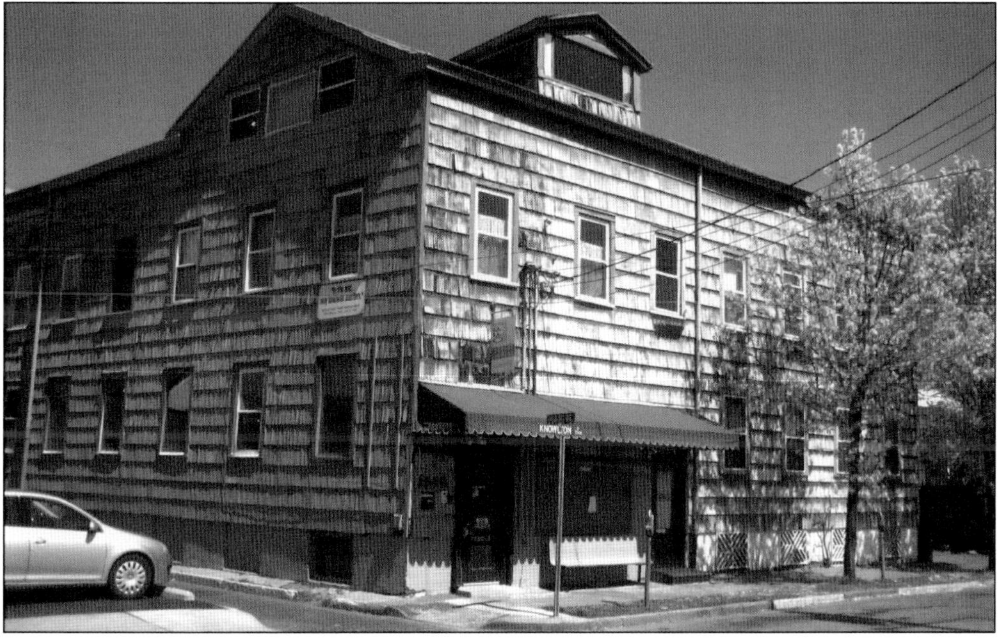

Parks Woodworking Machine Company operated here at 1501 Knowlton Street from 1887 to 1989. They manufactured band saws and planers, the tools needed to make the Victorian gingerbread trim common on Northside homes. The company employed 50–100 people per year during its operation. The owner, Louis F. Parks, was a pacifist and was edged out of ownership during World War I. It now houses Off the Avenue Studios.

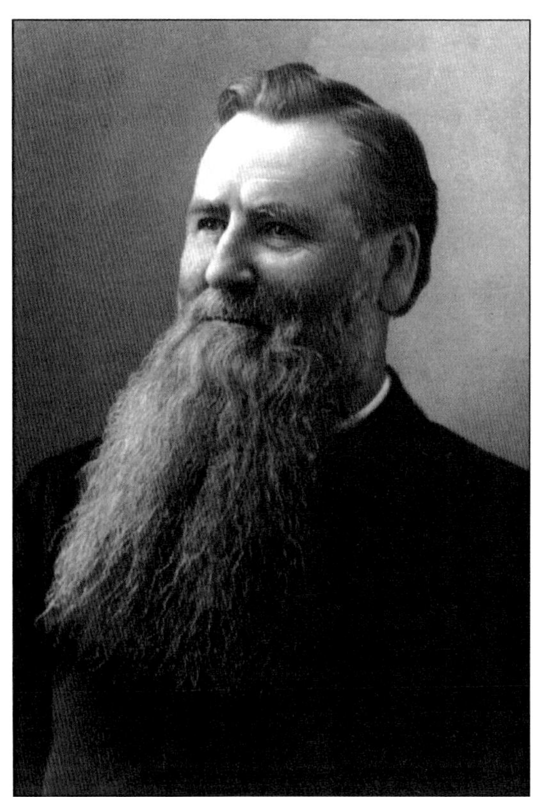

Robert Simpson came to Cincinnati in 1864 and purchased the Straub Mill Company, which sold a flour mill product nicknamed the "Queen of the South." Changing the name to Simpson and Gault in 1879, its product soon ground more than flour, including corn, spices, starch, and plaster. He passed the business to his son Orville, who had foresight to move the business in 1910 to a fast-growing Northside, naming it the Orville Simpson Company, later becoming today's Rotex. (Courtesy of Rotex Inc.)

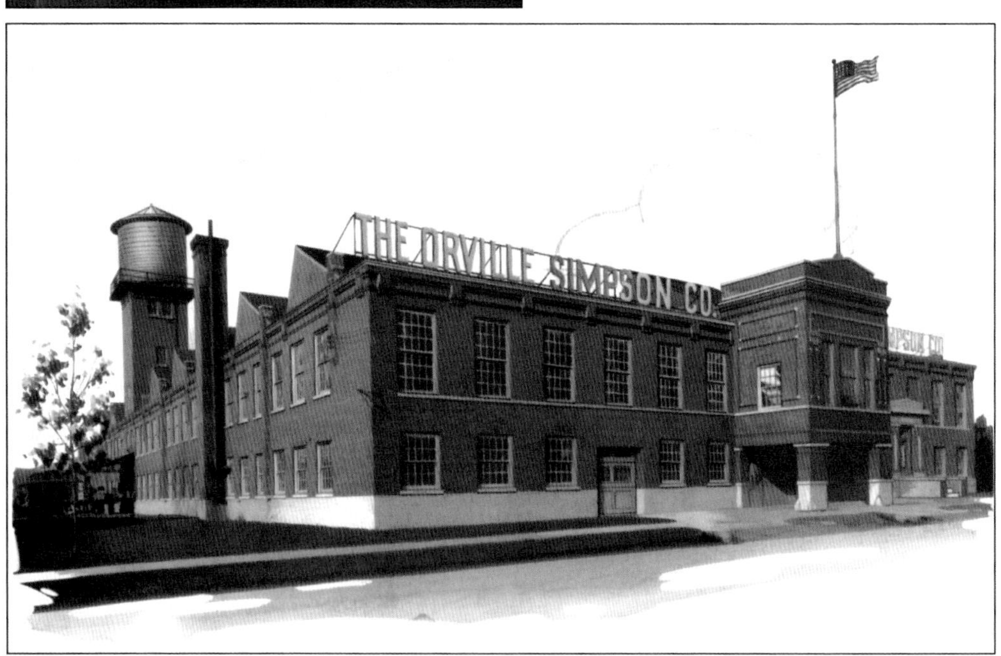

In 1910, the Orville Simpson Company came to Northside and constructed the building at Knowlton Street. It is shown here that first year, where "a continuous flow of innovation" keeps this engineered manufacturing company strong for over 165 years in Cincinnati. (Courtesy of Rotex Inc.)

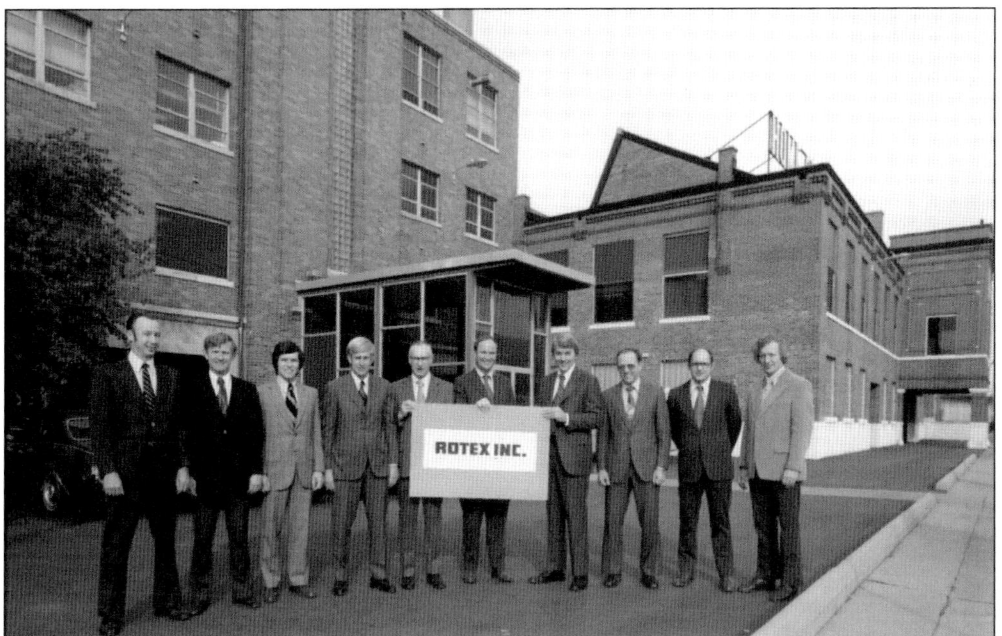

In 1974, the brand name Rotex became the company name, replacing the Orville Simpson Company. The management team in 1974 is, seen here from left to right, Dick Fox, Trez Folger, Pat McGuire, Bill Lower, Bob Westbrook, Jerry Simpson, Alex Young, George McFarland, Mike Quinn, and Nash McCauley. (Courtesy of Rotex Inc.)

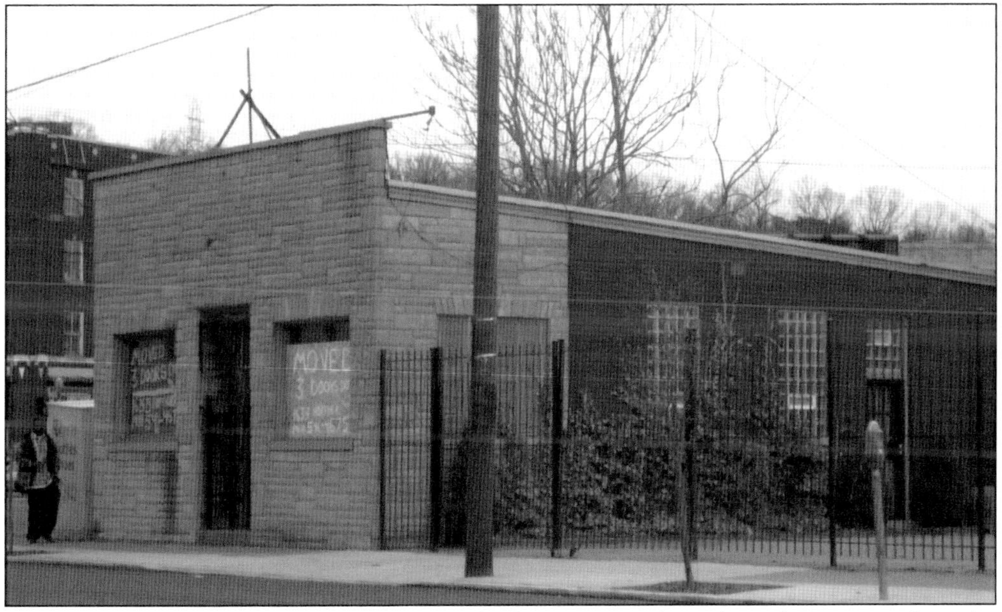

This 1609 Hoffner Street property, recently housing Cecil Lock and Key, was first the Workingman's Building and Savings from 1925 to the 1950s. This German institution helped many of the Hoffner Street Church members build homes. It was founded in the 1870s as the Cumminsville German Building and Savings Company. Former presidents were John Bruckman (1829–1887), August Gulow, and Gabriel Dirr (1838–1909). It was bought in the 1980s by the Brentwood Savings and Loan.

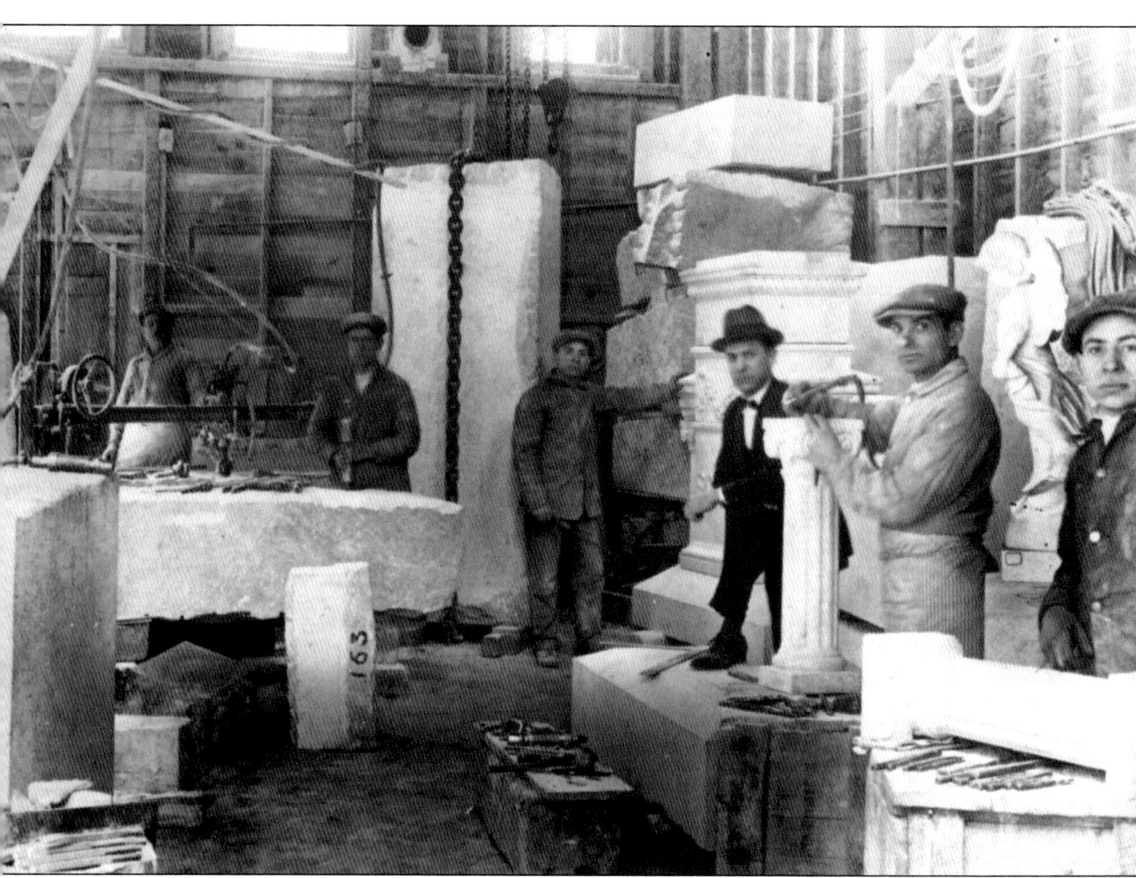

This 1925 photograph shows the interior of the Spring Grove Avenue monument factory of the Napolitano Brothers. Seen are, from left to right, two unidentified, Horatio, Joseph, Gaetano, and Peter Napolitano. In 1909, the five Napolitano brothers Peter, Joseph, Gaetano, Horatio, and Angelo, came to Northside from Modica, Sicily, with their mother Johanna and younger sister, Carmelina, in search of a dream. Trained in Sicily by their father, Emmanuel Napolitano, a master carver, they incorporated Napolitano Brothers Monuments in 1915, at 3835 Spring Grove Avenue, where they fabricated beautiful carved stonework and sculpture for funeral monuments, until they moved out of Northside in 1973. Today the original storefront is gone, but the Napolitano family is back, incorporated as Ascent, only a few buildings away from their original location. (Courtesy of Linda Naplitano Leidermeier.)

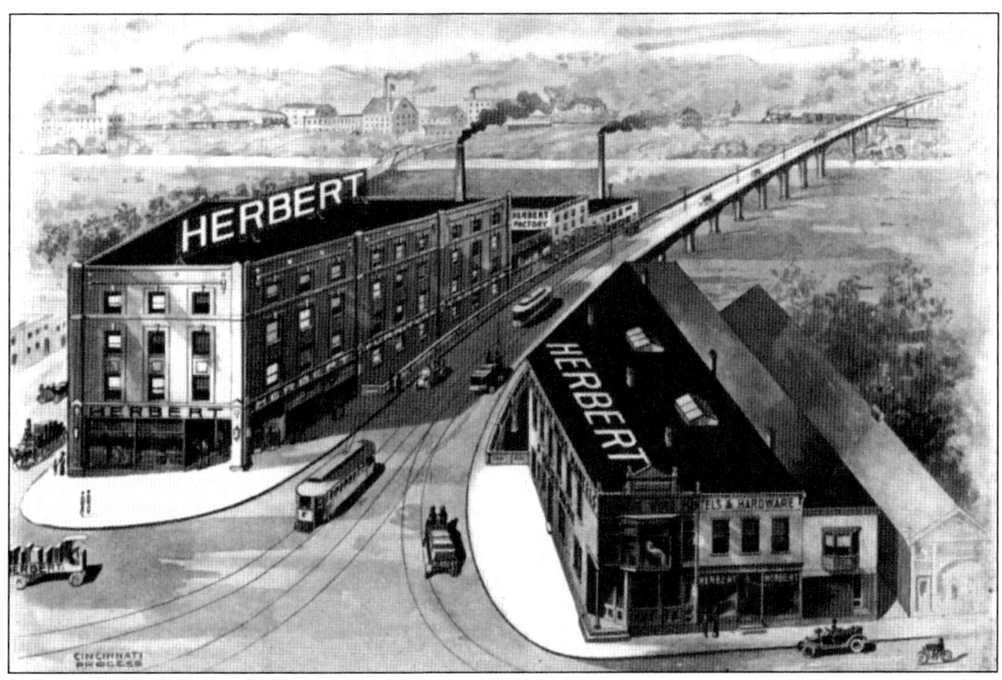

Peter Herbert (1847–1924), a German cabinetmaker, started a business in 1895, making wood mantels and hardware at 3944 Spring Grove Avenue. This 1914 etching shows the collection of newly built company buildings on both sides of the Ludlow Avenue Viaduct that was referred to as Herbert's Corner. U.S. furniture makers used Herbert's Corner, with its automatic elevator, electric lighting, and interchangeable loading system, as an example for their own facilities.

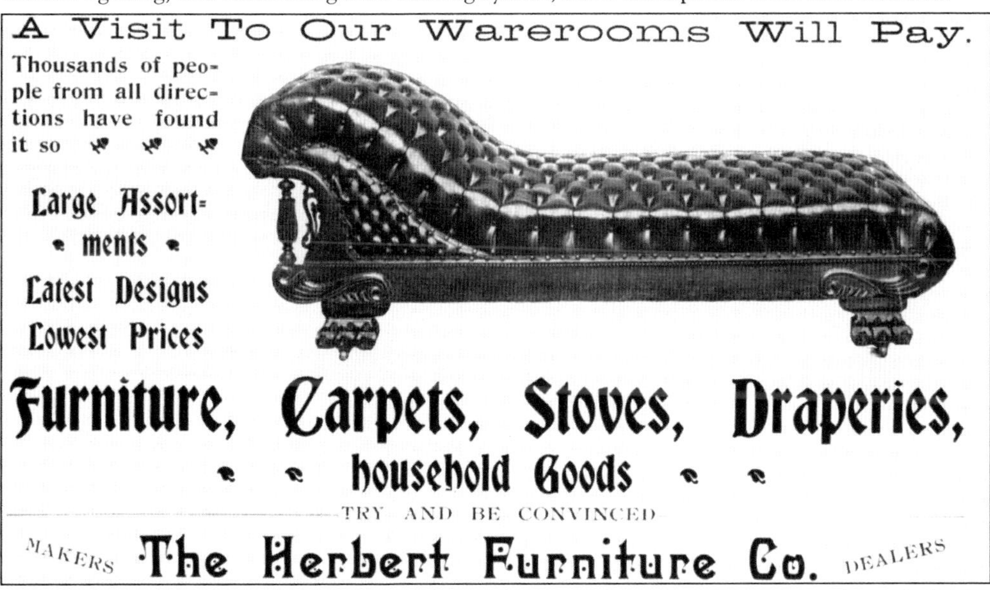

This advertisement from the 1905 *Northside Herald* shows a Victorian fainting couch, made by the Herbert Furniture Company. All of Peter's five sons, John A. (1875–1953), Frank A. (1878–1959), Georg F. (1883–1926), Edward F. (1887–1975), and Alonze E. (1890–1965), were involved in the business. John A. founded the Northside Business Association in 1907, and the Herbert descendants operate Herbert Motors on Spring Grove Avenue in Northside today.

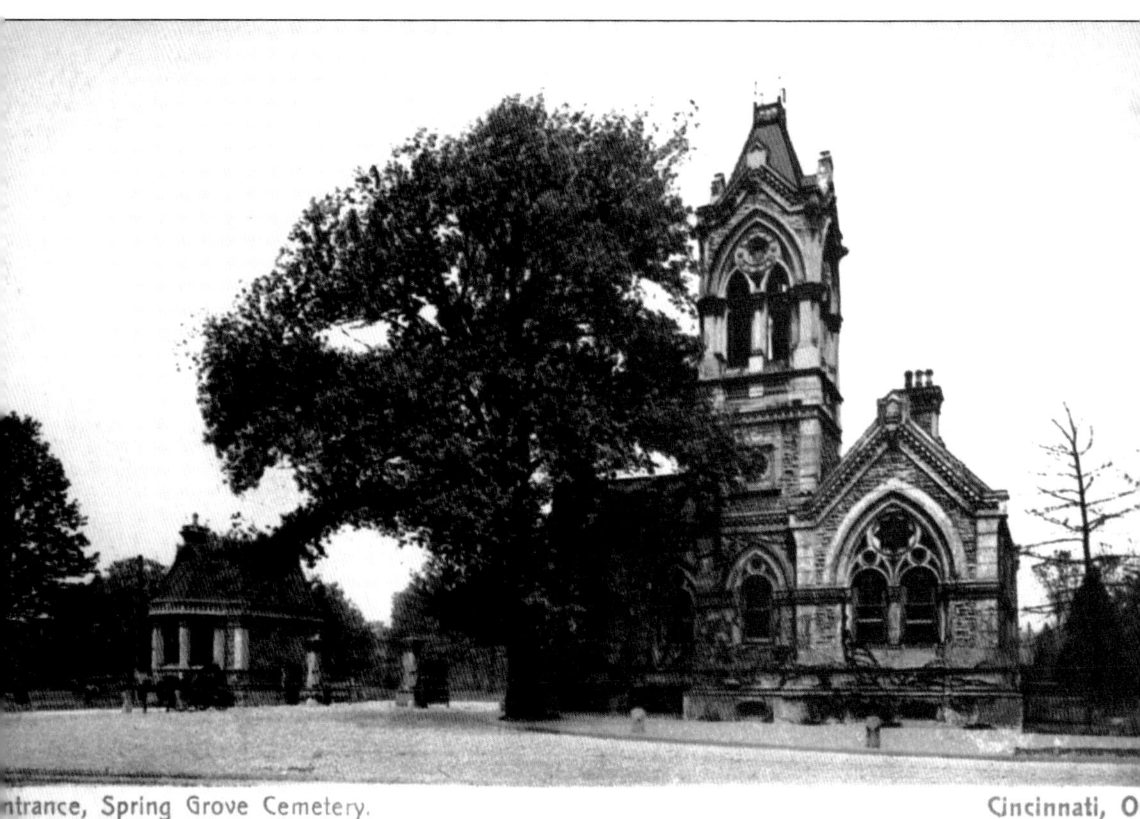

The entrance to Spring Grove Cemetery looks much like it did in this early-1900s postcard. The cemetery was founded in 1845 by a group of Cincinnati businessmen, including Salmon P. Chase. They wanted the natural setting to be a contemplative atmosphere conducive to consolation and commemoration. Its 733 acres of Adolph Strauch–landscaped grounds are the final resting place for numerous Northsiders and spawned a bustling funeral and monument business in Northside.

Eight

HIGH-QUALITY SHOPS

In Northside, there were four main business districts. These were Knowlton's Corner, Hamilton Avenue and Chase Avenue, Hamilton Avenue and Blue Rock Avenue, and Colerain Avenue and Spring Grove. The Knowlton's Corner and Hamilton Avenue and Chase Avenue business districts were the third-largest shopping district in Greater Cincinnati from around 1900 into the 1930s. One of four intersecting streetcars at Knowlton's Corner took residents from College Hill, North College Hill, and Mount Airy through Northside transfer points. People came to the high-quality dress and millinery shops and the large number of merchant tailors, jewelers, home furnishings companies, and eateries. There was nearly a grocery store or saloon on every corner in Northside. Several large pharmacies like Bristles, Meinengers, and Dow's were dotted throughout the business districts, each of which had a soda fountain that doubled as an entertainment spot. Knowlton's Corner was the intersection of four streetcar lines, and the completion of the Ludlow Avenue Viaduct in 1914 made access very easy from all directions of Greater Cincinnati. At the peak of the business district in the 1930s, stores were open three nights a week until 9:00 p.m. Many recall during this time that on Saturday night, when the stores were open until 10:00 p.m., sidewalks were so full that shoppers had to walk in the streets.

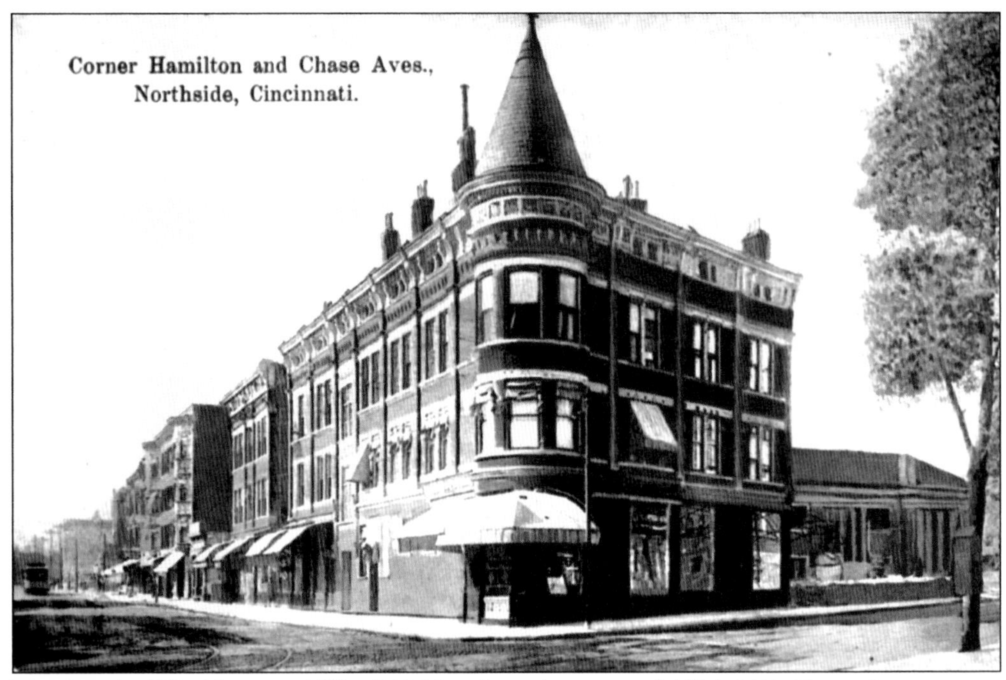

The Domhoff Buildings at 4203–4210 Hamilton Avenue and 1604–1614 Chase Avenue were built in 1893 by Charles H. Domhoff (1853–1920). Housing 17 apartments and 5 retail spaces, it was part of the building boom of high end apartments that swept the country after New York's Grammarcy Park. Now home to Happen Inc., it was added to the National Historic Register in 1980. (From the Collection of the Public Library of Cincinnati and Hamilton County.)

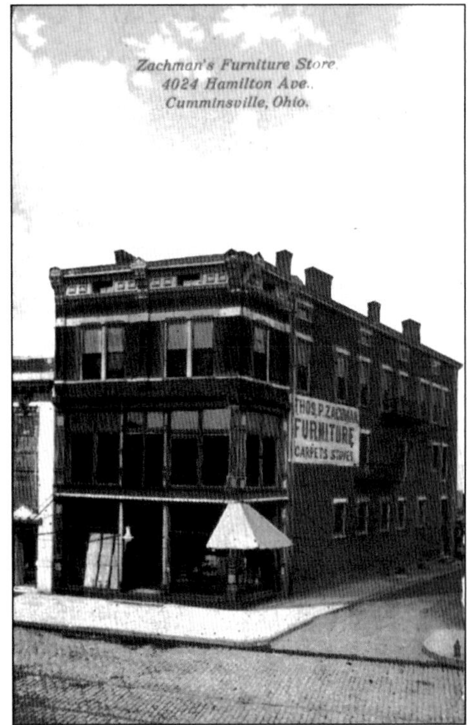

This photograph shows Zachman's furniture store at 4024 Hamilton Avenue in 1908. Thomas P. Zachman (1857–1956) took over the wallpapering and upholstering business from his German immigrant father, Phillip J. Zachman (1822–1893), when he died. Thomas expanded into furniture and built this Queen Anne Commercial with a unique two-story, cast-iron storefront in 1893 as his showroom. (From the Collection of the Public Library of Cincinnati and Hamilton County.)

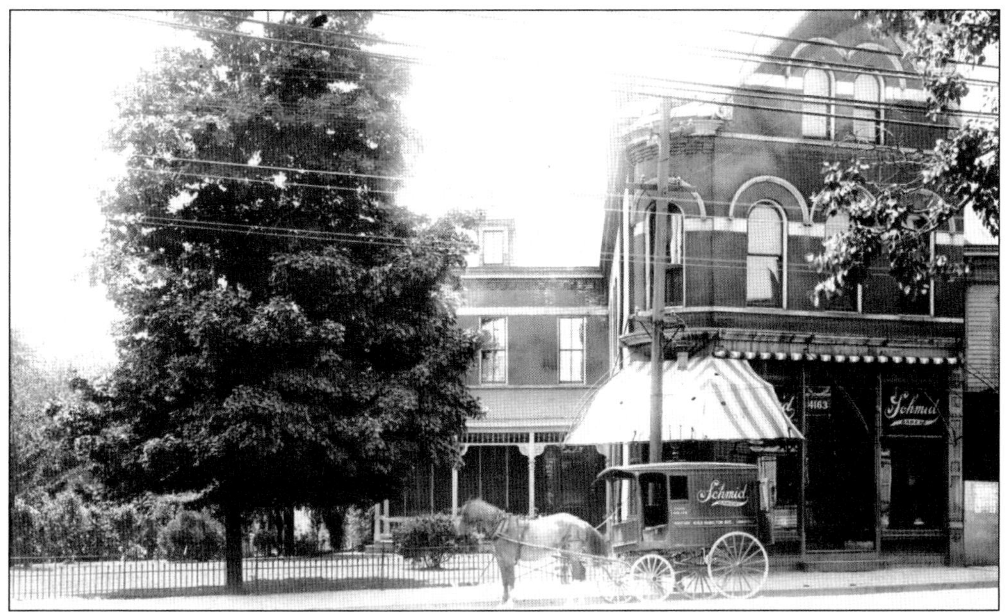

Schmid's Bakery and home at 4167 Hamilton Avenue is shown here in 1900. Built in 1893 by Andrew Schmid (1837–1914) from Wuertemburg, Germany, sons Chester (1879–1931) and Albert (1889–1965) ran it after his death. Schmid had the bakery delivery service for the east, while Volz Bakery cornered the service for the west side of Northside. It was sold to the Grote family in the early 1980s and now houses the Northside Tavern. (Courtesy of Bruce Demske.)

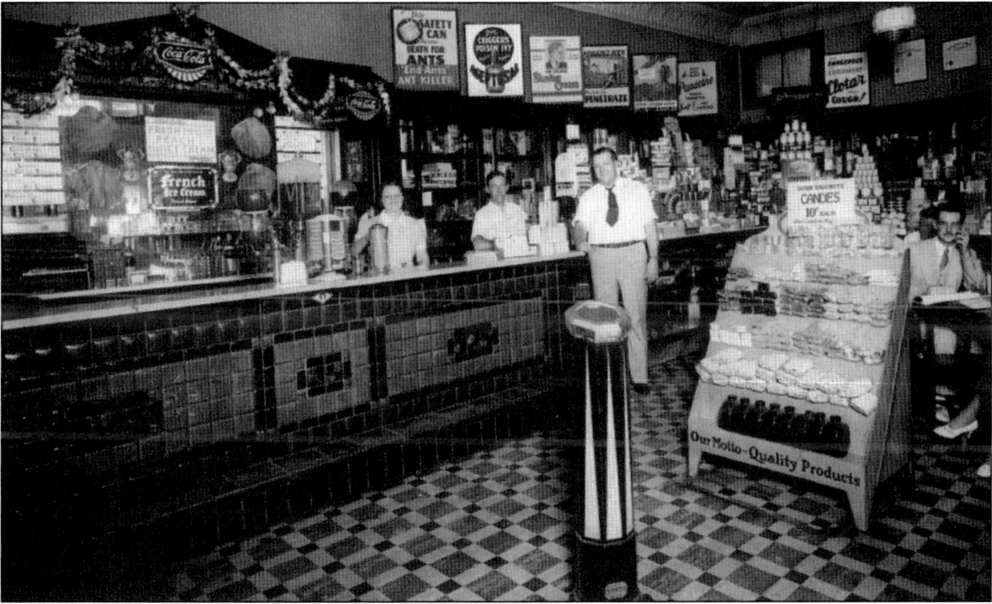

This 1930 photograph shows Herman and Helen Mueller and an unidentified worker inside Mueller's Pharmacy at the corner of Hamilton and Chase Avenues. Herman purchased the store from Harry C. Bristle in 1928, inheriting his soda fountain, and operated the store from 1928 to 1960. Harry's father, Charles D. Bristle, built the building in 1900 as a second location to his Knowlton's Corner location. Note the Peerless brand scale in the center, right next to the candy display. Sodas were made with Coca-Cola and French-Bauer ice cream. (Courtesy of Dorothy Knapp.)

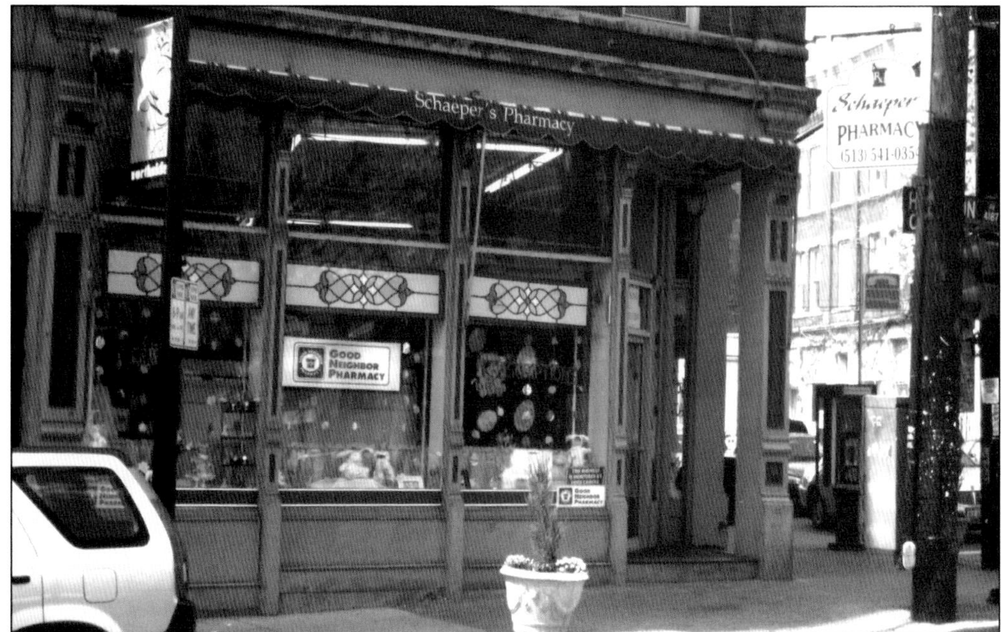

Gerald Schaeper bought Mueller's Pharmacy from Richard and Dorothy Knapp in 1985, owners from 1960 to 1985. Gerald's son Rick Schaeper took over the pharmacy in 1997 and continues its legacy as one of the last remaining family pharmacies in Cincinnati. The Schaepers moved the drug-filling counter inside the store from the small back room and are no longer serving French-Bauer ice-cream sodas. (Courtesy of Dorothy Knapp.)

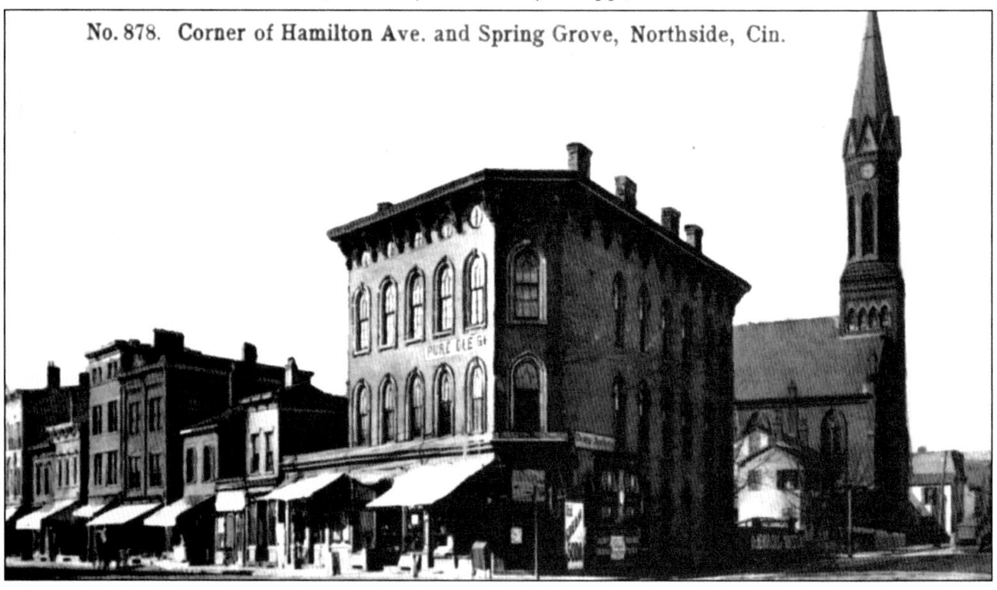

This photograph shows Bristles Pharmacy, at the current location of the BP gas station at the corner of Spring Grove Avenue and Hoffner Street. Built in 1851 as Dodsworth Hall, Bristles Pharmacy operated here from 1877 to 1928. A building sign reading *Deutsche Apotheker*, or "German pharmacist," refers to Charles Bristle. Before being demolished, it housed Erhardt's Meats, Alber's Grocery, and On Your Way. (From the Collection of the Public Library of Cincinnati and Hamilton County.)

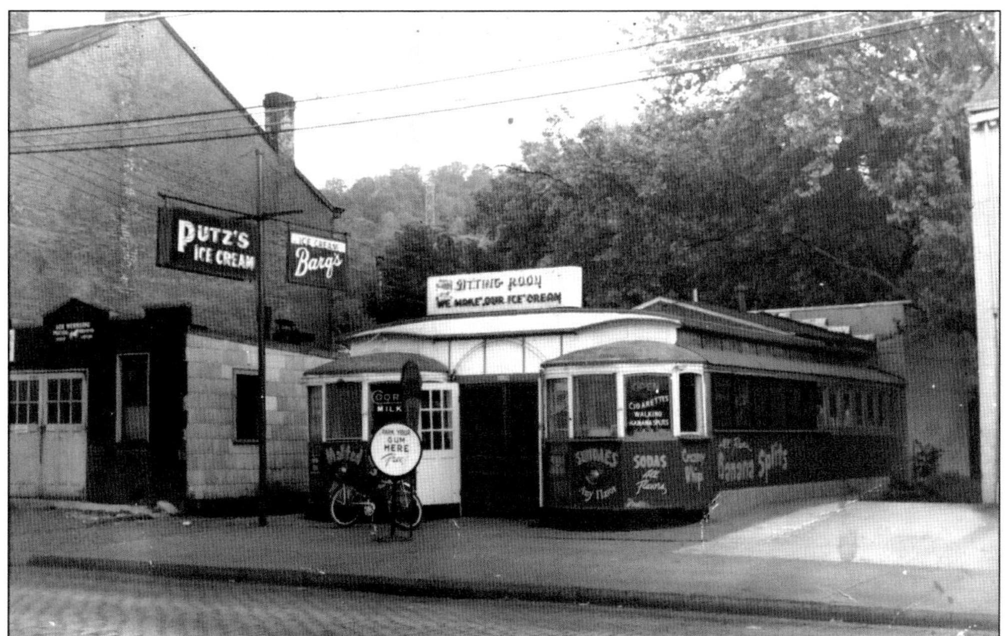

These trolley cars were the first location of Putz Creamy Whip at 4166 Spring Grove Avenue near Chambers Street. Started in 1938 by Constantine and Anna Putz, the creamery continues to be a Northside favorite, run by their great-granddaughter Donna Erhardt Borgman. The business sat next to George Wernsing's Practical Horse Saddling business, to the left. Note the Park Your Gum Here sign. (Courtesy of Donna Erhardt Borgman.)

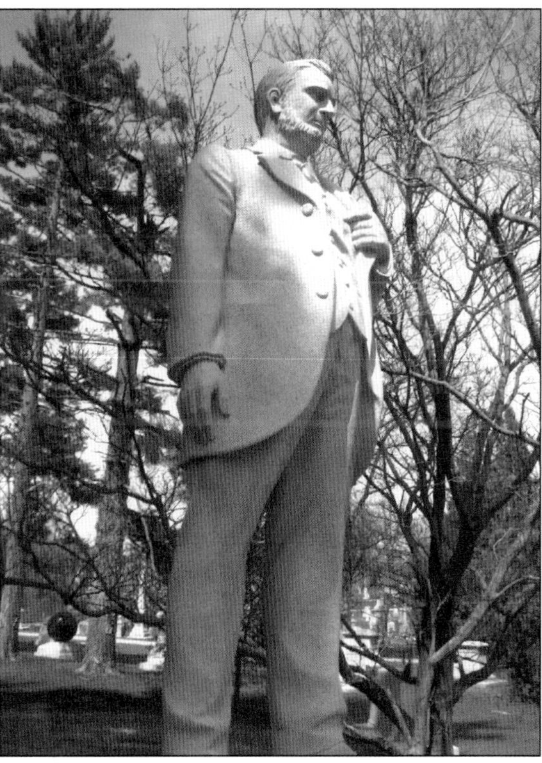

Befitting his long service to Northside mourners and his neighborhood philanthropy, Charles Anson Miller's (1842–1921) monument in Spring Grove Cemetery (section 15, lot 7) is one of only a few full-standing statues in the entire cemetery. Incorporated in 1866, Charles Miller's funeral business at 4318 Hamilton Avenue was one of the oldest continually operating businesses in Northside until 2008, when they moved to combine operations with Busse and Borgman.

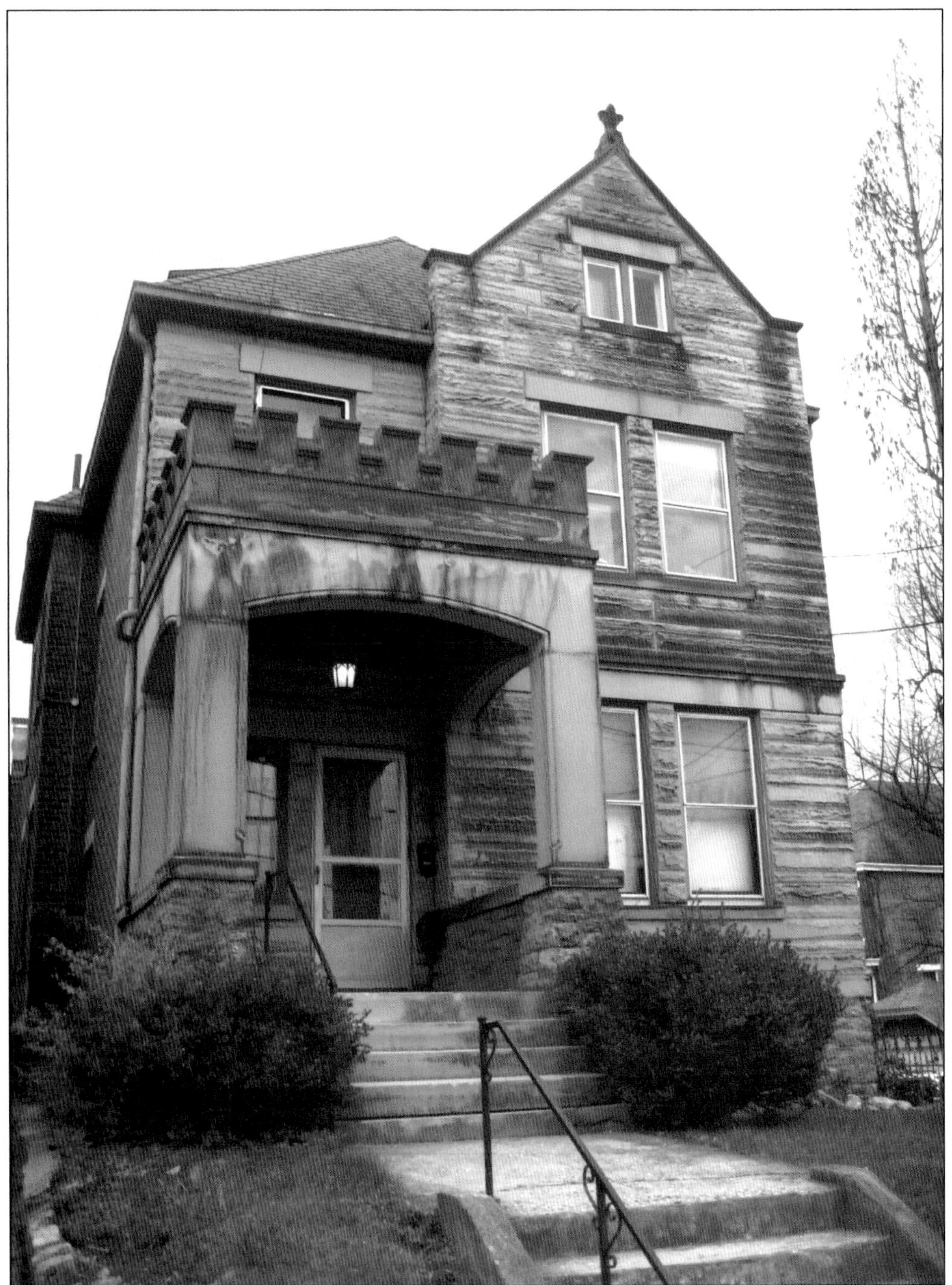

Charles Miller's home at 1817 Chase Avenue was built in 1890 by architect Samuel Hannaford and added in 1980 to the National Register of Historic Places. Miller was a Civil War veteran, director of the board of elections, and Cincinnati School Board president. Miller is also credited as being the go-to undertaker for the group of Scottish travelers, incorrectly known as Gypsies, who make an annual Memorial Day visit to Spring Grove Cemetery.

Nine

Frogtown Growers

Frogtown is the historic name given to the area around Springlawn and Crawford Avenues in Northside. The many natural springs in the area and the prevalence of frogs, known for their croaking, gave birth to this nickname. This area is a unique oasis in the center of Cincinnati, bounded to the south by Parker Woods and to the north and east by Spring Grove Cemetery. The gardening families of Frogtown on the Northside portion, and Wooden Shoe Hollow, on the Winton Place side of Spring Grove Cemetery, were a very close-knit group, and most were members of the Hoffner Street Evangelical Church. It was said that it was not advisable to talk bad about anyone at a dance or church event, as chances were that there was probably a family relation. The Kissel family is given credit for building the first greenhouses in Frogtown in about 1915, but the Hoeweller family, who raised 13 children in their small Gray Road home, are considered the grandparents of both the Frogtown and Wooden Shoe Hollow farming families.

Cincinnati Art Academy students would set up their easels every spring to paint the beautiful landscape. One artist in the 1970s created a calendar of his paintings of the area, titled with artistic license, "Frog Hollow Scenes."

The late 1950s brought intense competition with produce shipped from the southern and western states. This drastically reduced the profit made from vegetables. Those families that decided to convert their greenhouses to flowering plants, like the Kochs, were able to survive. Others left gardening altogether.

Although the Koch family is the only one still in the greenhouse business, all the houses in Frogtown are owned by original gardening families and are traded back and forth within the families.

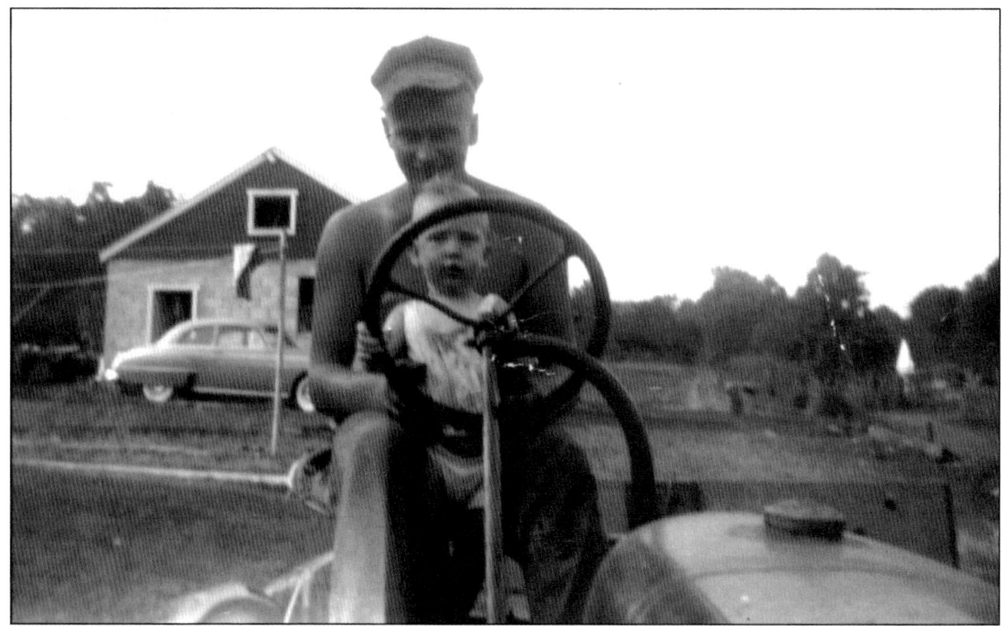

Fred C. Koch sits on the front of the tractor with his uncle Charles Koch in this 1953 photograph. Koch Greenhouses is a fourth-generation family-owned grower on Springlawn Avenue. Fred's great-grandfather Friedrich Christian Koch immigrated from Westphalia, Germany, in the late 1800s to Northside and started his truck farming business first growing vegetables like beet, leek, onion, celery, and rhubarb that they took to market for sale. (Courtesy of Denise Koch.)

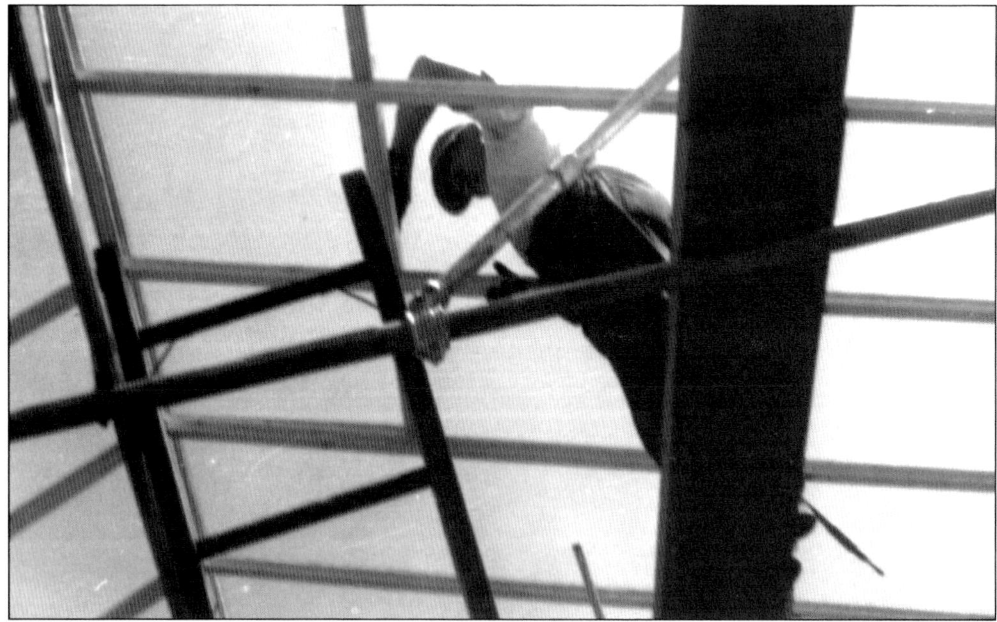

Fred's father, Albert, shown here framing in the greenhouses in 1953, transitioned to growing hothouse tomatoes and lettuce that were distributed through Cincinnati Greenhouse Vegetable Association and the Castellini Company. Albert's two brothers Wilbur and Charles both had their own greenhouse businesses. Wilbur owned the greenhouse property on Springlawn that still has the smokestack tiled with the Koch name. (Courtesy of Denise Koch.)

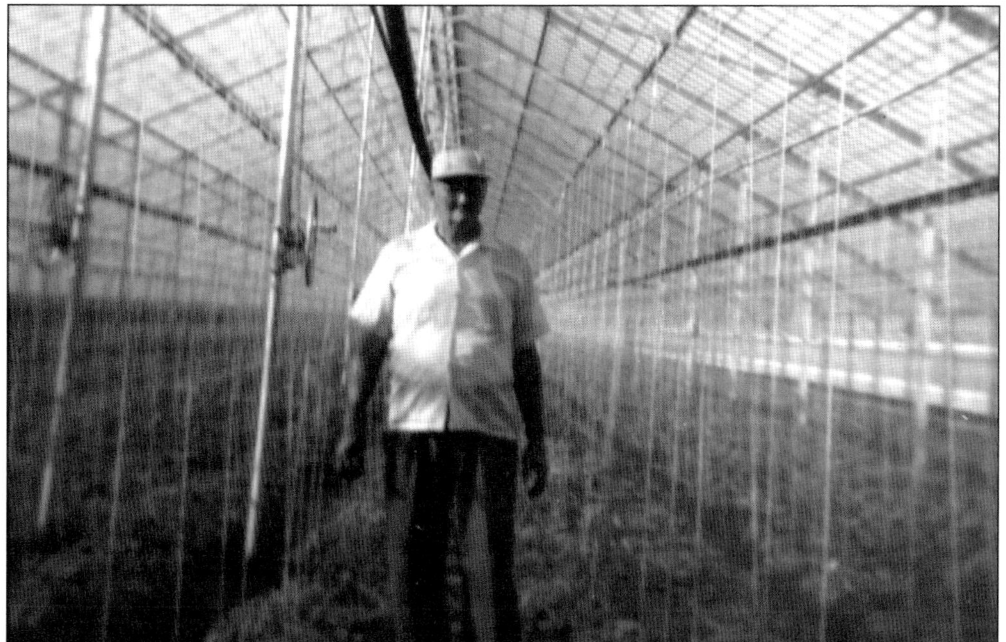

Fred's grandfather, Fred C. Koch, shown here in the greenhouses in 1953, was the second generation of the German immigrant farmers in the Frogtown area of Northside. Other German farming families in this area were the Kissels and the Hoewellers. Both the Kissels and Kochs intermarried with the Hoewellers and other families on the other side of Spring Grove Cemetery, in what was called Wooden Shoe Hollow along Gray Road, creating an interwoven set of gardening families. (Courtesy of Denise Koch.)

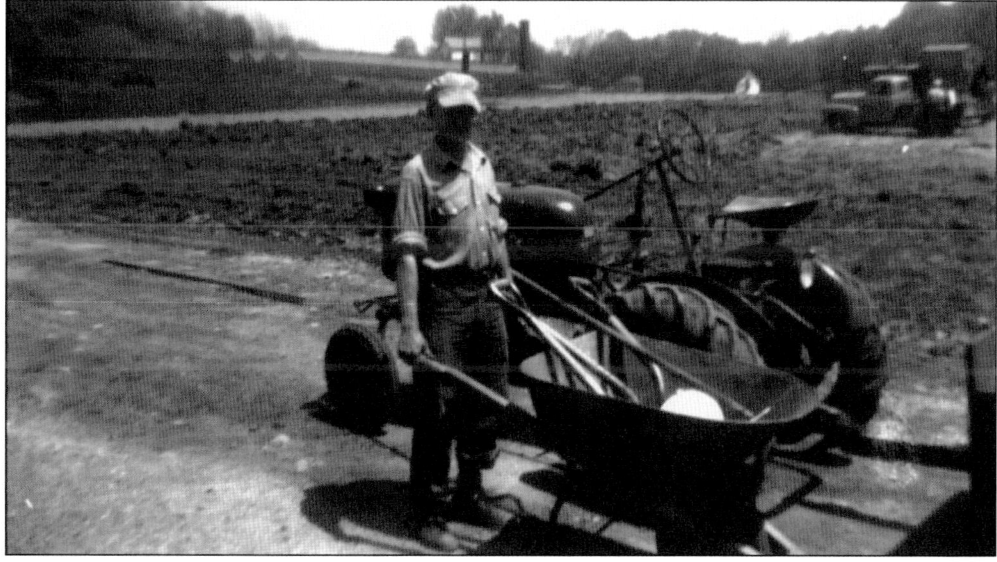

The rigors of truck farming are shown here in this 1953 photograph by Alfred Koch, the father of the current owner, Fred Koch. Aided by modern greenhouses and equipment, current owners Fred and Denise Dunham Koch have sustained a very labor-intensive, fourth-generation business, while college educating three daughters. Many Cincinnatians have spent summers or weekends working in the Koch greenhouses, including Nick Lache, of the band 98 Degrees. (Courtesy of Denise Koch.)

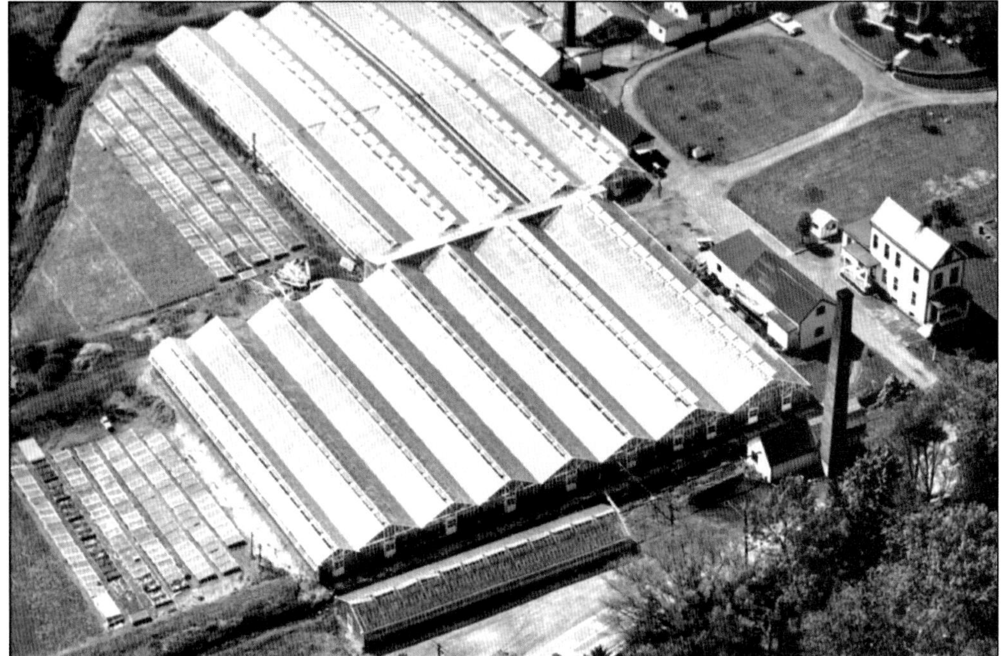

A 1950s aerial view of the Kissel Greenhouses on Crawford Avenue boasted one-and-a-half acres under glass. By 1957, the three families of Frogtown—Kock, Kissel, and Hoeweller, all descendants of the first settlers—had five acres under glass, growing produce and flowers. Albert Kissel removed these greenhouses in the 1980s and exited gardening, leaving the Koch family as the last remaining greenhouse business in Frogtown. (Courtesy of Dorothy Kissel.)

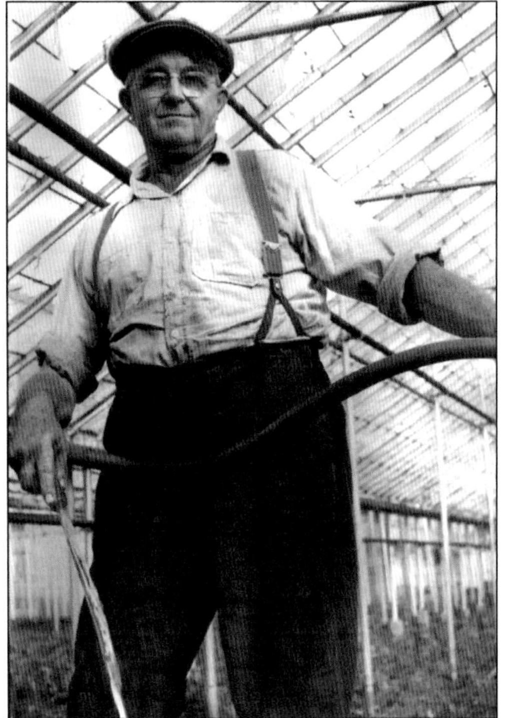

George Kissel is seen watering in this 1950s photograph, his favorite task. George's business included greenhouses, hotbeds, and field-grown vegetables. The gardeners produced vegetables mostly in the field and stretched out the spring and fall seasons by using hot beds—wooden frames with glass windows on top. George's sons, Albert and Edward, would haul manure from the nearby Springlawn Riding Club to make the hotbeds. (Courtesy of Dorothy Kissel.)

German immigrant Lorenz Kissel (1862–1913), shown here in the 1920s, was the founder of the Kissel family vegetable business in Frogtown. He and his wife, Henrietta Kettler Kissel, built their redbrick family home in the second decade of the 20th century on Springlawn Avenue near the corner of Crawford Avenue. Lorenz immigrated with his parents, George and Margaret Klaus Kissel, and two other brothers, Gottfried and Johann. (Courtesy of Dorothy Kissel.)

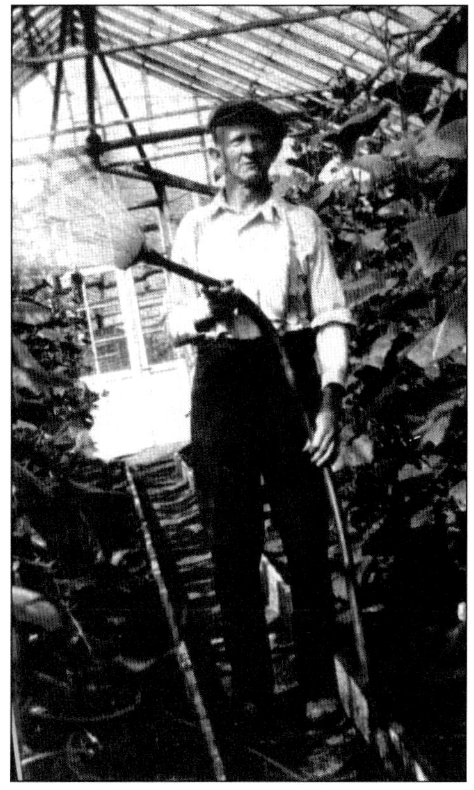

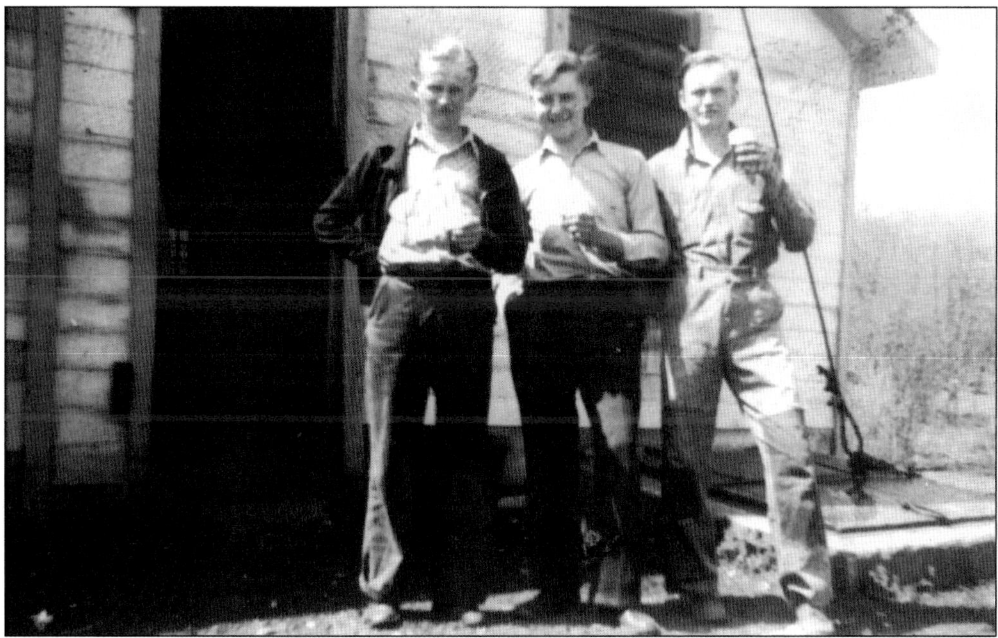

The men of Frogtown built their own card shack on the hill behind the Kissel family house on Crawford Avenue and hosted weekend men's-only card parties well into the night. William Kissel, son of Lorenz, was the leader of the group. This 1930s photograph shows, from left to right, Alfred "Whitey" Koch, Albert Kissel, and Wilbur Koch. (Courtesy of Dorothy Kissel.)

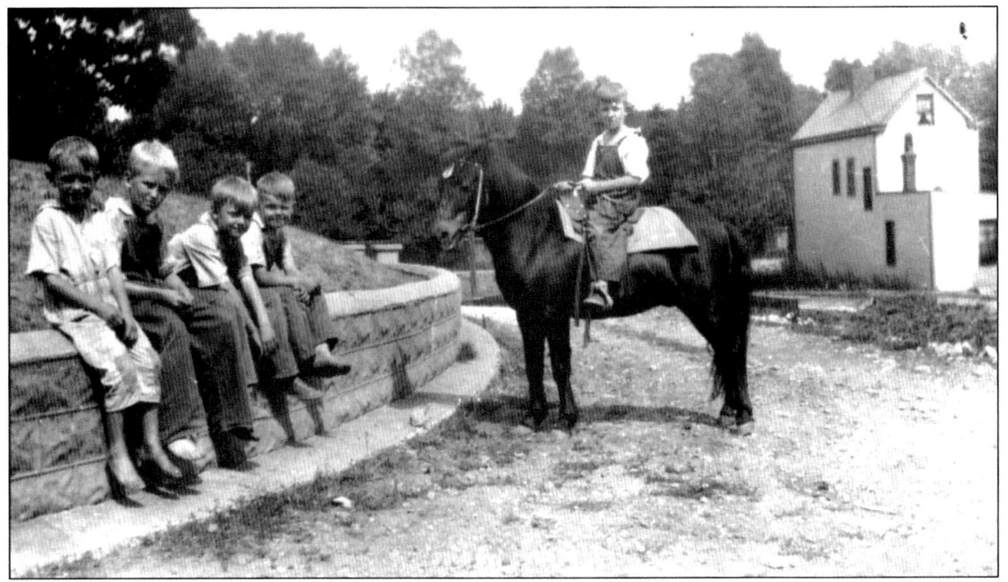

Frogtown children, shown here in the 1920s, enjoyed the closeness of the other children of gardening families in the Frogtown and Wooden Shoe Hollow areas around Spring Grove Cemetery. Wilbur Koch is on the horse, and Albert Kissel is the last child sitting on the wall. Indicative of gardening families in the area, Albert quit school at 17 to help with the family business. (Courtesy of Dorothy Kissel.)

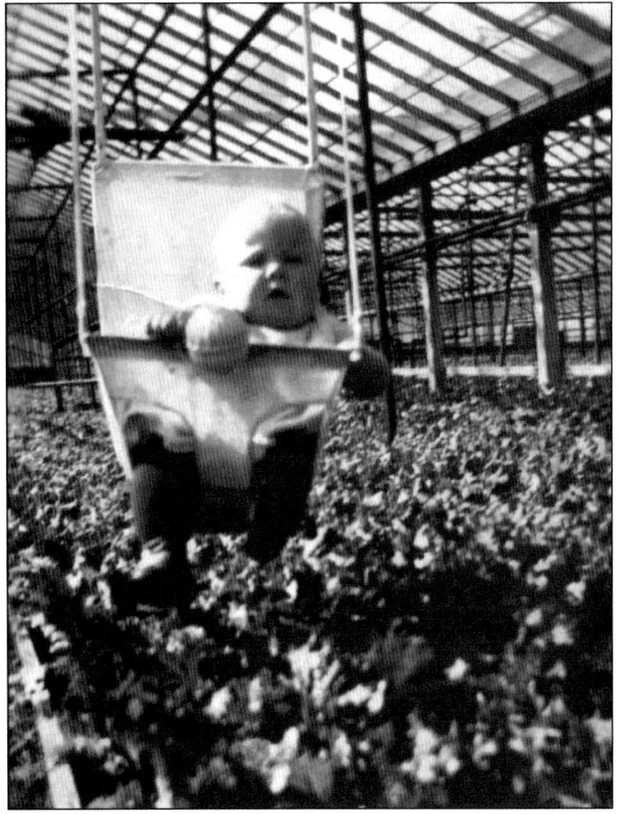

Albert (1923–2004) is shown in the early 1930s in his "jumpy" in the family greenhouse. All family members were involved in the business and gave the mother a watchful eye while working. Albert took over his father George's greenhouse business and, with his brother Edward, rebuilt the greenhouses in the 1950s with frames made from salvaged cypress beer tanks from the old Bruckmann Brewery. (Courtesy of Dorothy Kissel.)

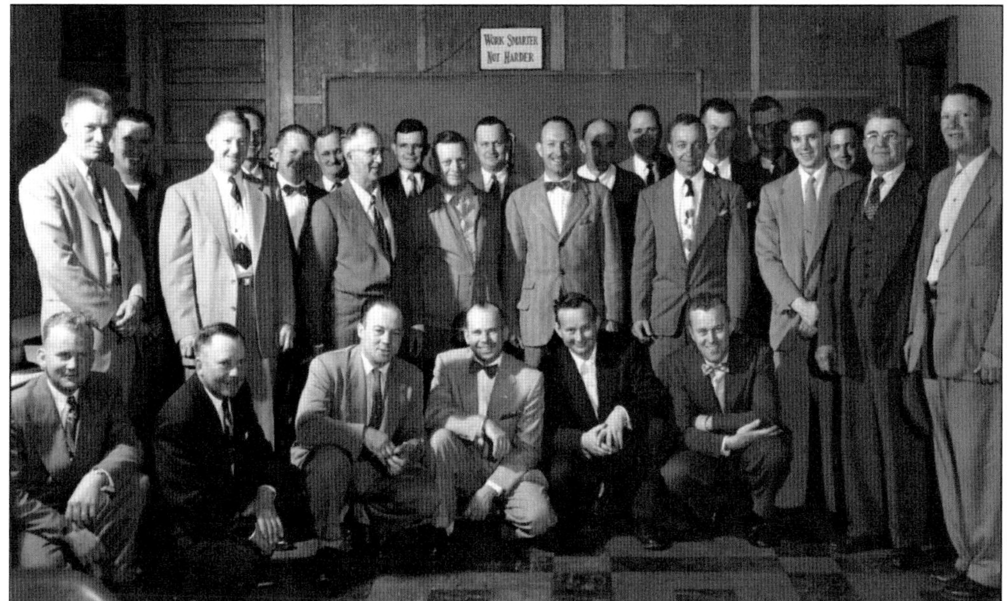

The Cincinnati Vegetable Growers Association, shown here in the 1950s, included not only the Frogtown and Wooden Shoe Hollow growers but also the Sietz family growers in Delhi and other growers farther out on the west side of Cincinnati. They met in the same room as the Northside Business Club in the 1950s, on the northwest corner of Hoffner Street and Hamilton Avenue at Knowlton's Corner. (Courtesy of Dorothy Kissel.)

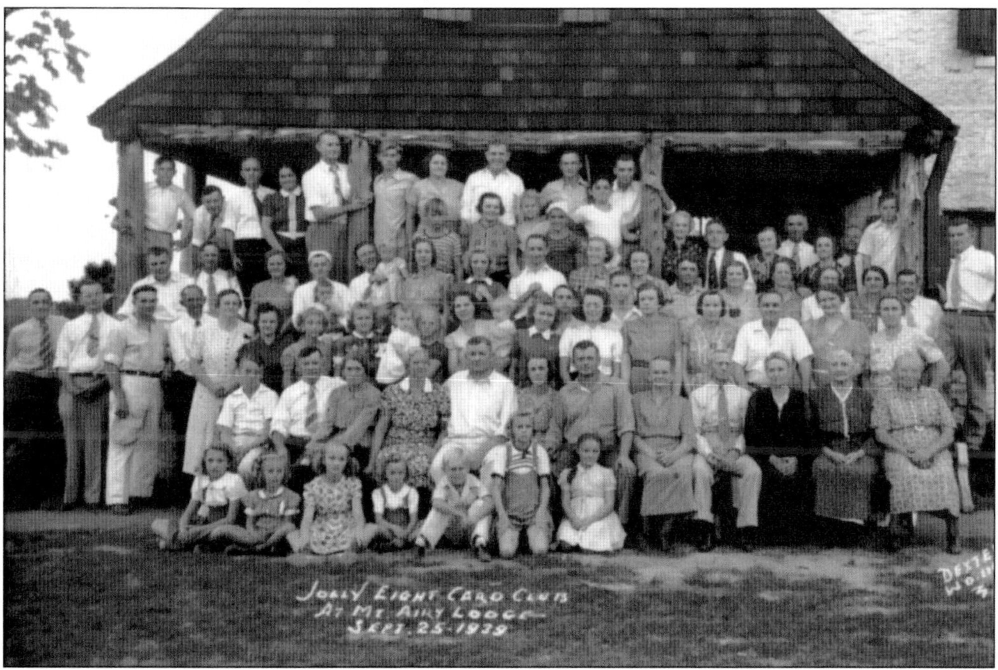

This 1939 photograph of the Jolly Eights Card Club at a shelter in Mount Airy Forest shows the close-knit community of all the gardening families of Wooden Shoe Hollow and Frogtown. Names like Kock, Funke, Rahn, Hoeweller, Kettler, and Kissel are in the list of this very large group. (Courtesy of Dorothy Kissel.)

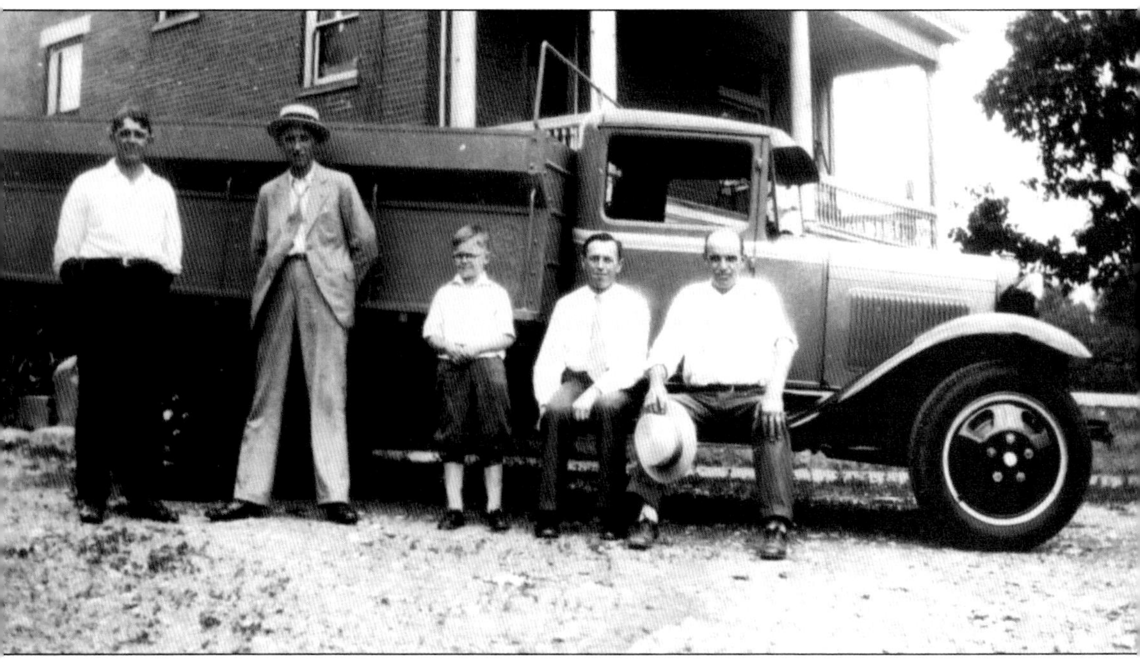

This 1930s photograph shows a young Albert Kissel in the center and workers in front of a vegetable delivery truck at the Kissel family house on Springlawn Avenue. (Courtesy of Dorothy Kissel.)

Ten

A MATURE COMMUNITY

In the 1920s, Northside's explosive growth began to slow. Most of the land use had not changed since the beginning of the 19th century, and there was only minimal new home building. The Depression brought the closing of several businesses, like the Liberty Theatre, and many changes in businesses. By the end of the 1930s, the Depression had taken its toll on independent businesses that made early Northside distinctive. Chain stores like Kroger and A&P Grocery started to join the other businesses. There was a brief surge in growth in the 1940s as several manufacturing businesses in Northside threw their production into the war effort. After World War II, most of the industry had left Northside and suburban flight began, as the older housing stock was viewed as out of date to younger families. By the 1960s, Northside businesses reflected a lower-spending clientele. There were a number of vacant stores and new shops like the Northside Bargain Center, and used furniture stores moved in. Long-standing neighborhood stores began to close and were replaced with service businesses that did not rely on Northside residents for business. In the 1970s, the Northside Business Association turned its focus to the preserved Victorian-era commercial structures along Hamilton Avenue, and in 1982, the City of Cincinnati designated the area as a local historic district. More recently, anchors to a newer renaissance of Northside were Crazy Ladies Bookstore and Hasselle Pottery, among many others. They led to a momentum that has been further accelerated with other successful newer businesses like Honeys and Slim's Restaurants, Northside Tavern, Shake It Records, and Take the Cake. Some of these new entries have flocked to Northside from neighboring Corryville, Clifton, and Over-the-Rhine, who see more opportunity in the supportive and active community. Northside continues to undergo renewal typical of historical neighborhoods that have become attractive to young, middle-income families and creative-class singles. Its residents exhibit a strong sense of neighborhood pride with active community organizations like the Northside Business Club, the Northside Community Council, and CAIN.

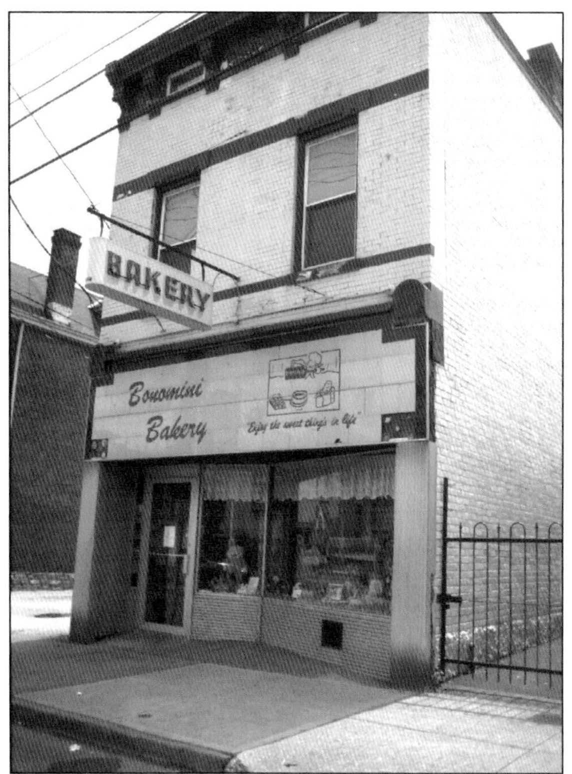

Bonomini Bakery, at 1677 Blue Rock Street was founded in 1976. Lenny and Virginia Volz Bonomini bought Blue Rock Bakery from Rudolph and Karoline Engler, owners since the 1950s. Lenny had inherited Volz Bakery at 4205 Virginia Avenue, from his father-in-law Joseph Volz, owner from the 1920s to the 1960s. In 1974, the City of Cincinnati bought Volz Bakery for the Hamilton-Colerain Connector, demolishing the property. Lenny's sons Joe and John Bonomini now carry on the family legacy.

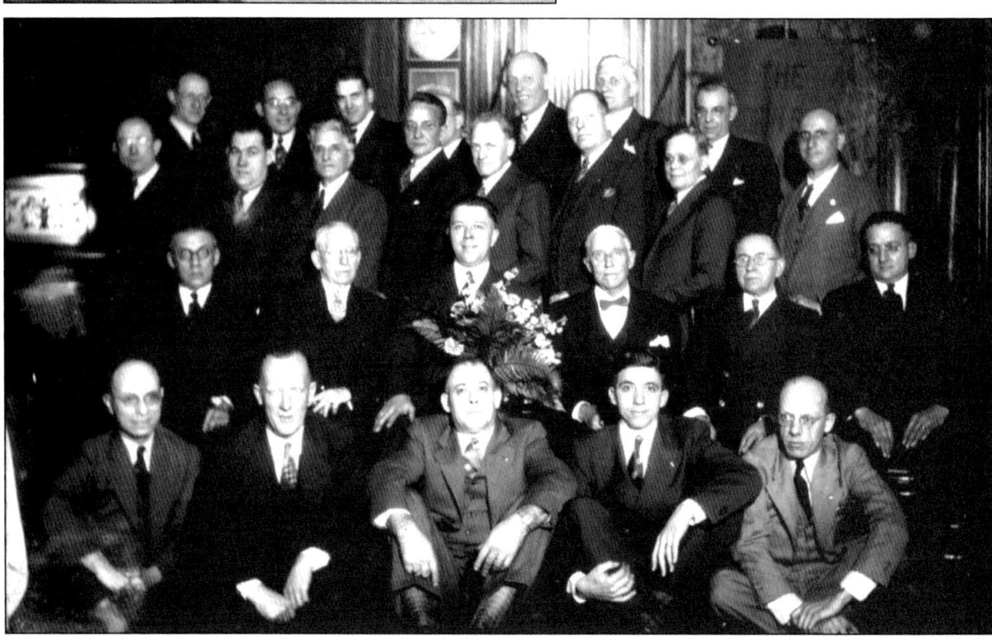

This 1930s photograph shows the Northside Business Association in its meeting room on the second floor of the building at the northwest corner of Hamilton Avenue and Hoffner Street at Knowlton's Corner. George Rehn was president then. The Northside Business Association was founded in 1907 by John A. Herbert, and the first president was William F. Ray. (Courtesy of Don Beimesche.)

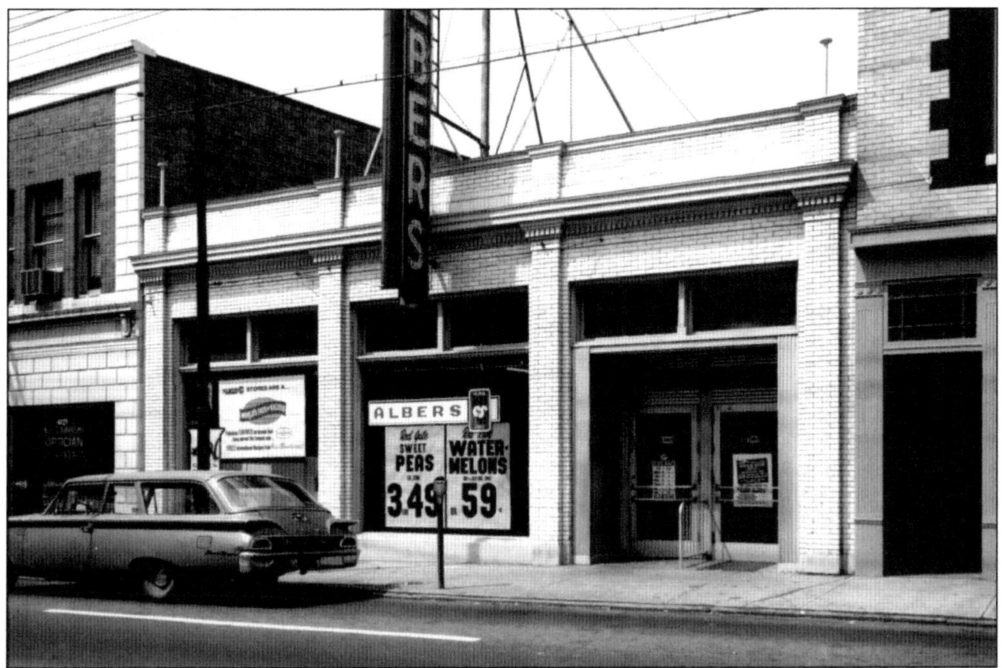

This photograph shows Albers Supermarket on Hamilton Avenue in the late 1950s. In the early 1930s, William H. Albers (1895–1944), a Kroger executive, severed his ties and opened one of the first "supermarkets" in Ohio. Selecting items from shelves, rather than asking a clerk, was what made Albers unique from other Northside grocers. Albers operated here until the 1960s, when a new store was built on Turrill Street. (Courtesy of Don Beimesche.)

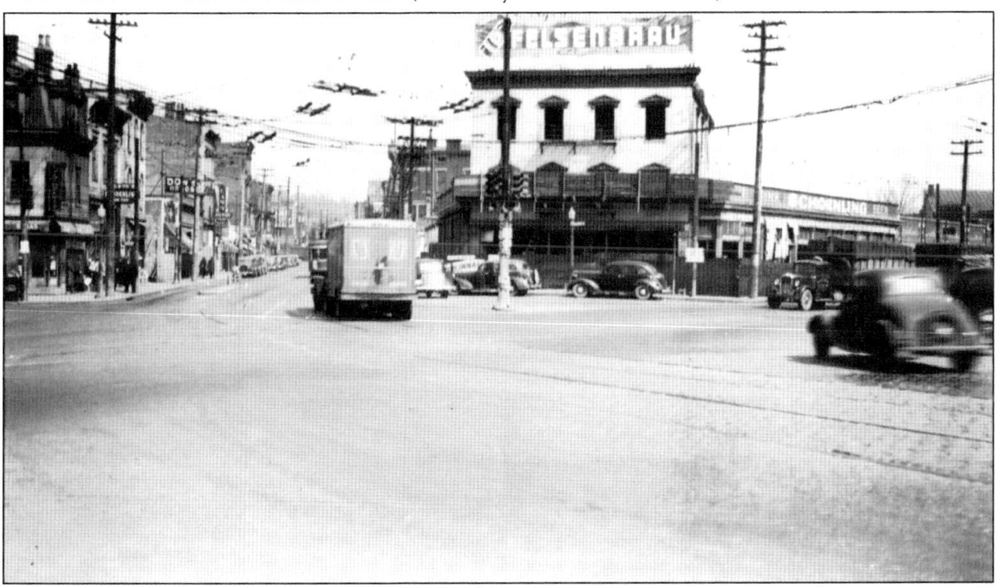

This photograph shows the last days of Knowlton's Stone Blockhouse in the late 1930s. The Felsenbrau Beer billboard above the blockhouse advertised the brand made by the local Clyffside Brewery in neighboring Clifton. The 1937 flood would cause severe damage to the building, causing it to be razed. A Checkers Store replaced the blockhouse and now houses Capazollo Printing. (From the Collection of the Public Library of Cincinnati and Hamilton County.)

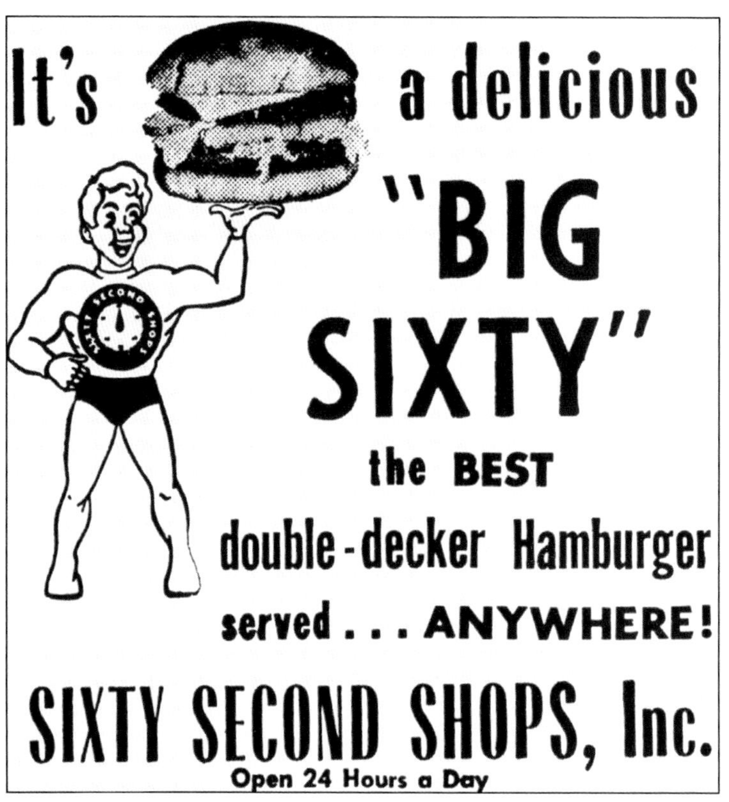

In the 1930s, all-night chili parlors and hamburger stands, like the 60 Second Shop shown here, the Kitchen, the Liberty, and the Tick-Top Sandwich Shop, abounded at Knowlton's Corner to cater to transferring streetcar passengers and late-night revelers, who took the "night owl" cars home from the Northside clubs. Small local chains of these burger stands dominated Knowlton's Corner even before Ray Kroc started his McDonald's empire in 1954.

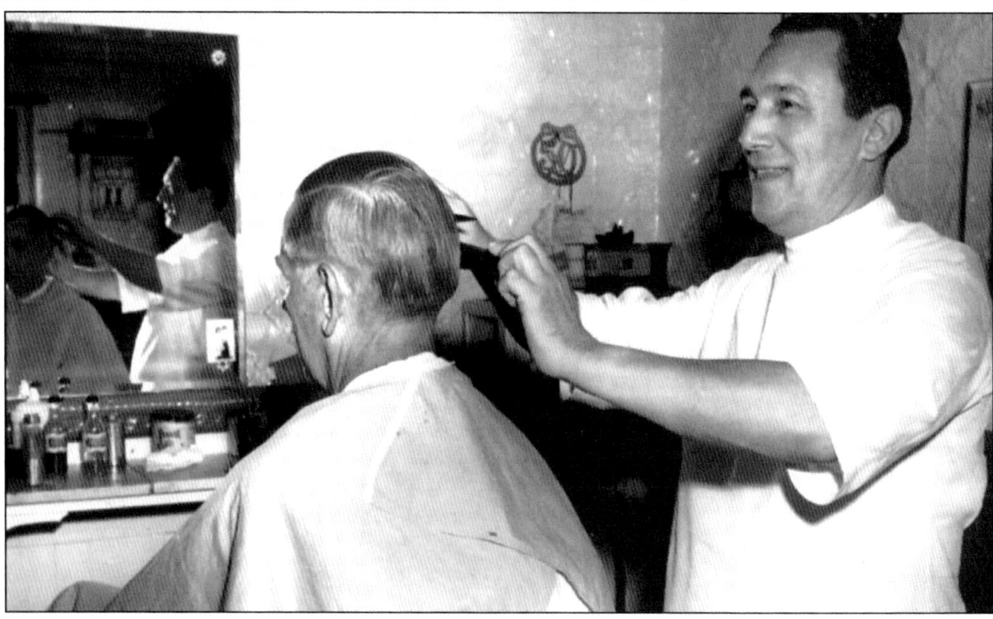

The Lipka Barbershop at 3850 Spring Grove Avenue near Powers Street was started in 1910 by German immigrant August Lipka (1877–1961). This photograph shows his son Oscar Lipka shearing a customer in the 1950s. Oscar quit school in the seventh grade to apprentice in the family business. He cut hair until midnight on weekends to meet the demand of Northside revelers. The shop survived until the 1970s. (Courtesy of Roberta Lipka Landwehr Watson.)

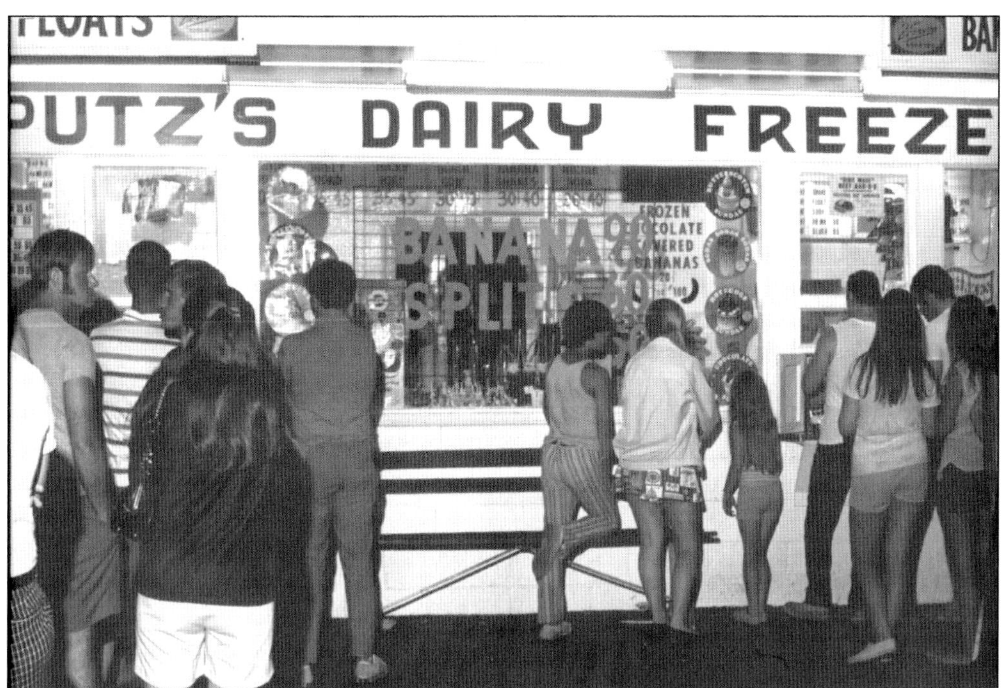

Seen here is a typical day for the Putz Creamy Whip in the 1970s at its new location on West Fork Road. Fourth-generation owners Ray and Donna Erhardt Borgman continue to serve lines of eager customers. They swear that their unique quality comes from using the original Electro-Freeze machines purchased in 1954 and 1955 by Ray and Gertie Putz Erhardt, Donna's grandparents. (Courtesy of Donna Erhardt Borgman.)

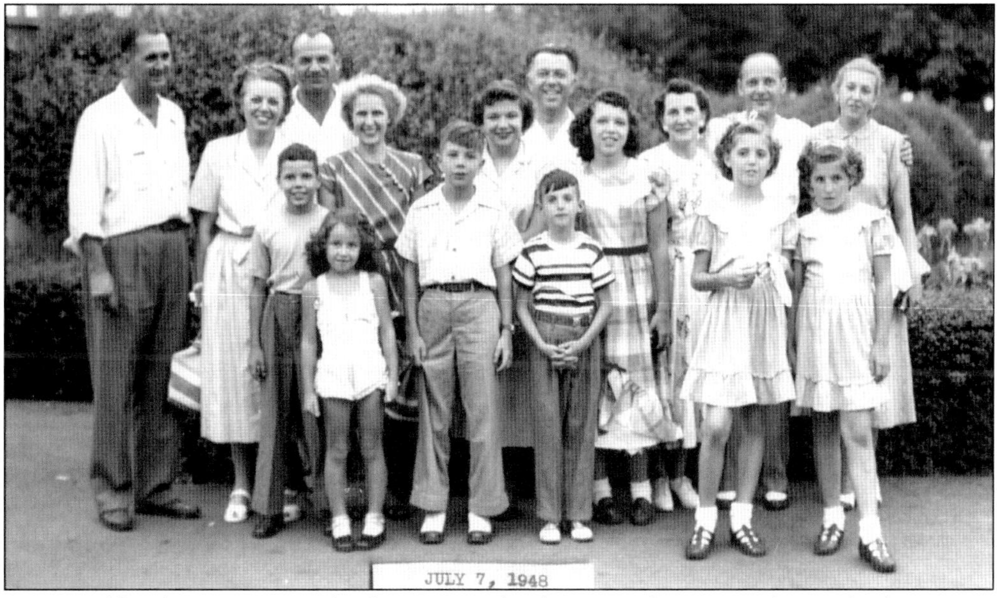

A group of families poses at Northsiders' Coney Island Day on July 7, 1948. The Northside Business Association hosted many picnics and outings from its inception in 1907. In 1925, they started their annual outings at the Cincinnati Zoo, with dance competitions, crowning of the festival queen, the better baby contest, and ball games and races. (Courtesy of Don Beimesche.)

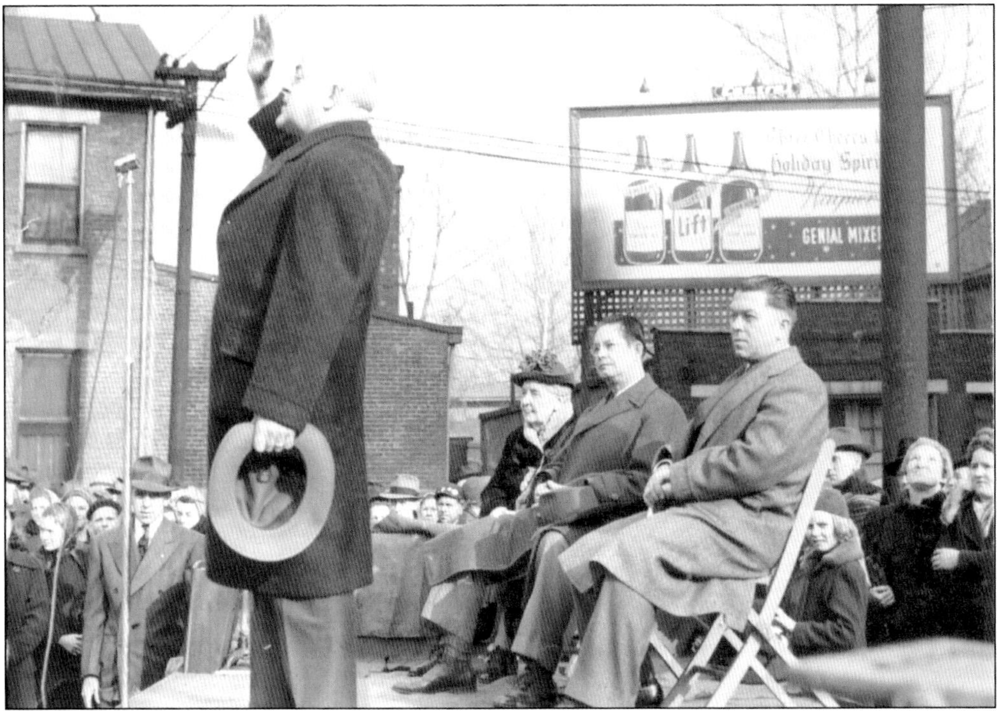

A flag raising at Knowlton's Corner on January 17, 1942, included distinguished guests (seated, from left to right) Annie Knowlton Zimmerman (1863–1948), born at Knowlton's Corner in the blockhouse of her grandfather Ephraim Knowlton; Jimmy Stewart Meyer; and Herman Gerbroth, business association president. (Courtesy of Don Beimesche.)

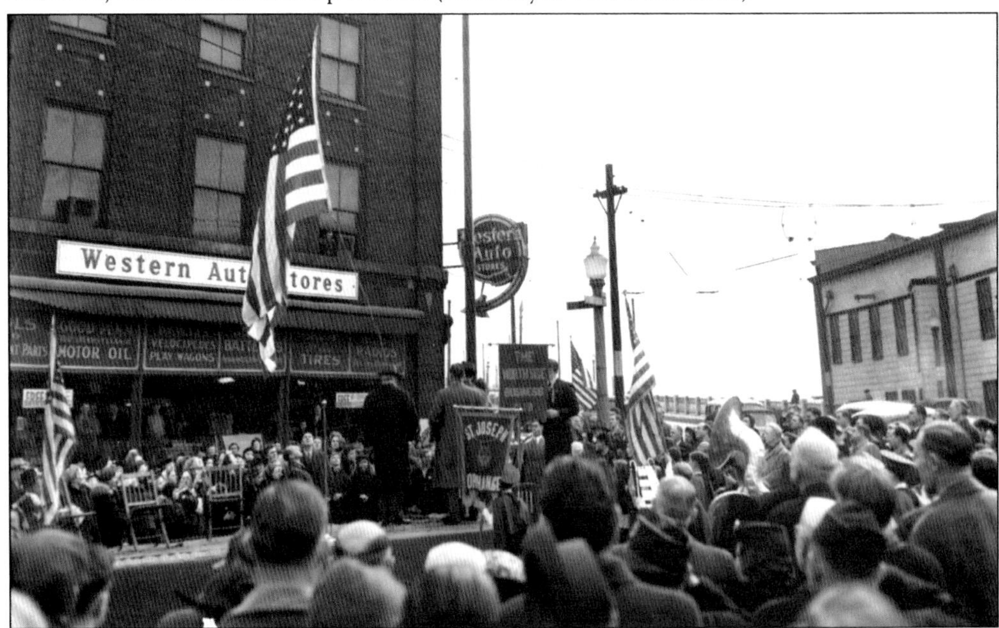

Another flag raising at Knowlton's Corner in the 1940s shows that the old Herbert Furniture factory and showroom at the viaduct now housed the Western Auto Stores. The St. Joseph's Orphanage Band accompanied the ceremony. (Courtesy of Don Beimesche.)

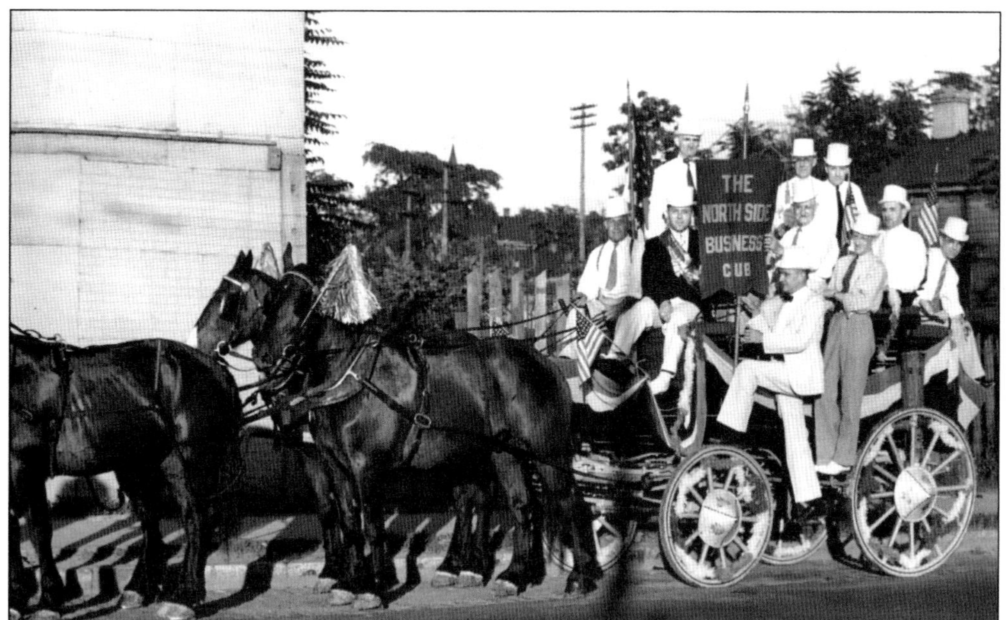

The Northside Business Club men line up for a parade on June 28, 1937, including, from left to right, William Batchler; Herman E. Gerborth, the grand marshal (owner of Gerborth Electric, and president of Ormande Savings and Loan); Warner Koops; Judge Nelson Schwab; William Fehrmann (grocer); John Heilman (owner of Heilman Motors, now the Ace Doran Building); Stanley Aston; Clifford Hengge; Fred Usinger (grandson of Usinger carriages); and William Kolhaven, in a carriage perhaps made by Fred's grandfather in Northside. (Courtesy of Don Beimesche.)

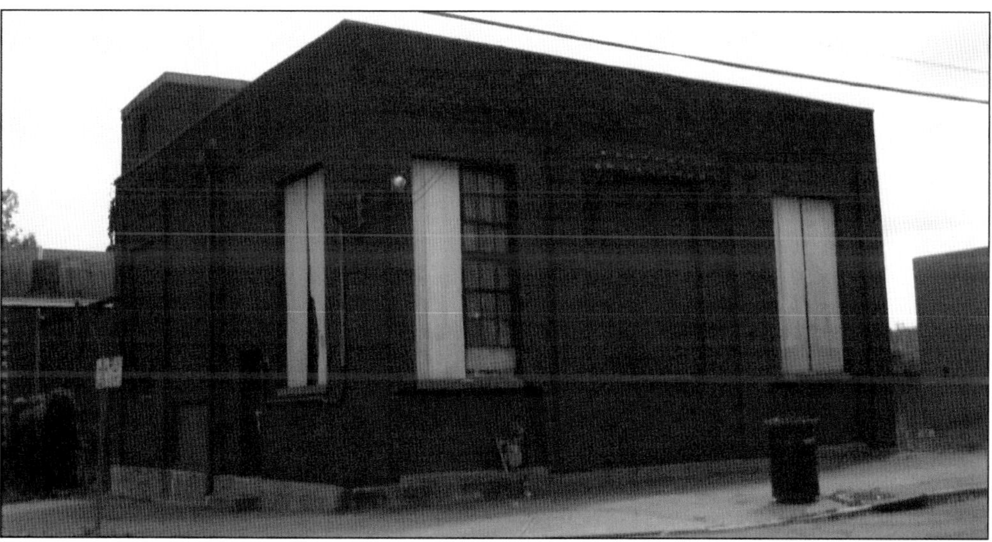

The power station for the Cincinnati Street Railway still stands at the corner of Chase Avenue and Turrill Street. It powered line 16, Colerain Avenue, which traversed Sixth and Vine Streets to Virginia and Colerain Avenues. The street stops were Sixth, Elm, Twelfth, Central Avenue, Clark, Baymiller, Liberty, Freeman, Central Avenue, Colerain, Spring Grove, Hamilton, Chase, and Virginia. Return street stops were Colerain, Central Avenue, Freeman, York, Linn, Clark, Central Avenue, Twelfth, Elm, Seventh, Vine, and Sixth.

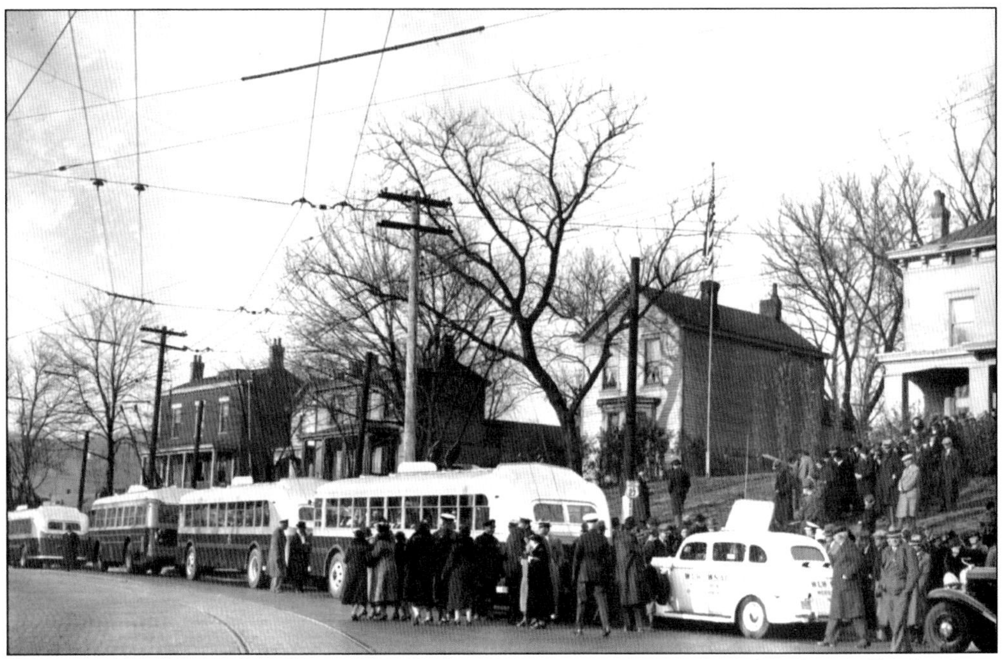

On November 30, 1936, the Cincinnati Street Railway company initiated its first trolley bus line, Route 15, to Clark Street from Colerain Avenue. This photograph shows the buses and people gathering on Colerain Avenue looking west. Many who have ridden trolley buses in Cincinnati recall the driver having to climb on top of the bus to reconnect to the trolley wires ahead after a wide turn such as this one. (Courtesy of Don Beimesche.)

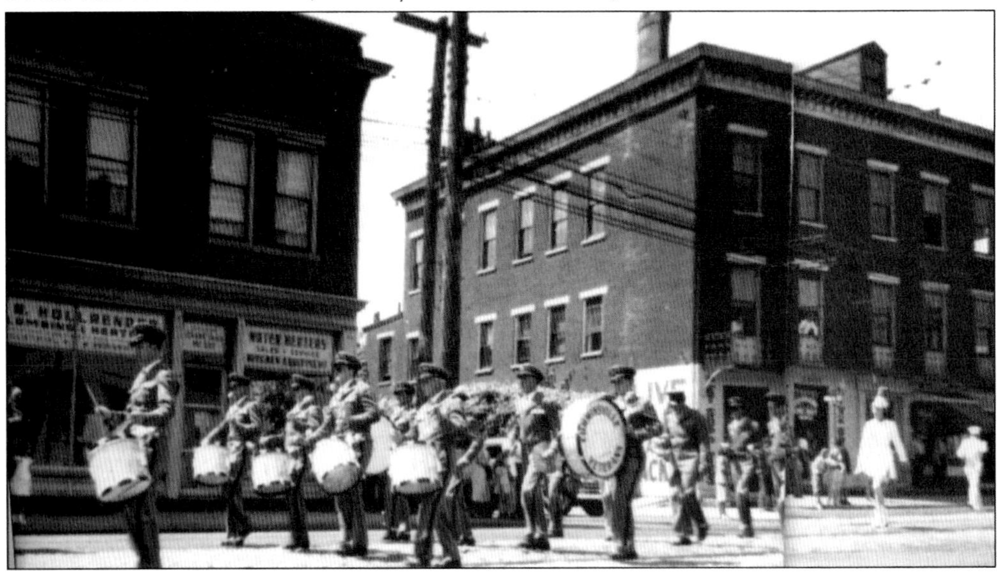

This 1948 Memorial Day parade photograph was taken in front of the original Spaeth Funeral Parlor at 3841 Spring Grove Avenue, then housing P. R. Hollrender Plumbing. The building to the right in the photograph is a former hotel that housed the Fehrman's live bait shop at 3901 Spring Grove Avenue. That building was razed, but the Spaeth building during World War II housed the Old Bar, which held female impersonation shows. The Spaeth building now houses the Visionaries and Voices Art Studio. (Courtesy of Roberta Lipka Landwehr Watson.)

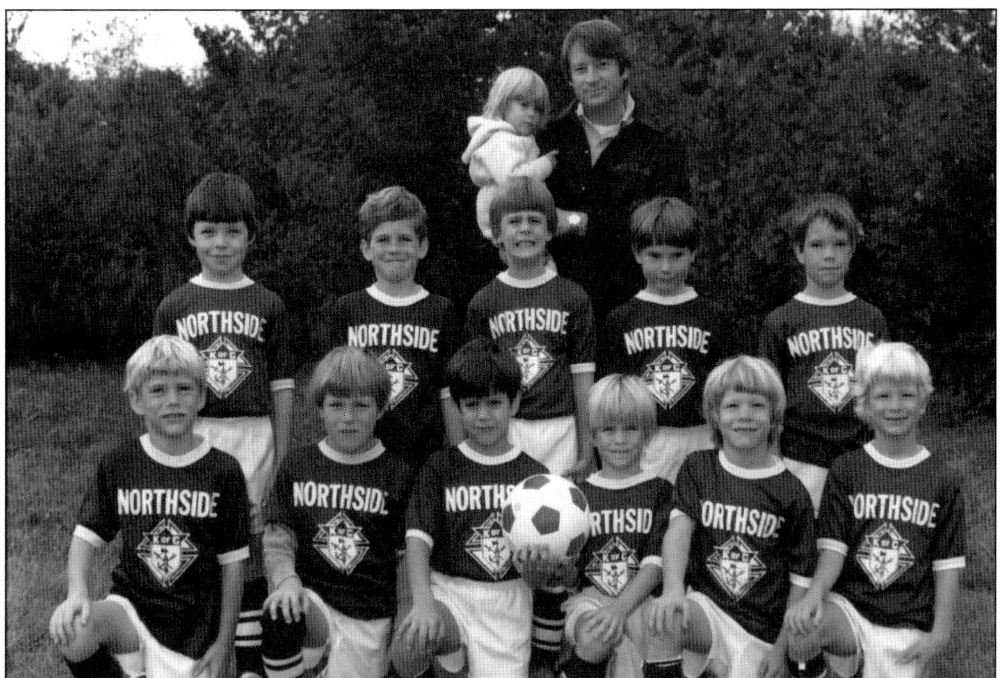

The Northside Knights of Columbus, headquartered for many years at the mansion at 4400 Hamilton Avenue at Haight Street, sponsored many sports teams like this 1978 soccer team, coached by Roger Woellert and a young Jen Woellert Uhl. Known team members here are, from left to right, (first row) Eddie McBride, two unidentified, Timothy Clayton, and Phillip and Paul Sterchi; (second row) second and third from the left, Mike Keegan and Dann Woellert.

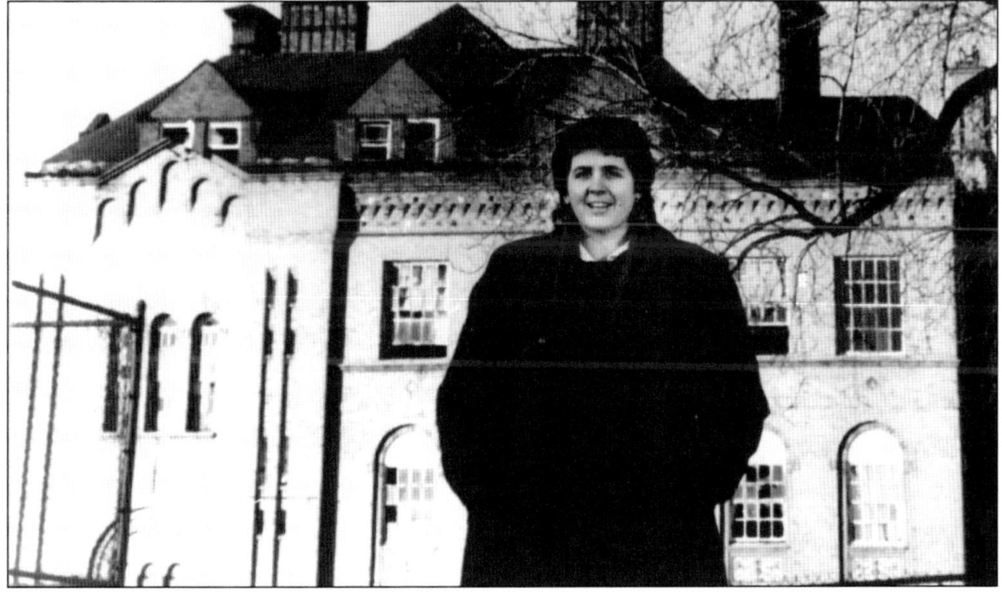

This photograph shows a South Cumminsville success story, Maureen Wood, standing in front of the vacant Garfield School. She led the development of Garfield Commons with Women's Research and Development Center, for the creation of a 47-unit apartment complex with community and day-care centers. (Courtesy of Maureen Wood.)

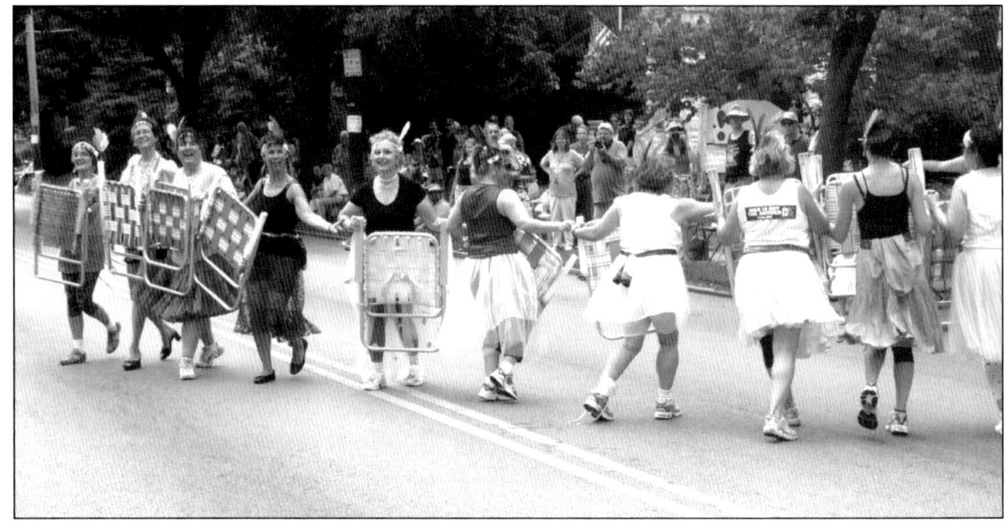

The Northside Fourth of July parade was started in 1970 by Northside Business Association president Fred Deubell. For many years, the feature of the parade was the Roger Bacon High School Marching Band. The group shown here, the Lawnchair Ladies, are also a parade favorite. Started in 1997 by Lynn Milosevich, Jacqui Phlipot, and Barb Boylan, they bring a smile to all with their themed chants and lawn chair choreography.

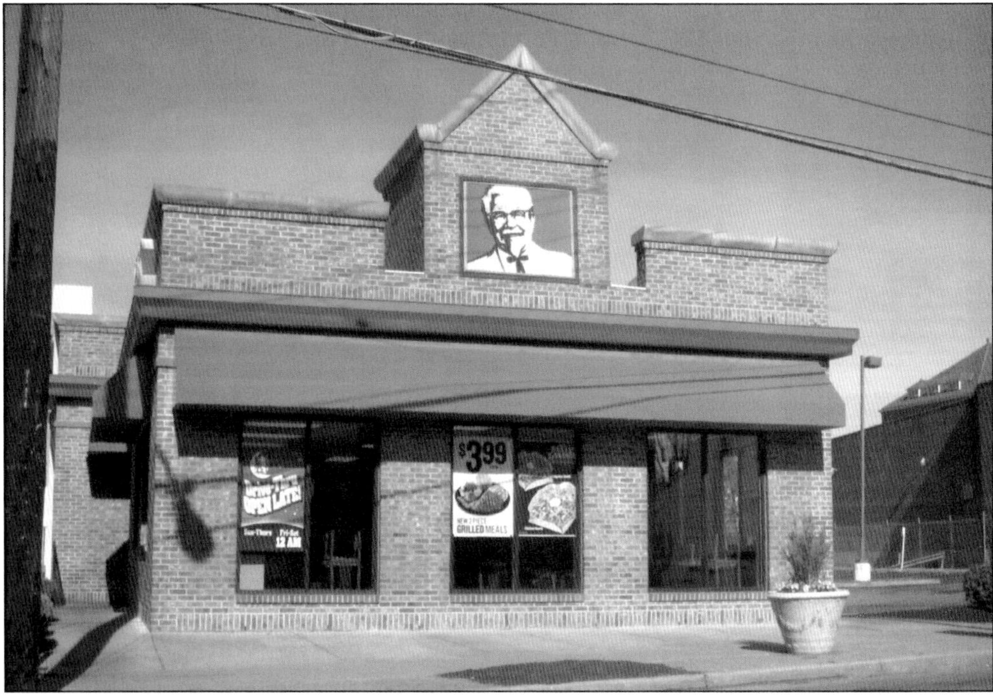

The Kentucky Fried Chicken at 4147 Hamilton Avenue, is the only example of "big box" development in Northside. Three properties from Knowlton Street to the Park Theatre were razed in 1970. One was the former Park Hotel, originally the Hotel Washburn. Another property housed Central TV, operated by partners Dave Oppenheimer and John Overhuls since 1953. Northside today does not invite such development. In 2005, the business association thwarted a Walgreens from coming into the Hoffner Historic District.

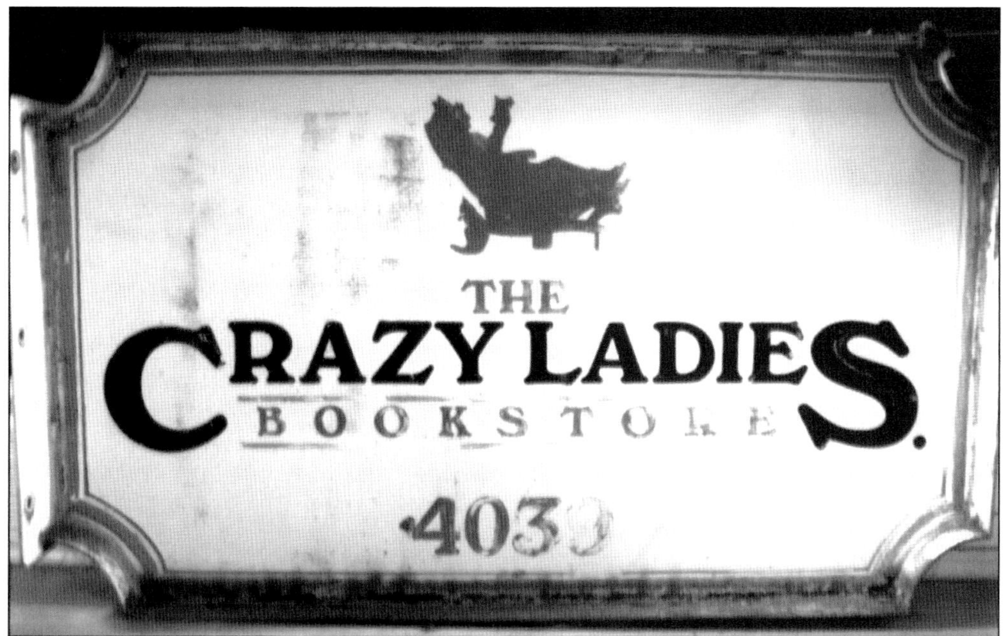

Carolyn Dellenbach Virginia, with the help of good friends, opened the Crazy Ladies Bookstore in Northside in July 1979 in a renovated William Todd building. This store at 4039 Hamilton and Vandalia Avenues was one of the first anchors in the recent neighborhood renaissance. Crazy Ladies was the only bookstore in Cincinnati to focus on feminist and women's literature. This original sign is an icon of Northside's rebirth.

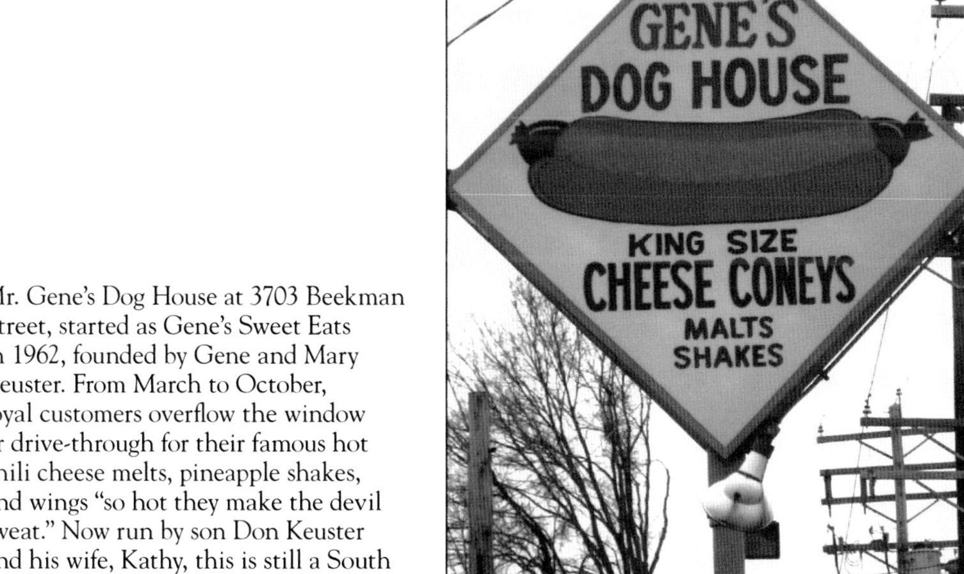

Mr. Gene's Dog House at 3703 Beekman Street, started as Gene's Sweet Eats in 1962, founded by Gene and Mary Keuster. From March to October, loyal customers overflow the window or drive-through for their famous hot chili cheese melts, pineapple shakes, and wings "so hot they make the devil sweat." Now run by son Don Keuster and his wife, Kathy, this is still a South Cumminsville neighborhood favorite.

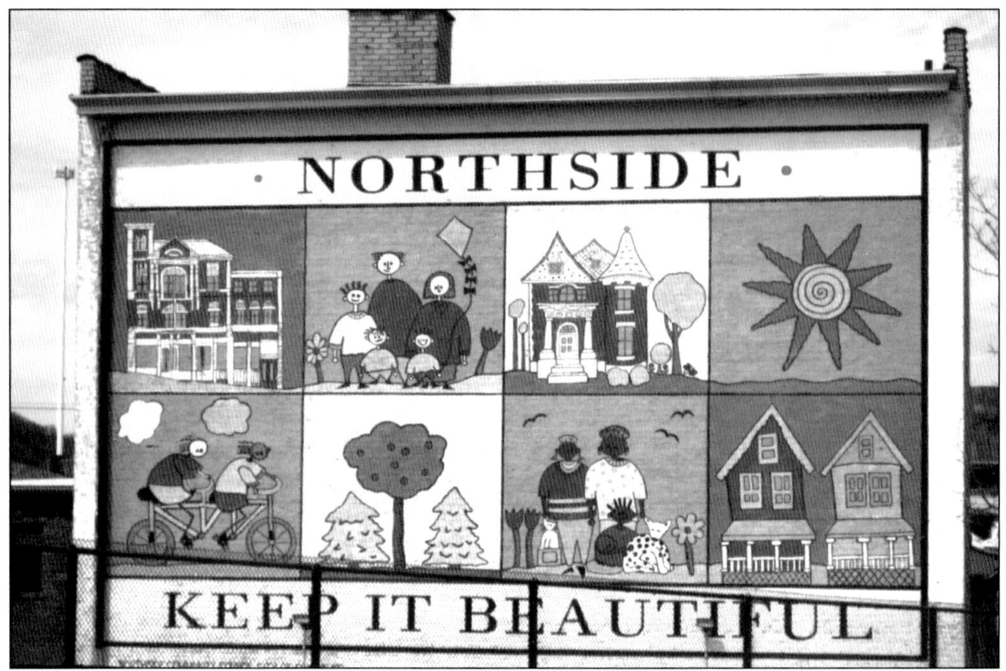

As visitors head toward Northside on the Ludlow Avenue Viaduct today, they are greeted by a mural on the back of the old Liberty Theatre. The checkerboard mural by local artist Ursula Roma gives a glimpse of the artsy and eclectic neighborhood they are about to encounter.

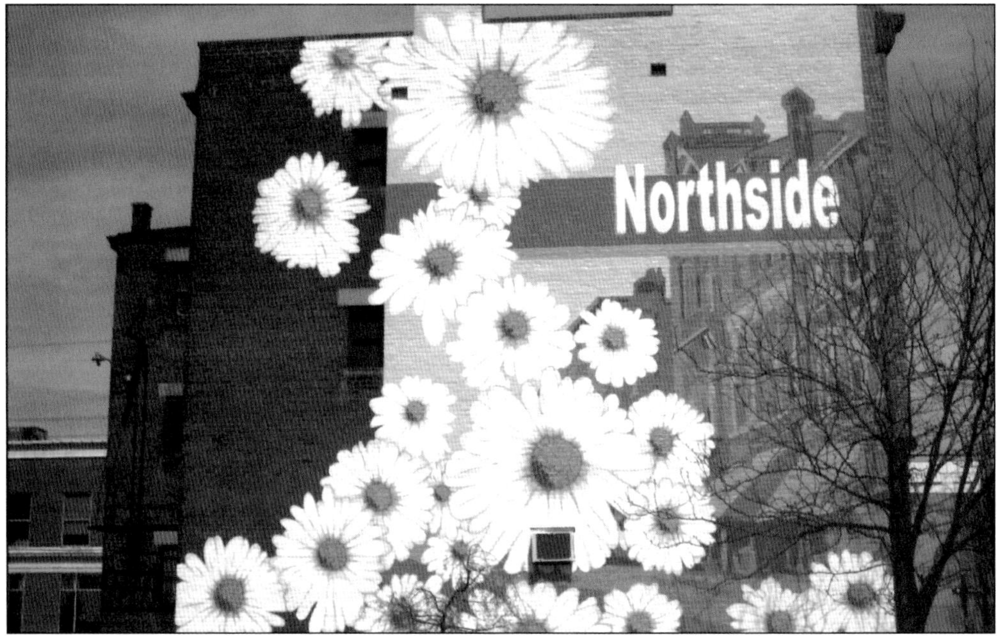

Turning right on Hamilton Avenue from the Ludlow Avenue Viaduct and heading north, travelers are greeted by a second mural created by Artworks in 2007 on the Palm Building at Hoffner Park. Lead artist Tim Parsley developed the image to acknowledge Northside's prosperous past and its current community energy. The mural presents flowers exploding from a historic view of a Hamilton Avenue streetscape.

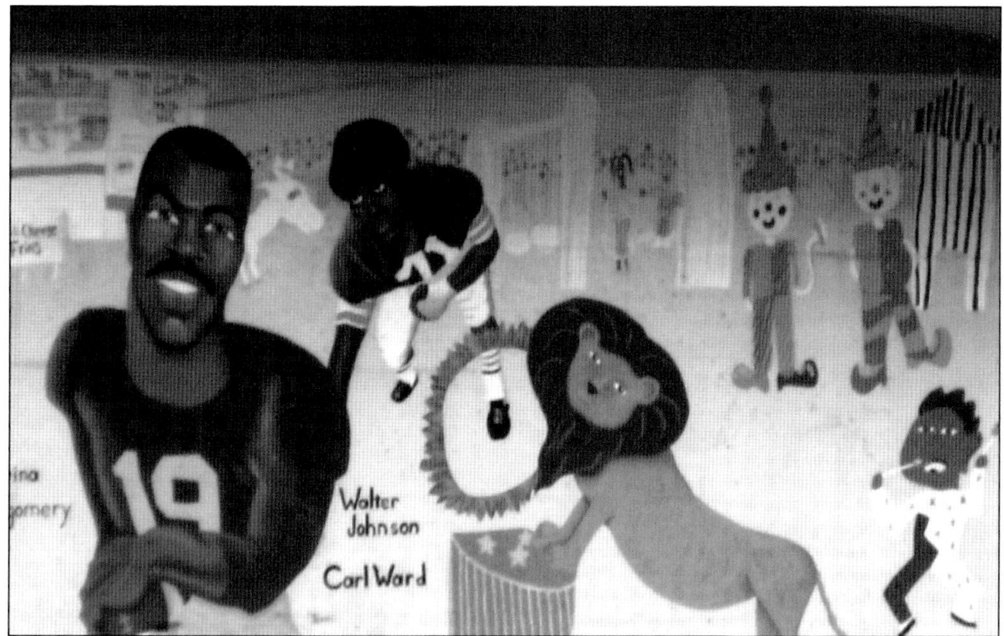

In 2005, artist Carol Anne Newsome, in collaboration with the South Cumminsville Community Council, created this 1,000-square-foot gateway mural next to the Garfield School overpass, celebrating the African American history of the originally German neighborhood. Neighborhood children created drawings to illustrate oral history shared by neighborhood elders, and these images were used to create the final design. This close-up notes the favorite topic of circus history.

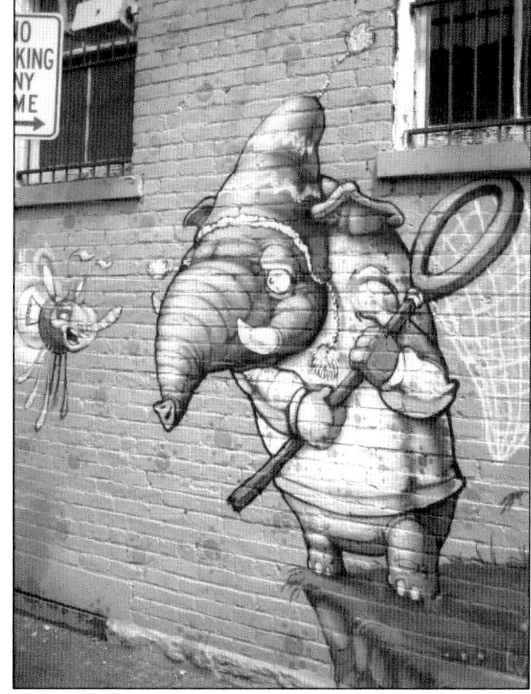

Kansas City graffiti artist Donald Ross, also known as "Scribe," created this mural on the south side of Wizard's Computers, the old Zachman Furniture Building. His style is self-described as "kind of a Garfield meets Cheech Wizard with a dash of Warner Brothers and Disney." Shake It Records in Northside has teamed with the artist to produce a children's book called *There's an Octopus in my Bed*.

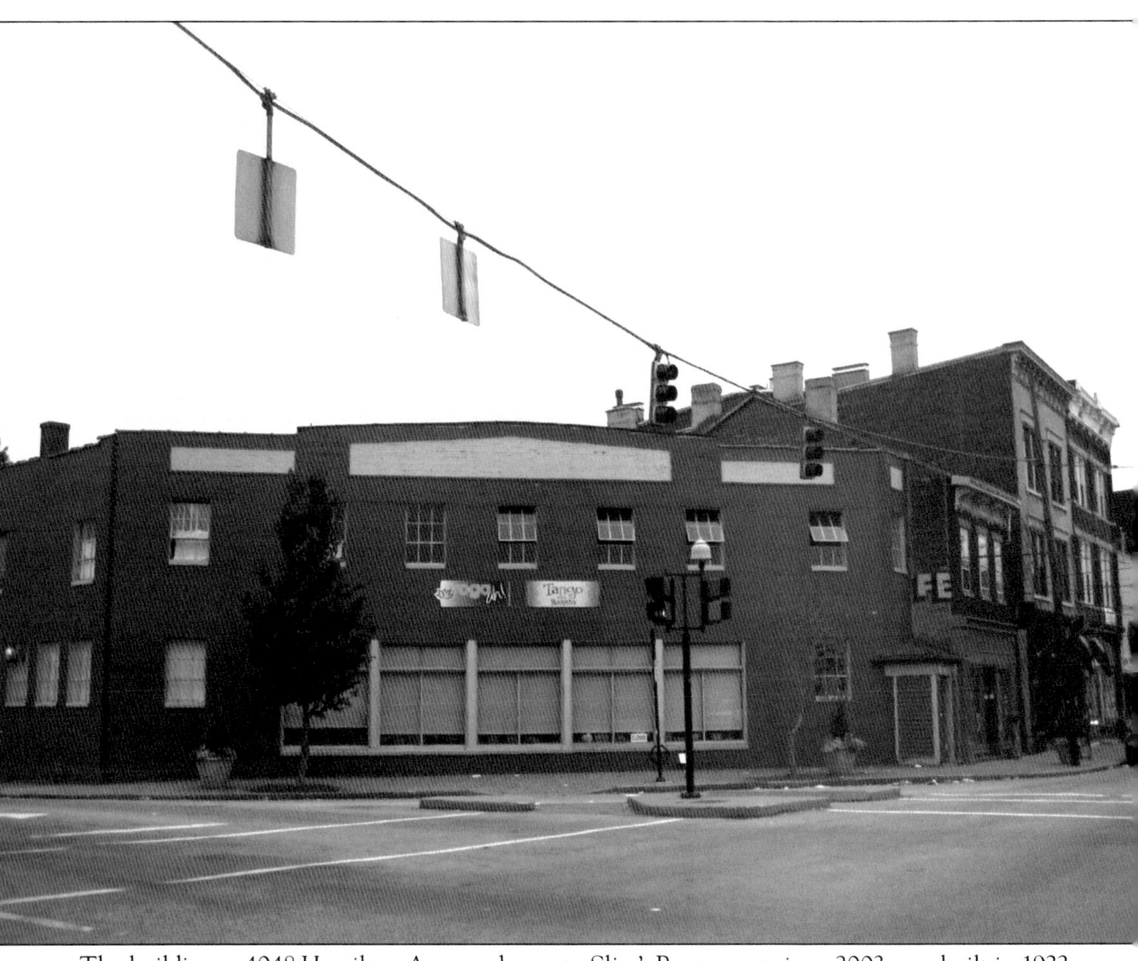

The building at 4048 Hamilton Avenue, home to Slim's Restaurant since 2003, was built in 1922 for the Benefit Steel Furnace Company because of its convenience to the railroad tracks. From the mid-1980s to the early 1990s, it housed the Hasselle Pottery of Bob Hasselle. Bob Hasselle was head of the Cincinnati Art Academy sculpture department in the 1970s, where he started the ceramics program. He provided a welcoming place for creatives with his retail pottery studio and, like Crazy Ladies Bookstore located across the street, was an anchor for the redevelopment of Northside. Hasselle rented the second-story loft of the building in 1990 to John Curley of Ultrasuede Studios. Curley and his studio partners recorded a number of local bands in this studio for the next few years, including his own band, the Afghan Whigs, and others like the Ass Ponys, Throneberrys, and the Love Cowboys. John Curley and his Ultrasuede Studios are responsible for making Northside an early haven for musicians.

Bibliography

Beck, Edwin R. *History of the Northside Methodist Church*. Cincinnati: Northside Methodist Church, 1967.

Burgheim, Max. *Cincinnati in Wort und Bild*. Burgheim Publishing Company, 1881.

Clubbe, John. *Cincinnati Observed: Architecture and History*. Columbus, OH: Ohio State University Press, 1992.

Dabney, Wendall P. *Cincinnati's Colored Citizens*. Cincinnati: Dabney Publishing Company, 1926.

Giglierano, Geoggrey J., and Deborah A. Obermyer. *Bicentennial Guide to Greater Cincinnati: A Portrait of Two Hundred Years*. Cincinnati: Cincinnati Historical Society, 1988.

Heyn, August, H. W. Felter, and William F. Ray. *The 1914 Souvenir History of Cumminsville*. Raisbeck and Company Printers, 1914.

Kollath, Rev. Karl B. *100th Anniversary of the First Evangelical Church, Hoffner Street, Cincinnati, Ohio*. Cincinnati: First Evangelical Church, 1955.

Northside: A Walk Through Neighborhood History. Northside Community Council, 1990.

100 Years: North Presbyterian Church. Cincinnati: North Presbyterian Church, 1955.

Roe, G. M., ed. *Our Police: A History of the Cincinnati Police Force*. Cincinnati: 1890.

St. Boniface Church Golden Jubilee Program.

Schade, Kristen. "Maitri Center: Place Identity and Identity Design." Master thesis, University of Cincinnati College of Design, Architecture, Art and Planning, 2005.

Schmitt, Robert C. "Cumminsville: A Study in Suburban Growth and Structure." Master diss., University of Cincinnati Department of Sociology, Graduate School of Arts and Sciences, 1947.

Turrill, M. S., and L. P. Rowe, eds. *Semi Centennial of the First Presbyterian Church of Cuminsville, Ohio*. Cumminsville, OH: First Presbyterian Church, 1905.

Workers of the Writers' Program of the Work Projects Administration in the State of Ohio. *Cincinnati: A Guide to the Queen City and Its Neighbors*. American Guide Series. Cincinnati: Wiesen-Hart Press, 1943. Reprinted with a new introduction by Zane L. Miller and a new preface by Harry Graff. Cincinnati: Cincinnati Historical Society, 1987.

Consistent with our mission to preserve history on a local level, this book was printed in South Carolina on American-made paper and manufactured entirely in the United States. Products carrying the accredited Forest Stewardship Council (FSC) label are printed on 100 percent FSC-certified paper.

MADE IN THE

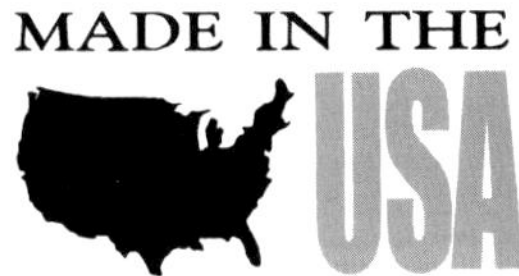